TEQUILA

A TASTING COURSE

TEQUILA

A TASTING COURSE

MILLIE MILLIKEN

CONTENTS

A FLAVOUR-FOCUSED APPROACH

This book is a celebration of the flavours of tequila.

Eating *birria* tacos and tequila-flavoured salsa in Atanasio's sprawling agave fields; snacking on *chicharrónes* and sipping a Cantarito on the streets of Tequila; or toasting the Day of the Dead to the sounds of a mariachi band – experiencing first-hand the culture of Mexico's national spirit brings it vividly alive.

But you don't need to go to Mexico to appreciate tequila – you can experience its myriad flavours from the comfort of your own home. In this book, you'll learn how an agave plant becomes the tequila in your glass: who makes it and how, and why it tastes the way it does. You'll also learn *how* to taste, get to grips with the language of tequila, and discover how to make some of its most iconic cocktails. You'll become familiar with the brands on retailers' shelves or behind the bar.

Many of us remember our first taste of tequila. For a long time, outside its birthplace in Mexico, it has, unfairly, had an identity crisis. Relegated to the party shot, and blamed for many a hangover, its colourful history, cultural importance, and the craftsmanship of its production were ignored for far too long. Its raw ingredient, the agave, spends more time in the ground than the raw ingredient of practically any other spirit. Tequila is identified geographically, much like Cognac

THE AGAVE SPIRIT IS HAVING A RENAISSANCE, AND DRINKERS ARE INCREASINGLY APPRECIATING THE COMPLEXITIES OF GOOD-QUALITY TEQUILA.

and Champagne, and its history spans hundreds of years. And yet, it has been one of the most misunderstood spirits in the global gamut.

Now, however, the agave spirit is having somewhat of a renaissance. Drinkers are increasingly appreciating the complexities of good-quality tequila, topics like *terroir* and sustainability are being discussed more fervently, and bartenders are creating more classics for us to enjoy at the bar and at home.

As someone who hasn't grown up in the culture of tequila's home, it's important to mention that this book would not have been remotely possible to write without the sharing of knowledge, generosity, and open arms of members of the tequila community, who live and breathe this historic spirit. This is their history, livelihoods, and story – one I have told through the lens of someone who is always learning about tequila.

ABOUT THE TEQUILAS IN THIS BOOK

I've tasted hundreds of tequilas to give you 100 of my favourites, split into six dual flavour categories: sweet/rich, grassy/herbal, citrus/floral, fruit/spice, earthy/mineral, and savoury/vegetal. Some stay distinctly in their lane, while others, it could be argued, fit across all of them. Note that these are my tasting experiences, which might vary from yours. Ultimately, though, I hope you'll find it a helpful starting point for building up your flavour library. One thing I think we can all agree on is that, when it comes to tequila, there is a wonderful world of flavour out there, both literally and figuratively.

WHAT
----------- <u>IS</u> -----------
TEQUILA?

WHAT MAKES TEQUILA, TEQUILA? It's one of the most misunderstood spirits on the market, and this section will equip you with the information you need to get to grips with what this agave spirit really is. We'll take a look at the legal, geographical, and categorical nuances of this very special spirit, and you'll gain an appreciation for the magic of the blue Weber agave, as well as the people and communities who have dedicated their lives and careers to celebrating this Mexican spirit over the centuries. We'll discover the difference between a *blanco* and an *añejo*, get acquainted with tequila's regulating body, the Consejo Regulador del Tequila (CRT), learn how to talk about tequila, and explore Tequila town. We'll also meet multiple generations of tequila families.

LEGAL DEFINITIONS OF TEQUILA

Legal definitions, although not the most fun part to consider, are arguably one of the most important when it comes to drinking high-quality tequila.

QUALITY AND PROVENANCE

Every spirits category has its own particular set of legal definitions, and tequila is no exception. These definitions ensure that what we are drinking is of good quality and has a transparent provenance, and are also the pillars on which experimentation is grounded. While you, the consumer, might not necessarily know what these definitions are when you're living your best life, ordering a Margarita at a bar or carefully selecting a bottle in a shop, they mean you can (on the whole) rest easy in the knowledge that someone has done that due diligence for you.

Having the full context of what you're spending your hard-earned cash on, however, is always a plus. The 20th century has seen what is and isn't allowed in the production of tequila change over time, and in the 21st century, a certain set of rules apply. We will dig into all of these definitions in more detail later, but here they are in a nutshell.

THE BASICS

Tequila can only be made in Mexico and with a minimum of 51 per cent blue Weber (or *azul*) agave (*Agave tequilana*). The remaining 49 per cent can be made using other sources of sugar, such as sugarcane or beet sugar.

If you see "100% agave" on a label, it means that 100 per cent of the sugars in this tequila come from blue Weber agave (see p14).

ACRONYMS TO KNOW

ABV This means alcohol by volume. In Mexico, tequila can be bottled anywhere between 35% and 55% ABV. When bottled in the US, it must be a minimum of 40% ABV, and in Europe, 37.5% ABV.
CNIT Founded in 1959, the National Chamber of the Tequila Industry represents, promotes, and defends the tequila industry's interests.
CRT The Consejo Regulador del Tequila (CRT, or Tequila Regulatory Council) was established in 1994 and is responsible for regulating and guaranteeing tequila's authenticity all over the world. Agave plants must also be registered with the CRT, and distilleries must record tests during production. Only CRT officials can seal barrels of aged tequilas.

MIXTO TEQUILA

Tequila must be made with at least 51 per cent blue Weber agave, and 49 per cent can be made with non-agave sugars, such as sugarcane or beet sugar. These are known as *mixto* tequilas.

Sugarcane

49% SUGARCANE/ BEET SUGAR

51% BLUE WEBER AGAVE

Sugar beet

Agave

THE FIVE LEGALLY DEFINED CATEGORIES OF TEQUILA

The rules and terms that apply to the ageing of tequila include the length of time it is aged, the wood used for the barrels, and the volume of the container.

BLANCO	JOVEN	REPOSADO	AÑEJO	EXTRA AÑEJO
Also known as silver or *plata*, these are tequilas that are aged for no more than two months and are usually free from additives. Not all *blancos* are aged.	Meaning "young", *joven* tequilas are also known as *oro* or gold. They can be a blend of aged tequilas or, quite often, are a *blanco* with added caramel colouring (see p82) and/or sweeteners.	*Reposados* are aged or rested tequilas that have spent from 60 days to no more than a year in oak, holm oak (*Quercus ilex*), or vats (*pipones*).	*Añejos* are aged from one to three years in oak or a container that holds no more than 600 litres (132 gallons). They can be labelled "extra aged" (not to be confused with extra *añejo*).	Otherwise known as "ultra aged", these tequilas have spent at least three years in oak or a container that is no more than 600 litres (132 gallons).

BLANCO, PLATA, OR SILVER TEQUILA **JOVEN, ORO, OR GOLD TEQUILA** **REPOSADO TEQUILA** **AÑEJO TEQUILA** **EXTRA AÑEJO TEQUILA**

DO Since 1974, tequila has had its own denomination of origin (DO), and was the first agave spirit to be assigned one. Tequila must be made with regulated methods and ingredients in specific regions of Mexico: the state of Jalisco and certain municipalities in the states of Guanajuato, Michoacán, Nayarit, and Tamaulipas (see pp16–17). **NOM** Tequila categories and classifications are defined in the

Norma Oficial Mexicana (Official Mexican Standard), regulated by the CRT. Every bottle of tequila has a NOM number that indicates the producer (see p87).

THE THREE As

Abocado The Spanish term for "mellowing", *abocado* refers to the use of certain additives in tequila (see pp82–83).

Additives The four additives often found in tequila are glycerine, caramel colouring, oak extract, and sugar-based syrup. Other additives can also be used. If the additives make up less than 1 per cent of the total weight, they do not have to be declared on the bottle.
Ageing Specific rules and terms apply to the ageing of tequila (see box above and pp22–29).

WHAT IS TEQUILA MADE FROM?

Tequila is made from the agave plant. There are more than 250 types of agave, but tequila is made from a specific species: blue Weber agave.

BLUE AGAVE PLANTATION
A plantation of blue agave grows in the Amatitán Valley in Jalisco, Mexico. The region is part of an area that was made a World Heritage site in 2006.

BLUE WEBER AGAVE

Since 1949, blue Weber agave (*Agave tequilana*), or *agave azul*, is officially the only species of agave that can be used in the production of tequila. The species was named by French botanist Frédéric Albert Constantin Weber (1830–1903), who took part in an expedition to Mexico in the mid-1800s.

Blue Weber agave is grown across numerous states in Mexico, mainly in the state of Jalisco. It became the preferred agave for making tequila for a number of reasons, including its relatively quick journey to maturity and its high sugar content, which is important in making tequila.

It reaches full maturity after five to seven years, when it is ready to be harvested for tequila, although it can be harvested later. Its heart is called the *piña*, a large, pineapple-like bulb that is processed for its inulin, a natural carbohydrate made up of glucose and fructose.

Its spiky leaves, which protrude from the head of the *piña*, can reach up to 2m (6½ft) tall. It also produces a stalk (*quiote*) after about five years, on which flowers (*floras*) appear. These stalks can reach 4.5m (15ft) or more.

Blue agaves are tended to and harvested by hand by farmers, called *jimadores* (see pp62–63). *Jimadores* cut down the flowering stalk so that sugars are diverted to the *piña*.

Bats are one of the agave's most prolific pollinators (see pp92–93), but farmers often clone blue agaves by cutting and replanting *hijuelos* (pups) from the parent agave, which reduces the genetic diversity of the species (see p92).

THE AGAVE PLANT

The blue Weber agave is the only species that is legally allowed to be used to make tequila.

FLOWERS
Yellow flowers appear on the stalk

STALK
The flowering stalk appears when the plant is about five years old, but *jimadores* cut it down before it grows tall

LEAVES
The spiky leaves can grow up to 2m (6½ft) tall

PIÑA
The *piña* is a large bulb that is used to make tequila

IT TAKES BETWEEN FIVE AND SEVEN YEARS FOR A BLUE AGAVE PLANT TO REACH MATURITY.

WHAT IS AN AGAVE?

Agave is a genus in the Asparagaceae family, which is native to the Americas and grows in hot, dry countries. Agaves are a succulent and are recognizable by their long, spiky leaves, which often get confused with cactus leaves. You might also see the word "*maguey*" used to refer to agaves, which is a Spanish word for large-leaved plants in the family.

WHERE IS TEQUILA MADE?

Mexico may be the home of tequila, but the spirit can legally only be made in specific areas in the country.

MEXICAN ORIGIN

Although tequila can only be made in Mexico, agave-based spirits can be made outside Mexico (see p85). But, just as English sparkling wine cannot be called Champagne, or sugarcane juice rum made in Florida can't be called *rhum agricole*, tequila is protected by the place in which it is made.

It was only in 1974 that Mexico actually became the official denomination of origin (DO) of tequila. That doesn't mean, of course, that is when tequila first started being made, only that Mexico was recognized as the area where tequila originated.

There are specific areas in Mexico that can legally produce tequila because of their suitability for cultivating the blue agave, their history, and traditional production processes. They are made up of

more than 180 municipalities in five Mexican states, covering a whopping 11 million hectares (27 million acres).

THE TOPIC OF *TERROIR*

The term "*terroir*" might be more commonly associated with wine, but its use in spirits terminology includes that of tequila. The fact that tequila has a DO tells us that microclimate, altitude, soil type, and surrounding ecosystem (encapsulated in the term "*terroir*"), as well as human influence, all have an important impact on the resulting flavour profile of the tequila (see also pp60–61).

CLIMATE
Variations in climate can make tequilas taste quite different from region to region across Mexico

TERROIR HAS AN IMPORTANT IMPACT ON A TEQUILA'S FLAVOUR PROFILE.

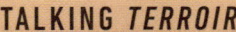

SOIL
Soil in the agave fields can contribute to a tequila's distinctive *terroir*

ALTITUDE
The altitude at which agaves grow affects their flavour

TALKING *TERROIR*

The altitude, microclimate, and soil, among other factors, of the agave's growing conditions all have an influence on the flavour profile of the finished tequila.

WHERE IN MEXICO?

The Mexican states in which tequila can legally be made are mainly located in the west of the country, with one outlier in the northeast.

I. JALISCO

The main area of tequila production, the entire state of Jalisco can produce tequila, and it is home to the town and municipality of Tequila. Bordering the Pacific Ocean, it is known for both its highlands and lowlands, which both produce differing styles of tequila. Before the 1974 DO, Jalisco had been the official home of tequila for 30-odd years.

2. GUANAJUATO

Bordered by Jalisco to the west and part of the wider Bajío region, Guanajuato is a state in which seven southwest municipalities can produce tequila. It's located between two different types of ecosystem – the drier north of Mexico and the lusher south – and is also part of the Trans-Mexican Volcanic Belt. The volcanic soil can have an impact on the flavour profile of the agaves grown in this area. Guanajuato is also becoming popular for wine production.

3. MICHOACÁN

Bordered by two other tequila-producing regions, Jalisco and Guanajuato, Michoacán has 30 municipalities that can make tequila. It is home to numerous Indigenous populations, including the Purépecha, Otomí, and Nahua people. It has a growing number of tequila distilleries, and is also known for its extravagant Day of the Dead celebrations on 1–2 November.

4. NAYARIT

Perhaps better known for its beaches and coastline of the Riviera Nayarit, this popular travel destination between the Pacific Ocean and the Sierra Madre Occidental has eight municipalities that can produce tequila.

5. TAMAULIPAS

An outlier of the tequila-making states, Tamaulipas is situated in the northeast of Mexico and has coastal plains along the Gulf of Mexico, as well as warm valleys and high sierras. It was inducted into the tequila-producing regions in 1977, with political reasons cited as the main driver, and it currently has 11 municipalities that can make tequila.

WHO MAKES TEQUILA?

As with any spirit, there is a daisy chain of people without whom your tequila wouldn't get made. So who are all the different people making our favourite agave spirit?

JIMADORES

The farmers who harvest agave do incredibly hard physical work in the heat of the agave fields. They head out early to beat the sun, and undertake the highly skilled task of identifying and harvesting blue agaves ready to be sent to distilleries. A *jimador* can unearth and trim the leaves off a mature *piña* (the part used to make tequila) in a matter of minutes, and can harvest around 100 mature *piñas* a day (see pp62–63).

Jimadores get paid per agave or by weight. Traditionally, fathers pass the role on to sons, but younger generations are turning their back on agricultural work, raising concerns about the future of the tradition.

HARVESTING PIÑAS
Jimadores perform the skilful and backbreaking work of harvesting *piñas* from the agave plants.

DISTILLERY WORKERS

When agaves arrive at a distillery, the hard labour continues, as workers go about splitting the *piñas* with axes to prepare them for the cooking process. They also tend to the agaves during cooking, assist with the crushing process, and oversee roller mills and *tahonas* (large stone wheels), preparing the agave juice for the fermentation process (see pp64–69).

TEQUILEROS

Tequileros or *tequileras* are the distillers or technicians who run and manage the distilling processes (see pp70–71). Depending on how manual or automated the distillery is, this could include monitoring the stills, recording data, charging the stills for first and second distillations, and testing or tasting.

MASTER DISTILLERS

Sometimes the owner of a smaller distillery, a *maestro tequilero* or *maestra tequilera*, is the person in charge of the makeup of the tequilas, and they are often the face of a brand or distillery. They usually have years of experience

READY TO COOK
A distillery worker loads an autoclave with agaves ready for them to be cooked.

in the industry, and this knowledge can be felt across the whole supply chain, from the quality of the agave to new releases. To spend time with a master distiller is an enlightening experience – a mine of information, they *are* tequila.

WAREHOUSE MANAGERS/ COORDINATORS

Taking care of those barrels of ageing tequila (see pp76–79) is, of course, an important job, but there is more to this than may meet the eye. Inventory, maintenance, supply, distribution, safety – they are all vital tasks to make sure that tequilas of the past, present, and future are all planned for.

DISTILLERIES AND BRANDS

Distilleries and brands aren't always the same. More often than not, one distillery is actually producing a number of tequila brands. The NOM number on a bottle will tell you who or which distillery actually makes your new favourite brand (see pp13, 87).

HIDDEN GEMS

There are some people you might not see on a distillery visit but who all play important roles.

Lab technicians Dressed in lab coats and conducting sensory and chemical analysis, these people have to constantly monitor the liquid coming out of a distillery, often filing reports regularly and ad hoc for the Consejo Regulador del Tequila (CRT; see p12).

Bottlers The people who bottle tequila are often doing repetitive work all day long. Some distilleries make sure to give them regular breaks, move them across different parts of the process, and encourage exercises to avoid injury.

Drivers The people who transport agaves from the field to the distillery, and bottles to distributors, bookend the process of getting tequila into your hands. Van heists aren't unheard of, so the role comes with certain risks and responsibilities.

BLANCO TEQUILA

Perhaps the most recognizable style of tequila, *blanco* is all about pure, unadulterated spirit with citrus, grassy, and vegetal notes.

WHAT IS *BLANCO*?

When it comes to talking about different categories of tequila, *blanco* is the place to start. *Blanco* is the first of the five main styles of tequila as stated by the Consejo Regulador del Tequila (CRT; see p12).

After going through the processes of fermentation and distillation (see pp68–71), *blanco* tequila is usually stored in stainless-steel vats and bottled. It does not usually undergo an ageing process, although it can be aged in barrels for up to two months.

Blanco cannot have anything added to it, except water, which dilutes it to bottling strength. More often than not, it is completely clear, although some *blancos* can have some colour. For many tequila lovers, *blanco* is the most "pure" of all the tequila categories.

OTHER TERMS

Plata or silver

FLAVOUR PROFILES

Grassy, vegetal, herbal, cooked agave, citrus

THE REGULATIONS

If stored in oak, it cannot be left for longer than two months.

The spirit can have a slight colour.

The use of *abocado* (Spanish for "mellowing"), such as caramel colour, oak natural extract, glycerine, and sugar syrup, is not permitted.

Casa Dragones Blanco is made with 100 per cent blue agaves

Don Fulano Blanco is matured for at least six months in stainless steel

Patrón Silver has a stopper made of the distillery's signature Portuguese cork

BOTTLED BLANCOS
Not all *blanco* tequilas are 100 per cent clear in appearance. Some distillers may label their *blanco* as *plata* or silver.

FOR MANY TEQUILA LOVERS, *BLANCO* IS THE MOST "PURE" OF ALL THE TEQUILA CATEGORIES.

COCKTAILS

Blanco tequilas are popular for mixing and appear in some of the most famous tequila cocktails.

MARGARITA
Combine with orange liqueur and lime juice to make the most widely known tequila cocktail in the world (see pp196–97).

PALOMA
Super simple and seriously refreshing, this highball brings *blanco* together with lime juice and is lengthened with grapefruit soda (see pp202–03).

TEQUILA MOCKINGBIRD
A particularly earthy *blanco* works well in this cocktail, alongside watermelon, lime juice, agave syrup, and jalapeños.

MIXERS

Blancos are easily lengthened with mixers, which really let the spirit itself shine.

TONIC WATER
Switch your gin out for *blanco* tequila and you have yourself a T&T (tequila and tonic). Add a pinch of salt to bring this to life.

COLA
The famous Batanga cocktail (see pp190–91) takes *blanco* and mixes it with lime juice and salt before lengthening with cola.

SODA WATER
Perhaps the simplest combo, just top a measure of *blanco* with soda water and a squeeze of lime for a lo-fi highball.

FOOD

Whether served straight up or in a cocktail, *blancos* are versatile and complement a huge range of food. See also pp120–21.

CEVICHE
Blancos are a match made in heaven with the citrus notes in this classic Latin American fish dish.

FRIED CHICKEN
Need something zippy to cut through the super savouriness of fried chicken? Clean and fresh *blancos* are perfect.

DARK CHOCOLATE
The bitterness of dark chocolate pairs beautifully with bright *blancos*.

JOVEN TEQUILA

Also known as *oro* or *gold*, *joven* (meaning "young") tequilas vary in their production methods and are great mixed in cocktails.

WHAT IS *JOVEN* TEQUILA?

Joven tequilas are young tequilas that can vary quite considerably in their makeup. The best are blends of unaged (*blanco*/silver) and aged (*reposado*/*añejo*) tequilas (see pp20–21 and pp24–27). These tequilas can, however, also be unaged and have caramel colouring added to give the illusion of age, as well as glycerine or sugar syrup to mellow the taste.

Perhaps *joven* tequila's most famous poster brand is Jose Cuervo, which has regularly topped the biggest-selling lists when it comes to the entire tequila category. Newer tequila brands are also embracing the *joven* category and ageing their liquid in former bourbon barrels to impart those sweeter, vanilla characteristics (see pp76–79).

OTHER TERMS

Oro/gold

FLAVOUR PROFILES

Honey, vanilla, pepper, oak, cooked agave, orange/ grapefruit citrus

THE REGULATIONS

They can be blended from aged (*reposado*) and unaged (*blanco*) tequilas, but can also be *mixto* tequilas that have caramel colouring and/ or sweeteners added to mimic aged tequilas.

Clase Azul Gold is a blend of *blanco*, *reposado*, and extra *añejo*

Cincoro Gold blends unaged *blanco* and aged *reposado*, *añejo*, and extra *añejo*

El Sueño Gold uses blue Weber agave and *piloncillo* (raw sugar) as its base

JOVEN TEQUILAS
Joven tequilas can contain some very special aged elements in their blend, but also may not, so make sure you know what you're buying.

THE BEST EXAMPLES OF *JOVEN* TEQUILA ARE BLENDS OF UNAGED AND AGED TEQUILAS.

COCKTAILS

Joven tequilas are used primarily in cocktails for their sweeter qualities.

MEXICAN MULE
A twist on a Moscow Mule, this replaces vodka with tequila, which is then mixed over ice with ginger beer and lime juice.

TEQUILA SUNRISE
Easy and delicious, this three-ingredient, layered cocktail consists of tequila, grenadine syrup, and orange juice, topped with a cherry and an orange slice (see pp206–07).

TOREADOR
The apricot liqueur makes this cocktail so special, and it mixes with tequila, lime juice, and simple syrup to make a clever riff on a Margarita (see pp208–09).

MIXERS

Mixing *joven* tequila is fuss free and top value too.

FLAVOURED TONIC WATER
Mixing *joven* tequila with flavoured tonics creates a more nuanced flavour and can really play with the sweeter varieties of tonic.

ROOT BEER
Perhaps not a classic choice, but certain *joven* tequilas work nicely with the sweet spice of a root beer, and it makes a great alternative to cola.

COLD BREW
Coffee and tequila work wonders together, and *joven* tequilas are perfect for lengthening with coffee – a touch of agave syrup can help the balance.

FOOD

Joven tequilas vary depending on their makeup, but when pairing with food, focus on whether the tequila is rich and sweet, or more light and citrussy. See also pp120–21.

SMOKY AUBERGINE
Aged elements in *joven* tequila are complemented by smoked aubergine, and the earthiness is the ideal companion to sweeter tequila notes.

STRONG CHEESES
Manchego, pecorino romano, Cotija – strong cheeses, especially hard ones, are the salty answer to a really good *joven* tequila.

HONEYCOMB
The sweet, honeyed, but also slightly bitter characteristics of honeycomb, in any form, are well matched with this style of tequila.

REPOSADO TEQUILA

Aged, or rested, this style of tequila spends no less than two months and no more than a year in oak, and is seriously versatile when it comes to cocktails.

WHAT IS *REPOSADO*?

Reposado (which means "rested" in Spanish) or aged tequilas have a very specific ageing timeframe: they can only be aged for at least two months up to a year. This style of tequila is where you really start to understand what the influence of oak has on what would have been a *blanco* before it went into the barrel (see pp76–79). The oak barrels or vats give this style of tequila a light straw colour.

The ageing process is also how *reposado* tequilas get their distinctive flavour characteristics – flavours such as vanilla, caramel, coconut, and whispers of spice are all imparted from the wood in which they have been aged. The contact with wood can also contribute to a softer, rounder mouthfeel for *reposados*.

OTHER TERMS

Aged

FLAVOUR PROFILES

Vanilla, caramel, coconut, fruit, spice, vegetal

THE REGULATIONS

Reposado tequilas must spend anything between two months and a year in oak, holm oak (*Quercus ilex*), or vats (*pipones*).

El Tequileño Reposado spends three months in American oak

Tapatio Reposado is a distinctly rounded tequila compared to the brand's *blanco*

Fortaleza Reposado is topped with its trademark *piña* stopper

REPOSADO TEQUILAS
Reposado tequilas benefit not only from the flavours that come from spending time in oak, but also added texture and a rounding-out of flavours.

AGEING IS HOW *REPOSADO* TEQUILAS GET THEIR DISTINCTIVE FLAVOUR CHARACTERISTICS.

COCKTAILS

Reposado tequilas are super versatile and are often perfect for swapping with other spirits in classic cocktails.

CANTARITO
Served in a clay drinking vessel, this Jalisco favourite mixes *reposado* with grapefruit, orange, and lime juice with salt and grapefruit soda (see pp192–93).

OLD FASHIONED
Using *reposado* in the place of bourbon or rye, this Mexican spin on the classic stirred-down-and-brown cocktail is just as delicious.

ESPRESSO MARTINI
Dick Bradsell's classic coffee Martini is given a twist using tequila instead of the traditional vodka (see p212).

MIXERS

Reposados are available at various ages, so make sure you don't mask their complexity with a mixer that overpowers the flavours.

RHUBARB SPARKLING WATER
The brightness and vegetal quality of the rhubarb works perfectly with a well-structured and young *reposado*.

LAGER
You read that right – lager makes an excellent lengthener with *reposado*. Mixing beer and tequila is technically a Corrido Prohibido cocktail.

PEACH ICED TEA
Iced tea is an underrated mixer, and the sweetness of peach and slight tannin from tea balance beautifully with a slightly aged *reposado*.

FOOD

One of the most versatile styles of tequila for pairing with food, *reposado* is at its most confident with bold ingredients. See also pp120–21.

GRILLED FOODS
Peaches, shrimp, steak, corn – the char on grilled foods complements *reposado* tequila beautifully.

PORK BARBACOA
This sweet, spicy, smoky sauce combined with slow-cooked pork makes a perfect pairing with *reposado*'s honeyed and caramelized notes.

CREAMY CHEESES
Soft and creamy cheeses, such as Camembert, brie, and ricotta, are like velvet when matched with the texture of *reposado*.

AÑEJO TEQUILA

Darker, richer, and fuller, *añejo* tequilas are all about the complexities of age. Those extra years in wood really start to make a difference here.

WHAT IS AÑEJO?

Añejo, or "extra aged", tequila, not to be confused with extra *añejo* (see pp28–29), has been aged for one to three years in oak. Ex-bourbon and Tennessee whiskey casks are often used for ageing, and they impart some tell-tale notes of coconut and vanilla that require some tempering to keep that agave character present in the final liquid (see pp76–79). There's a distinct change in the colour of this tequila compared to *blanco*, gold, or *reposado*.

Compared to *reposado* tequilas, *añejos* start to develop deeper levels of spice, darker fruit notes, and notes associated with other dark spirits like Cognac or Scotch. However, in the finest *añejos*, that underlying character of agave is still well and truly present.

OTHER TERMS

Extra aged

FLAVOUR PROFILES

Cinnamon, tobacco, dried fruit, butterscotch, chocolate, coconut

---

THE REGULATIONS

Aged for between one and three years in oak or a container that is no more than 600 litres (132 gallons).

Mijenta Añejo Gran Reserva is aged in American white oak, French oak, French acacia, and cherrywood casks

Arette Artesanal Suave Añejo is part of the brand's popular premium range

Rooster Rojo Añejo spends time in ex-bourbon barrels

AÑEJO TEQUILAS
Añejo tequilas can come with a heftier price tag, but that doesn't mean they can't be mixed in cocktails.

IN THE FINEST *AÑEJOS*, THE UNDERLYING CHARACTER OF AGAVE IS WELL AND TRULY PRESENT.

COCKTAILS

Añejo can be used in cocktails to bring real depth and body to the overall serve. Make sure it's well balanced, as it can be a rather bold player in the team of ingredients.

AÑEJO MANHATTAN
Swap American whiskey for *añejo* in this classic cocktail alongside vermouth and bitters, and garnish with a maraschino cherry (see p213).

AÑEJO SMASH
A seriously refreshing serve, this brings *añejo*, Grand Marnier, agave syrup, mint, and lemon together over crushed ice.

TEQUILA COLADA
A tequila twist to a tropical favourite, *añejo* works wonderfully with the flavours of pineapple and coconut.

MIXERS

The temptation to skip adding a mixer to an *añejo* is strong, but you'll be missing out if you do.

WATERMELON JUICE
Keep it simple or add some citrus, salt, or spice to really bring this fruity highball to life.

SODA WATER
Easily lengthened with soda, add a garnish of an orange slice or a jalapeño pepper to bring out some of the richer notes of the base tequila.

CHERRY POP
This feels kind of retro, but a cherry fizzy drink (preferably not too dark) is bright and perfumed and really makes *añejo* shine.

FOOD

Think depth and texture when it comes to drinking *añejo* with food. See also pp120–21.

STEAK
Dark meats, especially good-quality steak, work wonders with *añejo*, especially when served in tacos or fajitas.

MOLE
The depth and complexity of a classic Mexican mole sauce – rich with spices, chilli, chocolate, and more – is a worthy match for a super-deep *añejo*.

BAKED CHEESECAKE
Desserts go beautifully with *añejo*, and baked cheesecake is the ideal base for exploring its nuances, perhaps topped with figs or other dark fruits.

EXTRA AÑEJO TEQUILA

The most aged style of tequila, extra *añejo* has often spent much more than its minimum of three years in oak, and is revered for that.

WHAT IS EXTRA AÑEJO?

Deep orange or amber in colour, extra *añejo*, or "ultra aged", tequilas were classified only as recently as 2006 to recognize the growing number of super-aged and more premium tequilas on the market.

Extra *añejos* are aged for at least three years in oak, but many are older than that – hence their punchier price tags. These will often be sipped neat, but they can certainly be mixed if done deftly.

Extra *añejo* is the age range in which flavours become super concentrated, and the likes of leather, cacao, and dried fruits such as figs and raisins are matched with a rich and mouth-coating texture. If you like older whiskies, rums, or brandies, then extra *añejo* tequilas might well be the category for you.

OTHER TERMS

Ultra aged

FLAVOUR PROFILES

Leather, nutmeg, dried fruits, cacao nibs, vanilla

THE REGULATIONS

This tequila must spend at least three years in oak or a container that holds no more than 600 litres (132 gallons).

Fuenteseca Reserva 18 Years was distilled in 1995

Tierra-Noble Exquisito Extra Añejo has spent time in French oak

Código 1530 Origen Extra Añejo was aged in barrels that once held wine from Napa Valley

EXTRA AÑEJO TEQUILAS
You can pay anything from the low hundreds to the thousands for extra *añejos*, but remember that age doesn't always mean better.

EXTRA *AÑEJO* IS THE AGE RANGE IN WHICH FLAVOURS BECOME SUPER CONCENTRATED.

COCKTAILS

This style of tequila works best when substituted for other dark spirits, especially whisky, in classic cocktails.

EXTRA AÑEJO MANHATTAN
Replace whisky with tequila, and use mole bitters, such as Bittermens Xocolatl Mole Bitters, to really bring this boozy classic to life (see p213).

VIEUX CARRÉ
A New Orleans classic, swap in tequila for rye whiskey and combine with sweet vermouth, Benedictine, and bitters for a superb nightcap.

MEXICAN NAIL
Take extra *añejo* tequila, peated Scotch, and Drambuie, and you have the hallmarks of an excellent riff on the Rusty Nail cocktail.

MIXERS

It isn't sacrilege to combine old spirits with mixers, but go for quality to do them justice.

OOLONG TEA
A robust tea like oolong, cold brewed with a touch of agave syrup, makes a super-complex highball.

DANDELION AND BURDOCK
Earthy sarsaparilla and a touch of aniseed in this mixer add depth and complexity when mixed with extra *añejo* over ice.

GINGER BEER
A classic dark-spirits mixer, a good-quality ginger beer brings some fire and delicately enhances the tequila's spicy and sweet notes.

FOOD

Go big or go home when it comes to pairing food with extra *añejo* tequilas. See also pp120–21.

DUCK
Confit, Peking, or however you like it cooked, duck's richness works wonders with the texture and complexity of extra *añejo*.

MUSHROOMS
Bring some umami to the party – soy sauce, for example – and enjoy the juxtaposition of flavours.

SALTED CARAMEL
Whether this is in a dessert sauce or covered in chocolate, sweet meets salt, and the caramel notes are also complemented.

WHAT'S THE DEAL WITH CRISTALINOS?

Looks are deceiving with this clear, aged tequila. So why does it elicit such a strong response from some tequila aficionados?

CRISTALINO CONTROVERSY

There are plenty of subjects in tequila circles that can result in heated, but usually healthy debate. And one such subject is that of *cristalinos*.

Meaning "crystalline" in Spanish, *cristalinos* are aged tequilas, usually *añejos*, that have been either charcoal filtered or redistilled to remove the colour. Makers use the charcoal filtering process the most (see right). The resulting clear liquid should have all the flavour hallmarks of anything from a *reposado* (see pp24–25) to an extra *añejo* (see pp28–29).

WHY THE DRAMA?

Cristalino sceptics see the category as a dilution of tequila's identity. Why, they argue, would you spend time, skill, and money on making a beautiful aged tequila, only to strip out the visual and, some say, the flavour identifiers of it being just that?

Connected to that argument is the reasoning that if those aged characteristics are removed, at the very least the visual ones, it follows that some producers are (legally) using additives to bring those characteristics back (see pp82–83). It begs the question: why bother in the first place?

CHARCOAL FILTERING PROCESS

The aged tequila is either passed through a charcoal filter (shown here), or it has activated carbon added in a process called adsorption, which removes colour as well as other compounds from the liquid.

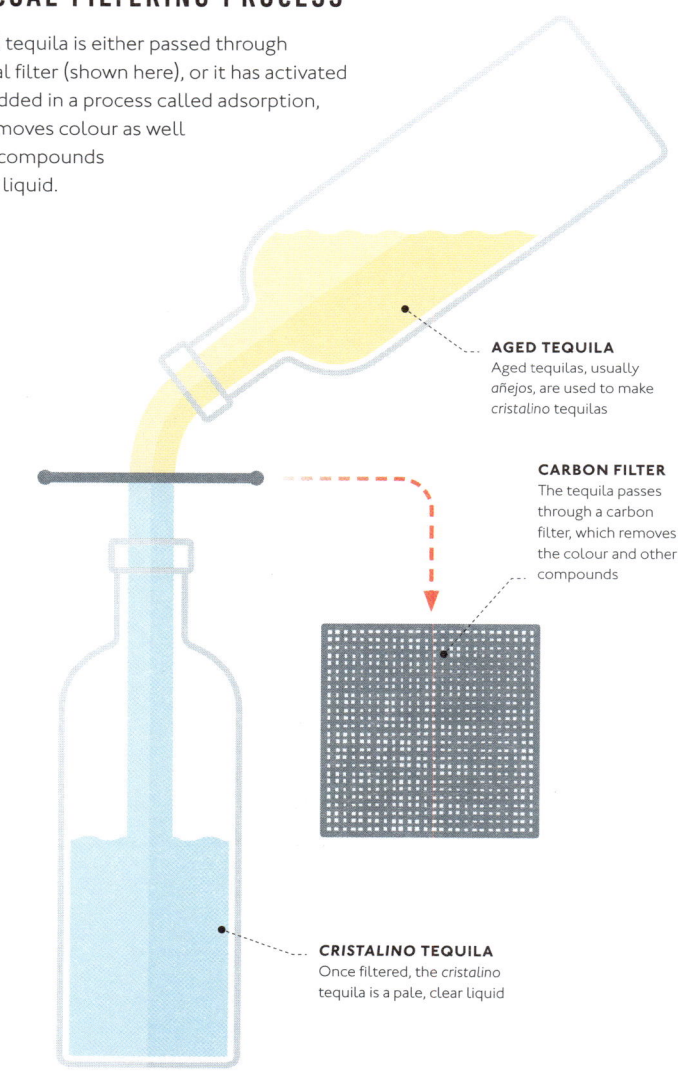

AGED TEQUILA
Aged tequilas, usually *añejos*, are used to make *cristalino* tequilas

CARBON FILTER
The tequila passes through a carbon filter, which removes the colour and other compounds

CRISTALINO TEQUILA
Once filtered, the *cristalino* tequila is a pale, clear liquid

THEIR COOL IMAGE, LUXURY ASSOCIATION, AND INNOVATIVE PROCESS ARE ALL FACTORS THAT MAKE *CRISTALINOS* POPULAR.

CRISTALINOS
A number of big brands have released *cristalino* expressions onto the market.

CATEGORY FIRSTS

It's widely accepted that Don Julio was the first brand to enter the *cristalino* game with its Don Julio 70 Añejo Claro, which has since been renamed as a *cristalino*. It was launched in 2012 to mark the 70th anniversary of Don Julio González's tequila career, and since then, this style of tequila has slowly taken hold.

So, why are *cristalinos* gaining traction? Their apparent cool image, luxury association, and innovative process are all factors that *cristalino* makers and fans argue make it worth their while. *Cristalinos* don't have a formal classification, yet, but premiumization – in which tequilas are perceived to have more value due to age, quality, and production processes – is driving sales of tequila as a whole. And *cristalinos*' popularity among people in Mexico is further cementing them firmly in the spirit category.

BIG MOVES

In a telling move, Patrón launched its first *cristalino* in 2024, driven by consumer demand and the lean towards premiumization. As a brand that prides itself on transparency and quality, it says a lot about what Patrón thinks of the selling power of the category.

Other brands followed suit in 2024, such as Mijenta with a limited-edition *cristalino reposado*, Milagro with its first *cristalino añejo*, and Komos, which launched a travel retail exclusive that is only available in travel retail stores such as at airports and not sold on the domestic market.

No matter what you think of *cristalinos*, it looks like there isn't any stopping them.

CURADOS AND LIQUEURS

Flavoured tequilas – *curados* – and tequila liqueurs have gained momentum in the last 20 years. Whether you're a fan or not, they can be an easy way to introduce newcomers to the tequila category, and when done well, can be handy for making easy at-home cocktails.

FLAVOURED EXPRESSIONS

Following in the footsteps of vodka and gin, the tequila industry has become no stranger to the concept of flavoured expressions, as well as liqueurs and cream liqueurs. From cocktail ingredients that bartenders use, to being served as shots and digestifs, flavoured expressions have become a relatively recent addition to the tequila category.

WHAT'S A *CURADO*?

Curados are tequilas that have been infused with natural flavours, and they were recognized by the CRT in 2006. Legally, they require only a minimum of 25 per cent agave spirit, and colourings and flavourings can also be added up to 75ml (2½fl oz) per litre (1¾ pints).

Macerating or infusing ingredients such as smoked pineapple or coconut is a popular method. However, brands like Tequila Ocho are doing things a little differently by infusing agaves other than blue Weber agave into tequila, such as *espadín* (*Agave angustifolia*) and *A. cupreata*.

CURADOS

Curados must contain at least 25 per cent agave spirit. Per litre (1¾ pints), 75ml (2½fl oz), or 7.5 per cent, can be colourings or flavourings.

75% OR LESS NON-AGAVE SPIRITS

AT LEAST 25% AGAVE SPIRIT

SMOKED PINEAPPLE

Curados may have macerated or infused ingredients, such as smoked pineapple or coconut

COCONUT

Some brands infuse agaves other than blue Weber agave, such as *espadín* (*Agave angustifolia*)

ESPADÍN

MACERATING OR INFUSING INGREDIENTS SUCH AS SMOKED PINEAPPLE OR COCONUT IS A POPULAR METHOD OF MAKING *CURADOS*.

FOR THE LOVE OF LIQUEURS

Tequila liqueurs have also emerged as a subcategory with legs. They are a minimum of 15% ABV and contain between at least 70 and 100g (2 ½ and 3 ½oz) of sugar per litre – whether honey, fruit, or jalapeño. These expressions can often be a handy string in your home-bar's bow. Cream liqueurs are also growing in popularity, with Tequila Rose, a strawberry cream liqueur, being an unlikely hero.

If the fallout of Patrón's discontinuation of its XO Café coffee liqueur in 2021 is anything to go by – it relaunched the product in 2024 – it seems that versatile and good-quality liqueurs are here to stay.

DO IT YOURSELF

Infusing your favourite tequilas with fruits, herbs, or spices is easy and can give another dimension to cocktails. Jalapeños, strawberries, grapefruit, pink peppercorns – there are plenty of possibilities. See p187 for more information on how to infuse your tequilas.

BEST OF THE BUNCH

Whether you're a Tequila Rose fan or like your tequila infused with other agaves, fruits, or spices, there is a slew out there to slake your thirst. Here are some of the more popular ones on the market.

LIQUEURS	COFFEE LIQUEURS	CREAM LIQUEURS	CURADOS
CAZCABEL Honey Liqueur	**PATRÓN** XO Café	**TEQUILA ROSE** Strawberry Cream	**ROOSTER ROJO** Smoked Pineapple Reposado
NO NAME Tequila Blanco Pineapple Liqueur	**VIVIR** Café VS	**TEQUILA BLACK 38** Chocolate Cream Liqueur	**1800** Coconut Tequila
TAKE Jalapeño Tequila Liqueur	**HERENCIA DE PLATA** Licor de Café	**MEX MELON** Cream Liqueur	**CURADO TEQUILA BLANCO** Infusión de Agave Espadín

THE LANGUAGE OF TEQUILA

How we talk about tequila has had an impact on the development of the category and how we understand it in the larger agave spirit realm.

VOLCÁN DE TEQUILA
The dormant volcano near the town of Tequila last erupted about 220,000 years ago. The lava left behind a rich volcanic soil, where the blue agave thrives.

MEZCAL CATEGORY

Before tequila was categorized as a distinct spirit in its own right, it was simply a category of mezcal (see p84), defined by its use of the blue Weber agave. It was included in the definition *vino de mezcal*, meaning mezcal wine, with "wine" referring to a distilled spirit.

The language that started it all is Nahuatl, also known as Aztec, which has been spoken in central and western Mexico since at least the 7th century. The word "mezcal" derives from the Nahuatl words "*metl*" and "*ixcalli*", which mean "cooked agave", reflecting how agave spirits are made.

THE MEANING OF "TEQUILA"

When tequila began to be made commercially in Amatitán, not far from the town of Tequila, it was transported with the word "tequila" stamped on the packaging and became known as *mezcal de tequila*.

So, where does the word "tequila" derive from? In Nahuatl, "*tequitl*" means work and "*tlan*" is place, so it may mean "place of work". Another meaning attributed to the word is "rock that cuts", a reference to the local volcanic rock from the dormant volcano that overlooks Tequila. The rock was used as tools called *tecatlis*, and the people who wielded them, *tecuilos*. Over time, this became the word "tequila". See p216 for a reminder of the terms used in tequila making.

DESTILADO DE AGAVE

If you see the term "*destilado de agave*" on a bottle of agave spirit, it means that while the spirit might be made out of, say, blue Weber agave, it cannot legally be termed "tequila" because it does not comply with the regulations – for example, it might be made outside of the DO (see p13). This doesn't necessarily make it of any less quality but just means that it legally cannot be called "tequila".

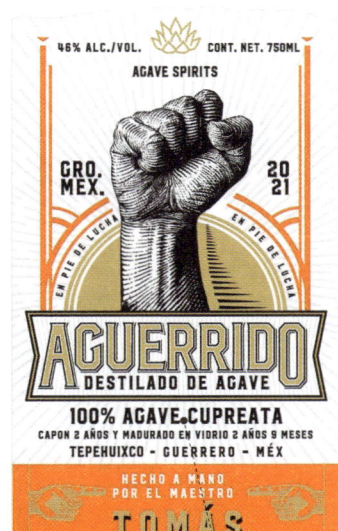

AGUERRIDO
Aguerrido Tomás is a *destilado de agave* made with *Agave cupreata*, so cannot be labelled as tequila.

Made with 100 per cent *Agave cupreata*

TALK TEQUILA AT THE BAR

Here are some handy words to bust out when ordering or drinking tequila.

LOS BESITOS
Meaning little kisses in Spanish, this is a term that can be used when tasting tequila in small sips. It also relates to Dos Besitos, a cocktail with a split base of *blanco* and *reposado* tequilas.

CABALLITO
Meaning little horse, this is the term for sipping (or shotting) tequila. It's also the name of the traditional tall sipping or shot glass with a wider mouth for serving tequila, also known as a *tequilito*.

CONCHAS
These are the bubbles that appear on the surface of tequila when it is shaken in the bottle. They are an indicator of the alcohol by volume (ABV).

SALUD!
Meaning health, this is a common way of toasting with tequila akin to cheers.

DISCOVERING TEQUILA COUNTRY

The area around Tequila town and Guadalajara is a hive of activity for making tequila, with many big-name distilleries making their home there.

A WORLD HERITAGE SITE

Tequila town is part of UNESCO's Agave Landscape and Ancient Industrial Facilities of Tequila, a World Heritage site listed in 2006. Located between the foothills of the Tequila Volcano and the valley of the Rio Grande river, the 34,658-hectare (85,642-acre) site is a landscape of blue agave fields and working distilleries.

The area also has traces of the pre-Columbian Teuchitlán culture, such as Los Guachimontones, an archaeological site that dates from 300 BCE to 450/500 CE.

TEQUILA AND ENVIRONS

In Tequila town, you'll find distilleries such as El Tequileño, Tequila Fortaleza, Sauza, and La Rojeña. Visitors to Atanasio can be taken to its agave fields to see first hand how they are cultivated.

A little out of town towards Guadalajara are the distilleries of Herradura, Volcan de Mi Terra, and Tequila Cascahuín. Further east near Arandas are the distilleries of Los Alambiques, where Tequila Ocho is made, and El Pandillo, where revered brands such as G4 and ArteNOM are crafted.

JALISCO DISTILLERIES

A number of renowned distilleries are located in or around Tequila town.

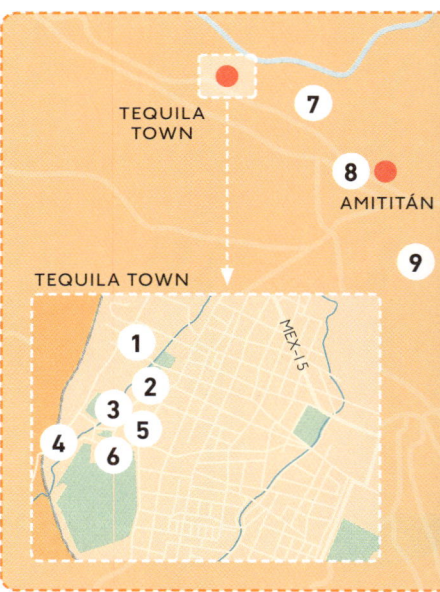

1. LA ROJEÑA
TEQUILA TOWN

2. CASA SAUZA
TEQUILA TOWN

3. EL LLANO
TEQUILA TOWN

4. TEQUILA ORENDAIN
TEQUILA TOWN

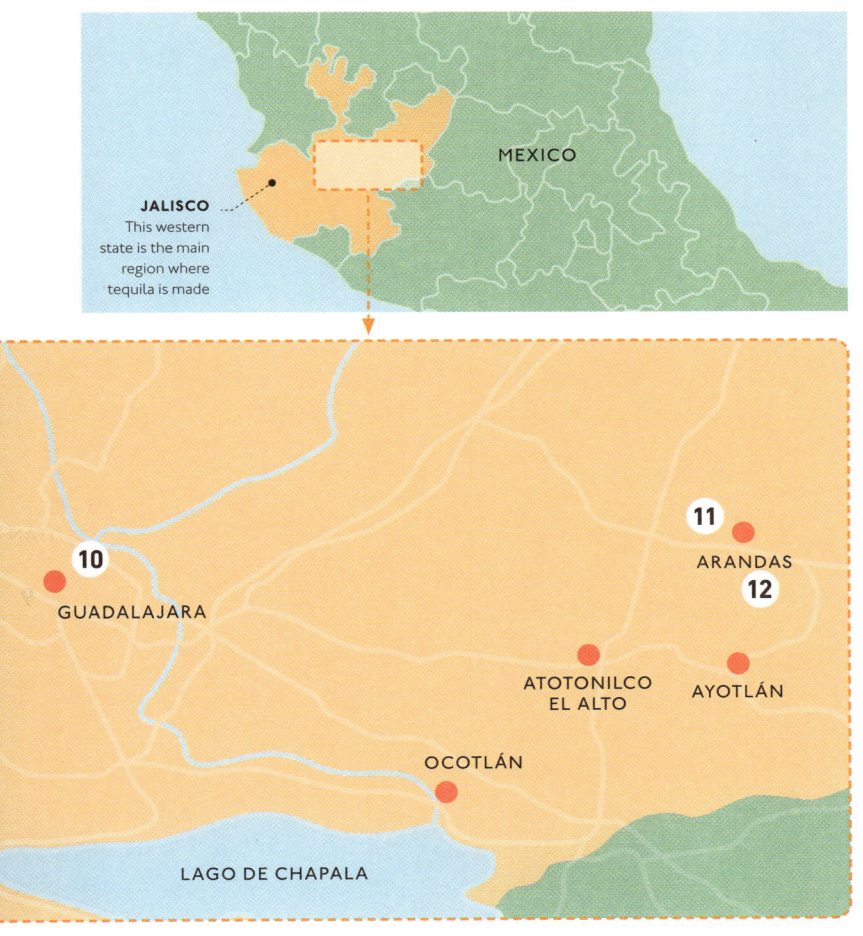

JALISCO
This western state is the main region where tequila is made

MEXICO

10 GUADALAJARA

11 ARANDAS
12

ATOTONILCO EL ALTO

AYOTLÁN

OCOTLÁN

LAGO DE CHAPALA

TEQUILA TOWN HIGHLIGHTS

LA CAPILLA This iconic bar (see p54) is the place to go for a Batanga (see pp190–91) for a truly authentic experience of Tequila town cocktail culture.

CHICHARRÓNES These traditional pork rind snacks are often sold from carts on the pavement and are served in a bag with spicy salsa. They're perfect for soaking up tequila!

CANTARITO People often walk around town drinking out of clay cups. These are Cantarito cocktails (see pp192–93) and are very popular with Mexicans.

DANZA DE LOS VOLADORES (DANCE OF THE FLYERS) This Mesoamerican ritual, in which costumed performers descend on ropes from a 30m (100ft) pole, takes place in the Plaza Principal. It's thought that it was originally a ceremony to call on the gods for rain in a drought.

NATIONAL MUSEUM OF TEQUILA The Museo Nacional de Tequila (MUNAT) is a good place to start on a journey in tequila history and education.

5. EL TEQUILEÑO
TEQUILA TOWN

6. TEQUILA FORTALEZA
TEQUILA TOWN

7. ATANASIO
SAN PEDRO DE LOS LANDEROS

8. HERRADURA
AMITITÁN

9. VOLCAN DE MI TERRA
HUAXTLA

10. TEQUILA CASCAHUÍN
EL ARENAL

11. LOS ALAMBIQUES
ARANDAS

12. EL PANDILLO
JESÚS MARIA

THE HISTORY
OF
TEQUILA

THE STORY OF HOW TEQUILA came to be is as complex as the spirit itself. From an Aztec goddess and the Spanish invasion, to a constantly shifting boom-and-bust cycle and a 21st-century resurgence, tequila encapsulates hundreds of years of sociological, political, and cultural change, all leading to the bottle on your table. In this section, you'll discover tequila's beginnings as a *vino de mezcal*, and how new distillation techniques, export abilities, and the necessities of war shaped the use of agave by the Indigenous people of Mexico into tequila. We'll also look at changes in more recent years, from the people who make tequila to those who serve it in bars around the world – they are all intertwined in the history of what we know as tequila today.

PULQUE AND THE LEGACY OF MAYAHUEL

How did a fermented agave sap drink set the foundations for tequila? The origins of tequila are intrinsically linked to Mexico's Indigenous people, and it's important to set this distilled agave spirit in the context of their lives, culture, and experiences.

THE STORY OF *PULQUE*

The story begins with *pulque* and its cultivation by the Aztecs in the Mesoamerican era, before the arrival of the Spanish (see pp42–43). This story gives us an idea of where using agaves to make drinks may have originated before the introduction of distillation. Made from fermented agave, *pulque* is often misconceived as the original tequila (or mezcal). While it is certainly a precursor of sorts, *pulque* is a drink entirely of its own merits.

The first documentation of *pulque* appeared in a mural from 200 CE (see below). It is made using *aguamiel* (honey water, or agave sap), which is tapped from *pulqueros* (agaves) and fermented naturally to produce a milky drink of about 4%–5% ABV.

In daily Aztec life, *pulque* was mainly used by priests in religious rituals and in sacrificial ceremonies. Over time, it was served in *pulquerías* where men (women were prohibited) would debate politics and put the world to rights.

In their book *Agave Spirits*, Gary Nabhan and David Suro Piñera write of *pulque* being a "prehistoric powerhouse" when it comes to the agricultural push of agaves.

MURAL OF *LOS BEBEDORES*
Los bebedores, or *The Drinkers*, is a large pre-Hispanic mural discovered in 1969 at the Great Pyramid of Cholula, near Puebla. Dating from 200 CE, it depicts a feast with revellers drinking what is most likely *pulque*.

MAYAHUEL
In the *Codex Borgia*, the goddess Mayahuel is depicted emerging from a *maguey* plant.

Pulque may have been eclipsed by its distilled counterparts in the 21st century, but even as recently as the mid-20th century, the people of Mexico drank *pulque* in its hundreds of litres per year.

Comiteco (distilled *pulque*) has been made since the 16th century. It is mooted to be a drink artisanal producers are interested in making, given the rise in international enthusiasm for agave spirits.

Pulque as a fermented drink is also enjoying a resurgence and being celebrated in Mexican bars such as Tlecān in Mexico City, which uses it to make an incredibly moreish Pulque Colada – a twist on the tropical rum-based classic.

PULQUE PITCHER
Today, *pulque* is served in a variety of vessels, including ceramic jugs, or *jarras*, such as this one.

THE LEGEND OF MAYAHUEL

Pulque is also intrinsic to the legend of Mayahuel, a goddess associated with the *maguey* (agave) and often spoken about or referenced in the history of agave-based drinks, including tequila. There are many different versions of her story, perhaps most prevalent being that she fell in love with a human and bore his 400 rabbit children, which she fed with *pulque* from her 400 breasts. Also seen as a goddess of fertility, her story represents the importance that was placed on the sacred agave plant and its ability to clone itself and provide for its people.

Depictions of Mayahuel can be found throughout history, including drawings, statues, and carvings. These include the *Codex Borgia*, a pre-Columbian 16th-century pictorial manuscript, and a carving in the Templo Mayor in Mexico City.

PULQUE IS INTRINSIC TO THE LEGEND OF MAYAHUEL.

THE SPANISH INVASION

The year 1519, when the Spanish invaded Mesoamerica, marks a pivotal moment in the history of tequila. It set in motion a change in alcohol production, eschewing traditional practices, and the advent of what we now know as tequila.

THE FALL OF THE EMPIRE

In the early 16th century, the Aztec Empire ruled over most of present-day Mexico. Led by the Spanish conquistador Hernán Cortés and aided by political rivals of the Aztec ruler Cuauhtémoc, the conquest of the Aztec Empire began with the fall of the capital, Tenochtitlán, in 1521. The Spanish conquerors established Mexico City on its ruins. Nearly a decade later, and the conquest of the town of Tequila in Jalisco and then the securing of the city Guadalajara began the Spanish intervention on alcohol production.

COMMERCIAL CHANGES

Recent evidence indicates that distillation for ritual drinks existed before the Spanish arrived, perhaps as early as 600 BCE, but the Spanish quickly put steps in place to accelerate the commercial production of distilled drinks.

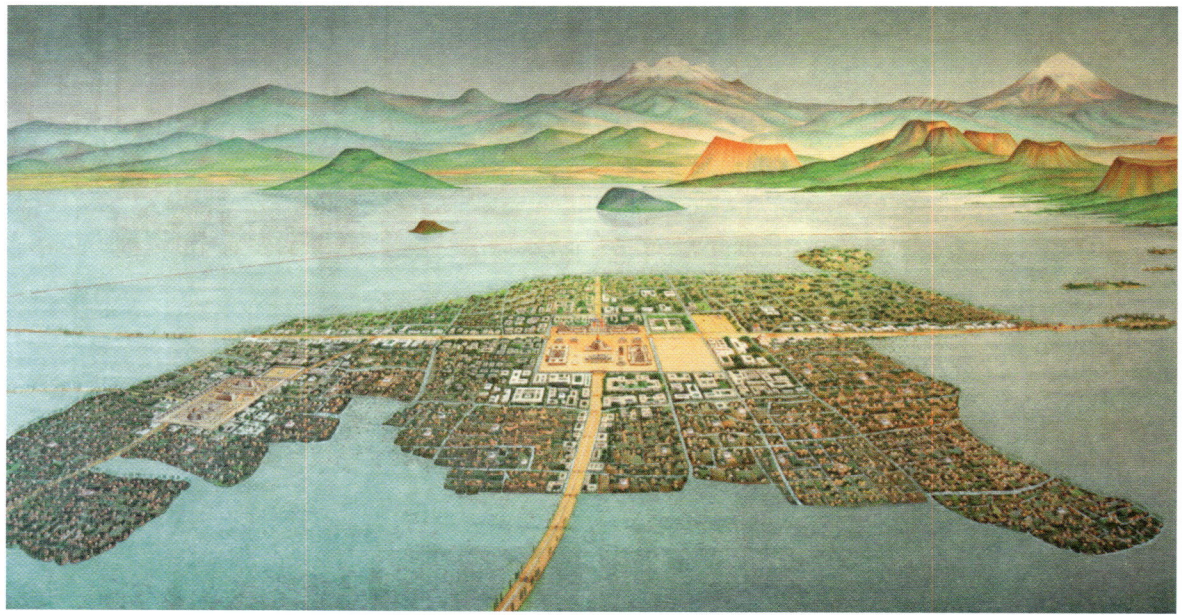

TENOCHTITLÁN AND LAKE TEXCOCO
A painting from about 1519 depicts the Aztec capital city of Tenochtitlán and Lake Texcoco. The city fell to the Spanish conquistadors under Hernán Cortés in 1521, who built Mexico City on its ruins and later drained the lake.

CASA SAUZA MOSAIC
A 30m (98ft) Venetian mosaic by Mexican artist José María Servín depicts the history of tequila at the Casa Sauza distillery in Tequila, Jalisco.

Initially, it's thought that the Spanish distilled agave in mud stills to quench their thirst for brandy. But the first big step was opening trade routes to colonies in Asia and America. Filipino migrants introduced stills more reminiscent of what we know today, and began distilling agaves into what was called *vino de mezcal* (see p84). By the early 1600s, the first distillery of scale was established in Tequila.

TIDAL CHANGE

By the mid-1700s, production was considerably ramped up. José María Guadalupe de Cuervo was given formal permission to start making *vino de mezcal* commercially by the Spanish King Carlos IV, having made the product since 1758. The Sauza family quickly followed, and were most likely joined by lesser-known, smaller, but by no means less pioneering makers (see pp44–45).

The next 70 years represented more change for tequila. The Mexican War of Independence (1810–21) threw production into flux as exports were compromised. But with the securing of Mexico's independence, *vino de mezcal* became more popular than ever and began its association with the word "tequila".

PRE-HISPANIC DISTILLATION

When talking about tequila, it's important to remember that Indigenous people's ways of working, culture, and production form the roots of this Mexican spirit. While the Spanish may have brought with them the formalization of the category, there is increasing new evidence that distilled drinks existed in pre-Hispanic Mexico. As with many colonized countries, its people get lost in the story.

LEADERS, THEN AND NOW

In the past 200 or so years, members of famous founding families and others have laid down and secured tequila's success, putting it firmly on the world stage.

THE ROLE OF THE LEADER

In the late 20th and 21st centuries, leaders in the tequila industry were laying down some of the fundamental principles of the spirit as we know it today, while cementing its place as one of the great international spirits.

While the history of tequila is dominated by men, it's worth noting that women's properties were often taken over or run by their husbands.

IN THE BEGINNING

- **Don Pedro Sánchez de Tagle**, known as the "Father of Tequila", was the first person to mass-produce tequila, in the 1600s.
- In 1795, **José María Guadalupe de Cuervo** was the first person licensed to produce and distribute tequila commercially.

PUTTING DOWN ROOTS

- **Eduardo Orendain González** acquired the Fabrica El Llano facility in 1926, while in 1944, his wife, **Mercedes Hernández Montaño de Orendain**, acquired La Mexicana property from **Don Cenobio Sauza**. In 1959, Eduardo became the founder and first president of the National Chamber of the Tequila Industry and had a role in founding the Tequila Regulatory Council (CRT) in 1994.
- **Don Francisco Javier Sauza** was the leading voice in securing tequila's denomination of origin (DO) in 1974.

MODERN MOVERS

- Known as the tequila ambassador, **Tomas Estes** brought tequila to Europe with his bar Café Pacifico (see pp54–55), while also championing *terroir* with his brand Tequila Ocho. His son, **Jesse Estes**, continues his father's legacy and has become one of tequila's most valued and educational voices.
- **Felipe Camarena**, founder of El Pandillo distillery, is a true innovator while still using traditional techniques.
- **Guillermo Sauza** founded Fortaleza in 2005 and is a true champion of tradition.
- **Bertha González Nieves**, the "First Lady of Tequila", is said to be the first *maestra tequilera* to be certified and is also CEO of Casa Dragones (see p50).

A TEQUILA TIMELINE

The businesses of two of tequila's most famous founding families – Cuervo and Sauza – have been running side by side with each other for the last two and a half centuries.

1888

JESÚS FLORES marries ANA GONZÁLEZ RUBIO, who takes over La Rojeña when Jesús dies

1964

JUAN BECKMANN'S nephew, JUAN BECKMANN GALLARDO, takes over Cuervo management

1970

JUAN ANTONIO SALLES joins El Tequileño

1758
JOSÉ ANTONIO DE CUERVO plants agaves

1795
JOSÉ MARÍA GUADALUPE DE CUERVO is granted the first licence to produce and distribute tequila

1805
JOSÉ IGNACIO FAUSTINO and MARÍA MAGDALENA DE CUERVO: siblings inherit Tequila Cuervo La Rojeña

1815
VINCENTE ALBINO ROJAS marries MARÍA MAGDALENA DE CUERVO and takes over the properties

1873
DON ELADIO SAUZA founds La Constancia distillery. DON CENOBIO SAUZA founds La Antigua Cruz (later La Perseverancia) distillery and Tequila Sauza is born

1870
DON CENOBIO SAUZA leases La Gallardeña distillery from LÁZARO GALLARDO

1860
JESÚS FLORES takes control of La Rojeña

1858
DON CENOBIO SAUZA finds employment in the tequila distillery of JOSÉ ANTONIO DE CUERVO

1900
ANA GONZÁLEZ RUBIO marries La Constancia master distiller, JOSÉ CUERVO LABASTIDA. He changes the name of the distillery to Jose Cuervo

1909
DON ELADIO SAUZA takes over the family business and industrializes Sauza

1914
ANA GONZÁLEZ RUBIO'S sister, VIRGINIA GALLARDO, marries JUAN BECKMANN, German consul in Guadalajara

1927
MARÍA ELENA "NINA" GUTIERREZ SALCEDO, a Cuervo cousin, marries DON FRANCISCO JAVIER SAUZA

1959
DON JORGE SALLES CUERVO, a great nephew of JOSÉ CUERVO, founds El Tequileño at La Guarreña distillery

1946
DON FRANCISCO JAVIER SAUZA inherits La Constancia

1943
DON FRANCISCO JAVIER SAUZA takes the Sauza helm and subsequently creates Hornitos tequila brand

1940
ANA GONZÁLEZ RUBIO dies and Tequila Jose Cuervo and La Rojeña distillery pass to her niece, GUADALUPE GALLARDO Y GONZÁLEZ RUBIO

1973
DON FRANCISCO JAVIER SAUZA creates the Tres Generaciones brand

1999
GUILLERMO SAUZA inherits land and a small distillery

2005
GUILLERMO SAUZA begins building and founds Destilería La Fortaleza. JORGE ANTONIO "TONY" SALLES joins El Tequileño

2008
JORGE ANTONIO "TONY" SALLES becomes manager and master distiller for El Tequileño

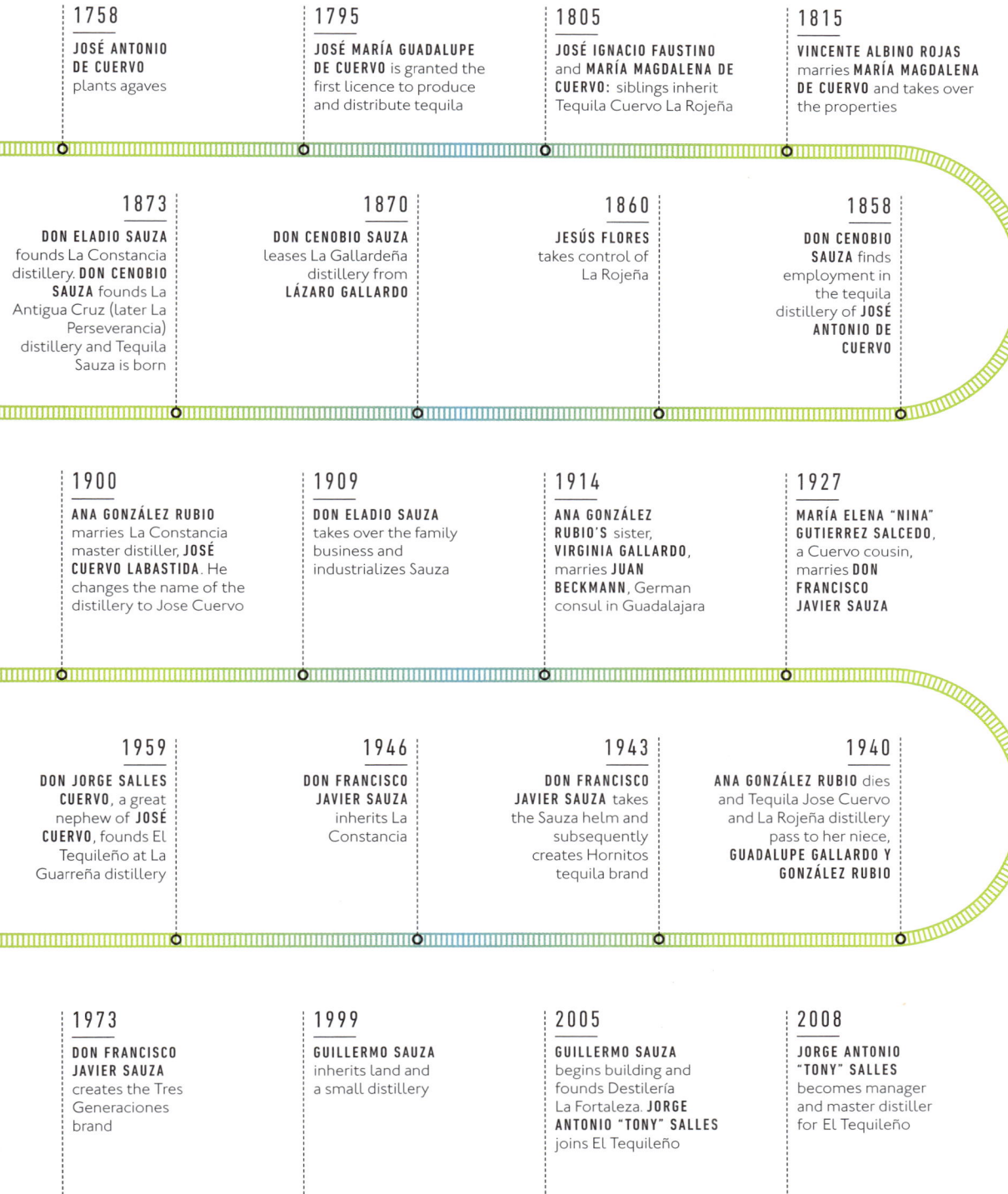

THE TEQUILA BOOM (AND BUST)

A familiar pattern for many spirits categories, the boom-and-bust cycle didn't spare tequila, and the 20th century marked plenty of ups and downs for our hero agave spirit.

20TH CENTURY

While the late 18th and 19th centuries marked the beginning of the tequila industry as we know it, the 20th century tested its resilience. Revolution, Prohibition, world wars, the Olympics, and even the Rolling Stones: over the course of 100 or so years, we saw tequila yo-yo in popularity and availability, which was marked in nearly every decade of the century.

Whether in or out of its control, the tequila industry spent the best

TEQUILA IN THE 20TH CENTURY TIMELINE

EARLY 20TH CENTURY

The beginning of the Mexican Revolution (1910–20) marks a development in Mexico's national pride. During turbulent times, Mexicans begin to turn to tequila as a drink of choice. World War I (1914–18) rages in Europe. In 1917, when the US enters the war, American soldiers stationed on the border of Mexico begin drinking tequila in local bars.

1920s AND 30s

Prohibition (1920–33) takes hold in the US, and Americans buy tequila over the border in Mexico, where it is more readily available and cheaper. The Great Depression (1929–39) signals a huge slump in the tequila industry, with a large number of distilleries closing. It also coincides with the end of Prohibition, which had boosted tequila's popularity.

1940s AND 50s

World War II (1939–45) sees a surge in demand for tequila. Exports increase from 21,000 litres (4,620 gallons) in 1941 to 4.5 million litres (990,000 gallons) by 1946. This, however, is followed by a huge slump when the war ends. While tourism to Mexico rises in the 1950s, agave supply diminishes.

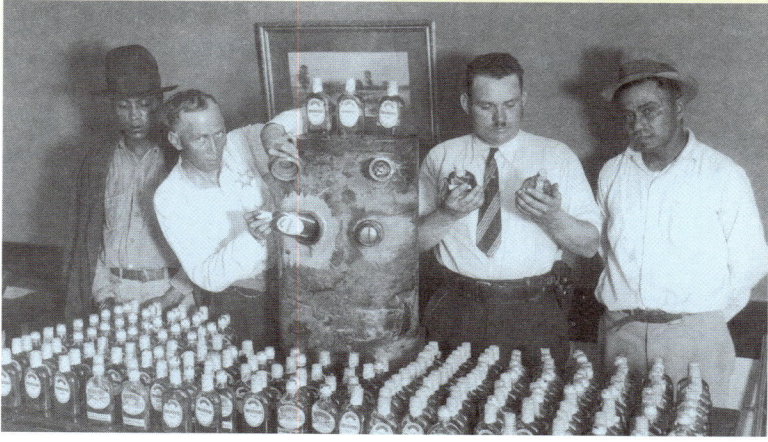

LOS TEQUILEROS
Los Tequileros smuggled tequila into the US from Mexico during the Prohibition era. Here, two Prohibition agents (in the centre) inspect a fuel tank that contained 250 bottles of tequila smuggled into the US in about 1930.

part of those 100 years navigating the ever-changing landscape it found itself in. Politics, economics, and social change all had a domino effect on the businesses that sustained the category.

Cocktail culture also had an impact on tequila, and some of the spirit's best-known cocktails were invented during this time.

ADVERTS CATCH ON
A magazine advert from the 1960s promotes Jose Cuervo Tequila. The 1960s, 70s, 80s, and 90s saw brands really dig into their advertising budgets.

1960s AND 70s

The Olympics in Mexico in 1968 marks a time of booming sales for tequila brands. Popular culture has an impact on the notoriety of tequila, as the Rolling Stones unofficially call their 1972 tour the Tequila Sunrise tour, having fallen in love with the cocktail on the road.

1980s

The 1980s see a rise in advertising and a steady growth in tequila consumption for some of the big-name brands. However, the Mexican economic crisis soon takes hold and sees sales take a nosedive as a result.

1990s

Despite continued interest and the emergence of tequila bars, this decade sees agave shortages hit the industry, both from underplanting as well as disease, which wipes out just over a quarter of the crop. The devaluation of the Mexican peso in 1994 leads to a currency crisis, informally dubbed the Tequila Crisis.

MEXICO OLYMPICS
The 1968 Summer Olympics, held in Mexico City, were the first Olympic Games to be hosted by a Latin American country.

THE 1980s
SEE A STEADY
GROWTH IN
TEQUILA
CONSUMPTION.

21ST-CENTURY RENAISSANCE

Mexico's cool factor, celebrity endorsements, and the rise of the Margarita have all contributed to the incredible ascent of tequila's popularity in the 21st century.

TRENDY TEQUILA

It's safe to say that the 21st century has seen tequila's popularity grow at a very healthy pace. Despite rumblings of a tequila crisis in 2000 and on other occasions, when demand for agaves outstripped supply, sales of the spirit and its popularity, not only among bartenders but also drinkers, burgeoned in the first decades of the century.

By 2024 in the UK alone, tequila's volume sales had risen by 83 per cent compared to pre-Covid levels, and according to the Wine and Spirit Trade Association, were up 94 per cent in value.

In its largest market, the US, tequila is set to overtake vodka – the biggest-selling spirit – in value. Premium and luxury tequilas – driven by desire for 100 per cent agave products – are having a moment and boosting tequila's dominance on the overall spirits sales landscape. According to Statista, in 2004, 8.7 million 9-litre (2-gallon) cases were sold in the US; in 2023, that had risen to 31.6 million 9-litre cases sold.

Exports started to rise in volume in 2009 and have been steadily bringing tequila to more markets around the world. So, what's driving drinkers so nuts for tequila?

THANK THE MARGARITA

It cannot be overestimated how much the Margarita, tequila's most popular cocktail, has done for the spirit's rapid rise to fame. It dances quite comfortably in the top 10 of many of the most popular cocktail lists, and increasingly it makes the top three. It was the best-selling cocktail in 2023 according to data by marketing research company NielsenIQ.

STAR POWER

Bars have clearly embraced tequila, and in 2024, *CLASS* magazine reported it at number two (behind gin) in its top 10 best-selling spirits in UK bars. But it's not just the biggest-selling brands that dominate the bar. In fact, Ocho, Fortaleza, and Tapatio were the top

RISE IN TEQUILA SALES

In 2004, 8.7 million 9-litre (2-gallon) cases were sold in the US; in 2023, sales had risen to 31.6 million 9-litre cases.

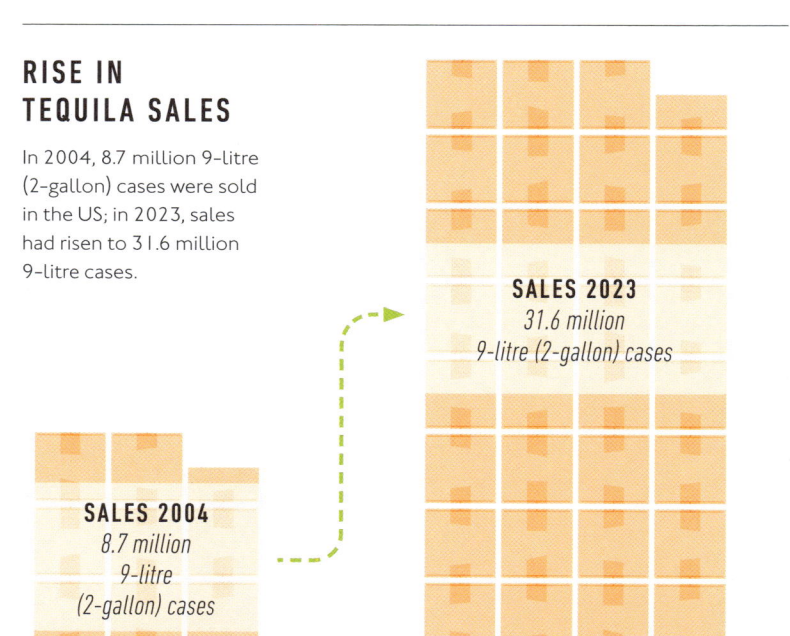

SALES 2023
*31.6 million
9-litre (2-gallon) cases*

SALES 2004
*8.7 million
9-litre
(2-gallon) cases*

EXPORTS STARTED TO RISE IN 2009 AND HAVE BEEN STEADILY BRINGING TEQUILA TO MORE GLOBAL MARKETS.

TOP TEN

CLASS magazine reported tequila as number two in its top-10 best-selling spirits in UK bars, after gin and before vodka.

VODKA

TEQUILA

GIN

MODERN MEXICO

Mexico is enjoying a surge in popularity worldwide, not just in tourism but also in its culture, with its food, drink, fashion, and film being celebrated.

Chefs such as Santiago Lastra are bringing the best of Mexican cuisine to London, while the film *Coco* (2017), inspired by the Mexican Day of the Dead, won two Academy Awards in 2018.

Mexico Fashion Week is said to be rivalling the Big Four – New York, London, Milan, and Paris.

Time Out magazine named Mexico City as the best city in the world for culture in 2023. In 2024, Handshake Speakeasy cocktail bar in the capital was awarded the best bar in North America and the world's best bar by the brand 50 Best. The country's star has never been brighter.

three favourites among bartenders. No doubt the Margarita's popularity has helped boost tequila's profile.

The resurgence of tequila and its popularity with consumers can also be aligned with the increasing adoption of the spirit by celebrities. George Clooney, Kendall Jenner, Dwayne "The Rock" Johnson, AC/DC, Rita Ora… the list of celebrities putting their name to

tequila is ever growing. Data from global drinks market researcher IWSR shows that, in 2022, the tequila annual growth rate was 13 per cent, while celebrity tequilas grew by 40 per cent.

Having famous faces associated with the category makes demand and sales skyrocket, but that does come with some issues too (see p96).

TRADE TARIFFS

At the time of writing, it's unclear what impact the United States' imposition of trade tariffs on Mexico will have on tequila exports to the US, which is the largest export market for tequila.

THE CHANGING FACE OF TEQUILA

From farming and distilling to education, women are now more part of the tequila conversation than ever before in what has traditionally been a male-dominated industry.

MASTER DISTILLER
Bertha González Nieves is the co-founder and CEO of Casa Dragones and a *maestra tequilera*.

LEADING THE CHARGE

While the term "*maestro tequilero*" (male master distiller) is widely recognized, "*maestra tequilera*" (female master distiller) is appearing more often. Said to be the first female master distiller in tequila, Bertha González Nieves of Casa Dragones, who is also the brand's founder and CEO, has set an example for women looking to work at the top of the industry.

Other pioneers are María Teresa Lara at Herradura, who was master distiller before she retired in 2017, and Alejandra Pelayo of Casa del Sol, who oversees production at the distillery.

SKIN IN THE GAME

There are more women-owned tequila brands on the market now than ever before. American Tiffany Capri Hainesworth became the first Black woman to solely own a tequila brand when she founded TCapri in 2019. Three American women are at the helm of 1953 Tequila – Shivam Mallick Shah, Lindsey Davis Stover, and Alison Kiehl Friedman – while French biochemist and engineer Sophie Decobecq became owner, founder, and maker of Calle 23 in 2003.

MEN'S WORK?

Farmed by men, made by men, and owned by men, historically, there has been little space for women to thrive in the tequila industry. But the tide is slowly turning: Cazcabel's new £37 million distillery has committed to making women 50 per cent of its 500 hacienda staff. And as more and more women make their mark on the category, the future of tequila's workforce and ownership is looking much more in balance.

Traditionally passed down from father to son, the job of a *jimador* is hard physical labour and has always been dominated by men. But Leticia Hermosillo Ravelero of Cava de Oro showed that things may be changing. She and her husband began farming agaves in the 1990s, and she remains one of the few women visibly doing this job. Today, there is more scope for women to take up the role, particularly as younger male *jimador* heirs are becoming less interested in the work.

THERE ARE MORE WOMEN-OWNED TEQUILA BRANDS ON THE MARKET THAN EVER BEFORE.

TEQUILA EDUCATION

When it comes to spreading the tequila message, from tastings to academies, women are at the forefront of education. Canadian-born agave expert Megs Miller and her partner, Sofia Barrera, who was born in Mexico City, teach all things agave from their Salón de Agave tasting room in Mexico City.

Mexican Ana María Romero Mena, one of the first official *catadores* of tequila (similar to a sommelier), has spent her career learning about and educating consumers on the category.

Sonia Espínola de la Llave was the first woman recognized by the National Chamber of the Tequila Industry and is one of tequila's best orators.

LEYENDA DE MÉXICO

When Melly Barajas founded her Leyenda de México tequila brand in 1999, it was, and still is, the only tequila brand owned and operated solely by women. With Barajas as the brand's master distiller, she hires women from all walks of life, from single mothers to grandmothers, to work at her distillery in the town of Valle de Guadalupe, Jalisco. It's no wonder she's known as the "Queen of Tequila".

WOMEN'S WORK
All the different roles involved in making tequila are performed by women at Leyenda de México, from harvesting the agaves, shown here, to distilling, tasting, and bottling.

TEQUILA IN MEXICAN CULTURE

Like many spirits, tequila has a wonderful way of bringing people together. It plays its part in some of Mexico's most important celebrations, and national festivals see tequila take a starring role.

CELEBRATIONS AND GATHERINGS

Food and drink play a large role in many of Mexico's celebrations and gatherings, and tequila is no exception. International Margarita Day is celebrated on 22 February, World Paloma Day on 22 May, and International Tequila Day on 24 July. From *lucha libre* wrestling matches, to weddings, baptisms, *quinceañeras* (girls' 15th birthday), and Christmas, tequila is never far from celebrating a good time.

HONOURING THE DEAD

Día de los Muertos (Day of the Dead), held on 1 and 2 November, is a time not to mourn but to celebrate the return of the dead. People set out offerings and altars in homes and public places, with photographs, sugar skulls, *pan de muerto* (sweet bread), *papel picado* (cut tissue paper) decorations, and *cempasúchils* (marigolds) to remember loved ones who have died. People often pour tequila into *copitas* as an offering to the spirits of the dead.

DAY OF THE DEAD
A memorial altar for the Day of the Dead includes a handicraft skull, marigolds, fruit, and offerings to the Virgin Mary.

TEQUILA PLAYS A ROLE IN THE RITUAL OF DRINKING LA BANDERA TO REPRESENT THE MEXICAN FLAG.

LA BANDERA
Mexicans drink La Bandera shots to celebrate Mexico's independence.

CELEBRATING MEXICO'S INDEPENDENCE

Mexico's independence from Spanish rule in 1821 is commemorated on 16 September every year, when Mexicans celebrate El Grito de Dolores (The Cry of Dolores), which marked the end of the 300-year rule. More celebrated than Cinco de Mayo, this day is a public holiday and full of festivities. Tequila plays a role in the ritual of drinking La Bandera (see p215) to represent the Mexican flag: lime juice for green, *blanco* tequila for white, and Sangrita for red.

MARIACHI MUSIC
Mariachi music features stringed and brass instruments. Here, a band plays in about 1950.

MUSIC AND TEQUILA

Tequila and mariachi music are inextricably linked, and Jalisco is said to be one of the areas where this traditional style of music, dating back to the 18th century, first originated.

Band members wear special outfits called *charros* and play instruments including violins, trumpets, guitars, and *guitarrónes* (six-string bass guitars). Lyrics and entire songs can be dedicated to tequila, and mariachi bands often play in *cantinas* and restaurants, like Cantina La Fuente in Guadalajara.

HOLY SPIRIT

Religion is an important part of daily life in Mexico, and almost 80 per cent of the population are Roman Catholic. Some tequila distilleries even have their own places of worship. The historic grounds of Casa Sauza are home to a small hexagonal chapel, and Hacienda Patrón built a chapel in honour of the Virgin of Guadalupe, which has been blessed by Pope Francis. Tequila town's most famous bar, La Capilla (see p54), translates as The Chapel, said to be because of its location near a small chapel.

TEQUILA BARS AROUND THE WORLD

Bars and their tenders have played an instrumental role in how tequila has become popularized all over the world. Here we pay homage to some of the best establishments to champion tequila across the globe.

FIVE OF THE BEST

These are some of the best-known establishments, old and new, for enjoying tequila neat or in cocktails.

LA CAPILLA
TEQUILA, MEXICO

A trip to Tequila town is not complete without a visit to the famous La Capilla. The oldest bar in this historic town, and opened by Javier Delgado Corona (aka Don Javier) in 1940, the walls of this characterful bar pay homage to the people who've been drinking in it for the last 85 years. It is also the official birthplace of one of tequila's most famous cocktails, the Batanga (see pp190–91).

CAFÉ PACIFICO
LONDON, ENGLAND

London has Tomas Estes and Phil Bayly to thank for bringing the flavours of Mexico to the UK. In 1982, they opened Café Pacifico, a Mexican restaurant that has been pioneering tequila in London for more than 40 years. Now run by co-owner Carlos Londoño, Café

LA CAPILLA
La Capilla is the birthplace of the Batanga cocktail. Don Javier is depicted in this mural using his trademark knife to mix ingredients.

CAFÉ PACIFICO
In 2024, Café Pacifico won the prestigious Timeless International Award, a category in Tales of the Cocktail Foundation's Spirited Awards.

Pacifico has never faltered in its commitment to delivering one of the world's best offerings of tequila with its award-winning Margaritas and extensive selection of bottles behind the bar. A favourite among the industry too, this is a home away from home for the tequila community.

TOMMY'S MEXICAN RESTAURANT
SAN FRANCISCO, US

If you've heard of Tommy's Margarita, then you need to pay a visit to Tommy's in San Francisco. Here, Tomas ("Tommy") and Elmy Bermejo have been serving Yucatán cuisine since they founded the restaurant in 1965. It has won multiple awards, including ones for its spirits selection. Their son, Julio Bermejo, is the man to thank for the creation of Tommy's Margarita (see p196), which is a classic in its own right, at his family's restaurant.

BARRO NEGRO
ATHENS, GREECE

Barro Negro (meaning "black clay" after the traditional Oaxacan ceramics) was Athens's first *tequilaria* when it opened in 2019. Co-founders George Kavaklis and Stelios Papadopoulos launched it to educate guests on agave spirits. Behind the bar soars a wall of bottles on display for customers to choose from, while cocktails are also a showcase of tequila's (and mezcal's) versatility. Its Paloma Embassy, in partnership with Three Cents, is a celebration of this famous cocktail (see pp202–03), while other serves combine tequila with mezcal for the full agave experience.

COA
HONG KONG

Opened in 2017 by Jay Khan, Mexican-inspired cocktail bar Coa has been no stranger to the higher echelons of best-bar lists. Named after the tool used to harvest agaves (see p63), Coa houses Hong Kong's largest collection of tequila and mezcal – about 200 bottles – and a 41-page spirits menu to boot. Be sure to order the Ancho Highball with *blanco* tequila, salted plum, ancho chilli, and guava soda, or its signature cocktail La Paloma de Oaxaca with tequila *blanco*, mezcal *joven*, lime, grapefruit soda, and worm salt (a spicy condiment made from agave worms, chillies, and sea salt).

FARMACIA RITA PÉREZ
Customers will find not only a wide range of tequilas but also other national spirits, such as *raicilla* and *sotol*, at Farmacia Rita Pérez.

THE BEST OF THE REST

Wherever you are in the world, here is a handy checklist of bars to get your tequila fix.

MEXICO

FARMACIA RITA PÉREZ, Guadalajara
A relative newbie to the Guadalajara scene, Farmacia Rita Pérez is one of the most fun spots in the city. A dive bar crossed with a *cantina*, it's full of retro knick-knacks, an extensive tequila list, and a strong repertoire of tequila cocktails, with delicious original recipes and riffs on the classics too.

OTHER MEXICAN BARS TO TRY

686 BAR, Mexico City
CANTINA LA FUENTE, Guadalajara
EL GALLO ALTANERO, Guadalajara
HANDSHAKE SPEAKEASY, Mexico City
HANKY PANKY, Mexico City
VIETNAM BAR, Guadalajara

UNITED STATES

LEYENDA, New York
Opened in 2015 by two of New York's (and the industry's) most knowledgeable bartenders, Ivy Mix and Julie Reiner, award-winning Leyenda is a pan-Latin American bar where agave takes centre stage. House classic cocktails and their agave flights are musts, alongside snacks like *chicharrónes* (fried pork rind).

OTHER US BARS TO TRY

BAKAN, Miami, Florida
EL CARMEN, Los Angeles, California
LA PIÑA, Milwaukee, Wisconsin
LAS PERLAS, Austin, Texas
MAYAHUEL, Astoria, New York
WHITE BUFFALO BAR, Marathon, Texas

EUROPE

EL CAMION, London, England
El Camion restaurant is a late-night institution. Its extensive list of Margaritas is more than solid, and it also turns out proper classic tequila cocktails and food with a fun and laidback vibe. Head downstairs and you'll find the dinky Pink Chihuahua bar for more cocktails, music, and mingling.

OTHER EUROPEAN BARS TO TRY

CALLE OCHO, Amsterdam, Netherlands
HACHA, London, England
LA PERLA, Paris, France
SIDE HUSTLE, London, England
THE BARKING DOG, Copenhagen, Denmark
THE CHUG CLUB BAR, Hamburg, Germany

CANTINA OK! IS CONSIDERED TO BE ONE OF THE BEST AGAVE BARS OUTSIDE MEXICO.

CANTINA OK!
This tiny bar describes itself as a "micro mezcal mecca" and serves an array of cocktails in addition to its legendary Margaritas.

REST OF THE WORLD

CANTINA OK!, Sydney, Australia
Laying claim to Sydney's best Margarita, Cantina OK! is considered to be one of the best agave bars outside Mexico. Hand-sourced agave spirits are presented on its incredible agave index, with tequila among the impressive range. The Margarita OK! is the cocktail to go for, but stay for the rest too.

OTHER BARS IN THE WORLD TO TRY

CAT BITE CLUB, Singapore
CATA AGAVE BAR, Tamarindo, Costa Rica
LOS ATICO, Bangkok, Thailand
MESA VERDE, Melbourne, Australia
THE TACO BAR, Beijing, China
UNA MÁS, Cape Town, South Africa

HOW IS

----- TEQUILA -----

MADE?

WHILE ALL DISTILLED SPIRITS GO through a similar process, each category has many different production nuances. Tequila remains one of the most labour-intensive and time-honoured spirits in the world, and there is still a lot about making tequila that stays true to its entrenched traditions, alongside more modern techniques. It all begins in the field, where agaves are harvested for their sugar-rich *piñas*. The *piñas* are cooked to convert the sugars for fermentation, and crushed to squeeze out the sugary juice. This liquid is left to ferment, before heading to the stills for two or sometimes more distillations. Some tequilas are aged before being blended, diluted, and bottled. So, let's get deep into each stage of the tequila-making process.

LOCATION MATTERS

Where agaves grow, where tequila is made, and local resources all impact flavour. Let's dig a little deeper into how climate change, soil, water, and local agriculture can influence the tequilas from any given distillery.

CLIMATE CHANGE

Climate change is affecting the production cycle of tequila. Generally speaking, Mexico's climate, especially in tequila-making states, is dry and warm all year round – perfect conditions for agaves, which need minimal water.

However, as the effects of climate change begin to raise average temperatures, farmers are harvesting agaves earlier because the plants reach the optimum sugar levels for making tequila at a younger age. This means the agaves spend less time in the soil, which means less time to absorb minerals, as well as less time exposed to the elements, which inevitably alters their flavour profiles for the worse.

PERFECT
pH 6–7

SOIL pH
Agaves prefer a slightly acidic to neutral soil of around 6–7 pH.

SOIL TYPE

Agaves grow best in free-draining loam soils with a pH of around 6 or 7. Farmers and their clients carefully monitor the soil in agave fields to make sure both these elements are stable so that agaves grow as healthily as possible. We've seen how *terroir* impacts the resulting flavours (see p16), and soil particularly has an effect on the flavours of the final tequila (see below).

AGAVE SOIL

Agaves grown in iron-rich highland soil produce more florality and fruit flavours, while those grown in the lowlands have more vegetal character.

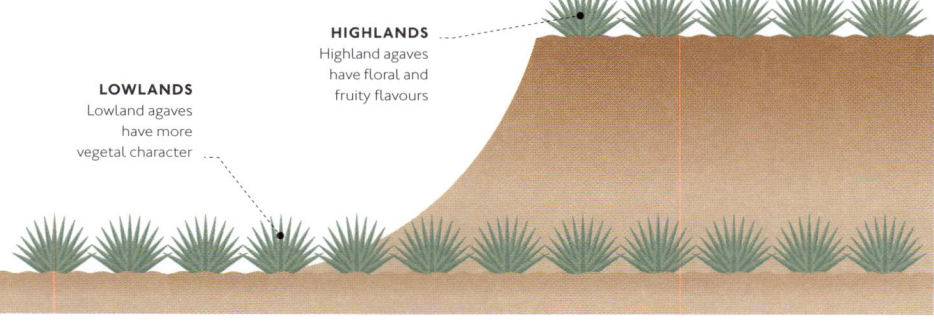

HIGHLANDS
Highland agaves have floral and fruity flavours

LOWLANDS
Lowland agaves have more vegetal character

WATER USE

The tequila industry is reliant on a clean water source, needing 15 litres (3 gallons) of water to make 1 litre (1 ¾ pints) of tequila.

1 LITRE (1 ¾ PINTS) TEQUILA

15 LITRES (3 GALLONS) WATER

THE SINGLE-RANCH APPROACH

More brands are beginning to release tequilas that are made from agaves grown on a single ranch or estate, with Tequila Ocho leading the charge in this area. Try them alongside other expressions from the same distillery, but using agaves from different estates, in order to taste the difference in the one varying factor – where the agave was grown.

TEQUILA OCHO
With its commitment to *terroir*, all Tequila Ocho's expressions are from single estates.

WATER SUPPLIES

It can take 15 litres (3 gallons) of water to make just 1 litre (1 ¾ pints) of tequila, so sourcing water is important for the production process. Water quality in Mexico is a considerable issue, with 57 per cent of the population lacking access to clean water, and droughts and scarcity common.

Distilleries have to think cleverly about where they source their water from, be it deep well water, collected rainwater, or natural spring water, particularly if they want to implement sustainable practices (see pp90–91).

WILD YEAST

The majority of tequilas are made using cultivated yeast, but when open or spontaneous fermentation is allowed to occur, the presence of wild or ambient yeast can impart tell-tale flavours on a finished tequila (see p69).

The 150-year-old mango trees near El Tequileño's distillery have had an influence on the yeast used during fermentation and on the resulting flavours. The agaves for Tequila Ocho's Los Mangos expressions grew in former mango and cherry orchards, and the expressions speak of both fruits.

HARVESTING AGAVE

We know what blue agave is, where it grows, and how it's farmed. But how do we know when it's ready to be made into tequila, and how is it unearthed from the ground?

READY TO HARVEST

Blue Weber agaves take between five and seven years to mature, so once they've reached maturity – and with monitoring from the farmers – they are ready to harvest for making tequila. Farmers who know their agave well will be able to spot the tell-tale signs that it's good to go: its leaves grow heavy, its base may change colour, the *piña* might have deep red spots, and the leaves at its centre stop growing.

Knowing the sugar content is key to when an agave is ready too.

Farmers test sugar content using an optic refractometer, which measures the agave's Brix. Brix is a scale used to measure the amount of dissolved sugars in a liquid. One degree Brix is equivalent to 1g of sucrose in 100g of solution, or 1 per cent sugar. By subtracting

THE HARVESTING PROCESS

Harvesting often takes place in the first five months of the year. Particularly proficient *jimadores* can harvest nearly 1 tonne of *piñas* per day.

COA
The *coa* is a versatile tool that helps with unearthing the agave and cutting the roots free

CUTTING THE LEAVES
Jimadores use a *coa* to cut off the leaves from the agave

1

After testing the sugar content, the *jimador* selects the agaves to be harvested.

2

The *jimador* cuts the agave from its root using a *coa*, often needing to loosen it with their foot.

3

Then the *jimador* cuts off the agave's long, spiky leaves, called *pencas*.

THE AVERAGE WEIGHT OF A *PIÑA* IS 30KG (66LB), BUT THEY CAN BE MUCH HEAVIER.

20 per cent from the Brix score, farmers obtain the amount of reductive sugar. Ideally, sugar content should be no less than 21 per cent when the agave is cut. Once the agave has been tested and is in the perfect condition, it's time to harvest.

Unlike a lot of other spirits, tequila's harvesting (*jima*) process is done by hand by *jimadores* (farmers). They undertake the backbreaking task of removing the all-important *piñas* from the blue agave plant, which contain the sugars needed for making tequila.

WHAT IS A COA?

Also known as a *coa de jima*, a *coa* is the machete-like spade that the *jimadores* use to release the agave from its roots and also to cut the leaves off.

ROUND HEAD
The round head of a *coa* has a sharp edge that facilitates cutting

SHARPENER
Jimadores sharpen the *coas* before each use

LONG HANDLE
A *coa* has a long handle like a hoe

PIÑA
The central core of the agave is known as the *piña* (Spanish for "pineapple")

TRANSPORT
The *piñas* are usually transported by lorry, but donkeys may be used in rough terrain

4

The *jimador* cuts away the leaves close to the *piña*. How closely they cut the leaves depends on the distillery and the desired final flavour.

5

The *piñas* are then transported to the distillery for the next stage of the process: cooking.

COOKING THE *PIÑAS*

Once those freshly cut *piñas* arrive at the distillery, it's time to get cooking, which marks the second stage of the tequila-making process.

WHY COOK?

When they arrive at the distillery, the delivery lorries are weighed, and receivers select *piñas* at random to test their sugar content. Next, the first stage of the cooking process is to split the *piñas*.

In their raw form, agave carbohydrates are difficult for yeasts to ferment. By cooking the *piñas*, the carbohydrates are turned into sugars that can be fermented, which is exactly what you need to make any kind of alcohol.

In modern tequila-making, there are two main ways of cooking agaves: either in *hornos de mampostería* (masonry ovens) or in autoclaves. Both methods use steam.

HORNOS

Hornos are a more traditional method of cooking, and can be made of brick, concrete, or clay. Workers stack the *piñas* inside and inject steam from the top or bottom (or both in the case of El Pandillo distillery), which cooks

the agave for anything up to three days. The bitter agave juice, or "honey" (*aguamiel*), that comes off the agave in the first few hours is discarded as it contains undesirable flavours and textures. Once the cooking has finished, the agave is left to cool down in its own juices for 6 to 12 hours.

AUTOCLAVES

Autoclaves are pressurized cookers and are much larger than *hornos*. They can complete the cooking

HORNO

A brick, clay, or concrete *horno* is the traditional way of cooking *piñas*.

INJECTED STEAM
Steam is injected into the oven from the top or bottom (or both)

OVEN WALLS
Hornos can be made of brick, as here, concrete, or clay

STACKED PIÑAS
The *piñas* are split in halves or quarters and stacked inside the oven

AUTOCLAVE

Autoclaves are pressurized cookers made of stainless steel.

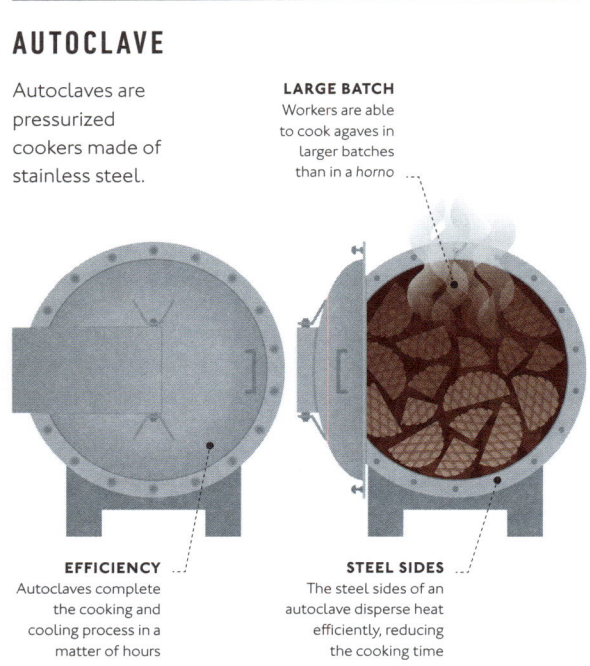

LARGE BATCH
Workers are able to cook agaves in larger batches than in a *horno*

EFFICIENCY
Autoclaves complete the cooking and cooling process in a matter of hours

STEEL SIDES
The steel sides of an autoclave disperse heat efficiently, reducing the cooking time

and cooling process as quickly as eight hours. Autoclaves can also be customized to cook more slowly. While not the preferred method for tequila purists, the autoclave is much more efficient for a huge distillery.

THE CONTROVERSY OVER DIFFUSERS

Another way of extracting sugars is the use of diffusers (see below) – a word that elicits heated debate in the tequila industry. Some people argue that the use of diffusers strips the agave of its flavour, and means that additives (see pp82–83) need to be used later to bring them back.

DID YOU KNOW?

THE WORD "MEZCAL" COMES FROM THE NAHUATL WORDS *"METL"* AND *"IXCALLI"*, WHICH MEAN "COOKED AGAVE".

WHAT DOES COOKED AGAVE TASTE LIKE?

If you visit a tequila distillery, be sure to ask to try some cooked agave. It is not only delicious, but also it will help you identify it as a flavour in the final product. Think caramelized sweet potato skins, dates, and dark honey.

HONEY   SWEET POTATO   DATES

IN MODERN TEQUILA-MAKING, THERE ARE TWO MAIN WAYS OF COOKING AGAVES.

DIFFUSER

Distillery workers shred the uncooked *piñas*, and then add water and sometimes acids to extract the juice, which is then cooked.

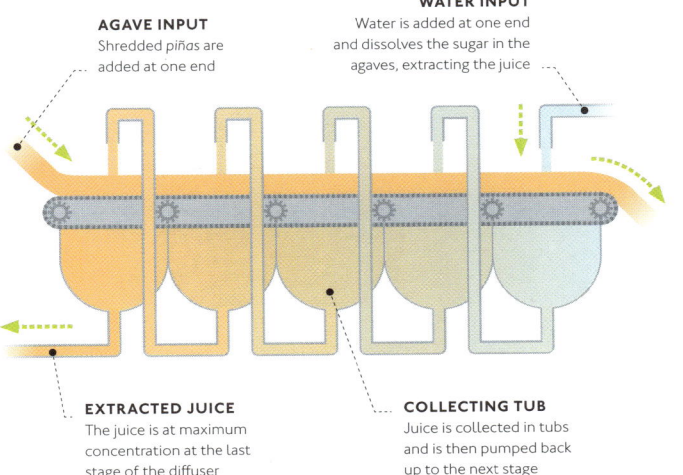

AGAVE INPUT
Shredded *piñas* are added at one end

WATER INPUT
Water is added at one end and dissolves the sugar in the agaves, extracting the juice

EXTRACTED JUICE
The juice is at maximum concentration at the last stage of the diffuser

COLLECTING TUB
Juice is collected in tubs and is then pumped back up to the next stage

CRUSHING OR MILLING THE *PIÑAS*

Once the cooking and cooling process is complete, tequila makers crush or mill the *piñas* to extract the juice from the agave fibres to prepare it for fermentation.

TAHONAS AND ROLLER MILLS

The oldest method of extracting juice from the *piñas* is pounding the agave in a small sunken hole in the ground with a hand mallet. These days, however, there are two main ways tequila makers do this: the *tahona* or roller mill. Of course, if they've used a diffuser, this process has already been done (see p65).

A *tahona* is a large, heavy, volcanic stone wheel that can weigh as much as 2 tonnes. Before modern technology, these wheels were pulled around a circular pit by donkeys. The weight of the wheel on top of the cooked agave separates the fibres and the juice. These days, *tahonas* are motorized or pulled using tractors. They are the most time-consuming way of crushing the *piñas*.

Roller mills or milling machines are a more efficient method, in which the cooked agaves run through a series of rollers, extracting the juice along the way.

TAHONA

Today, *tahonas* are motorized or pulled by tractors to crush the *piñas* in the pit below.

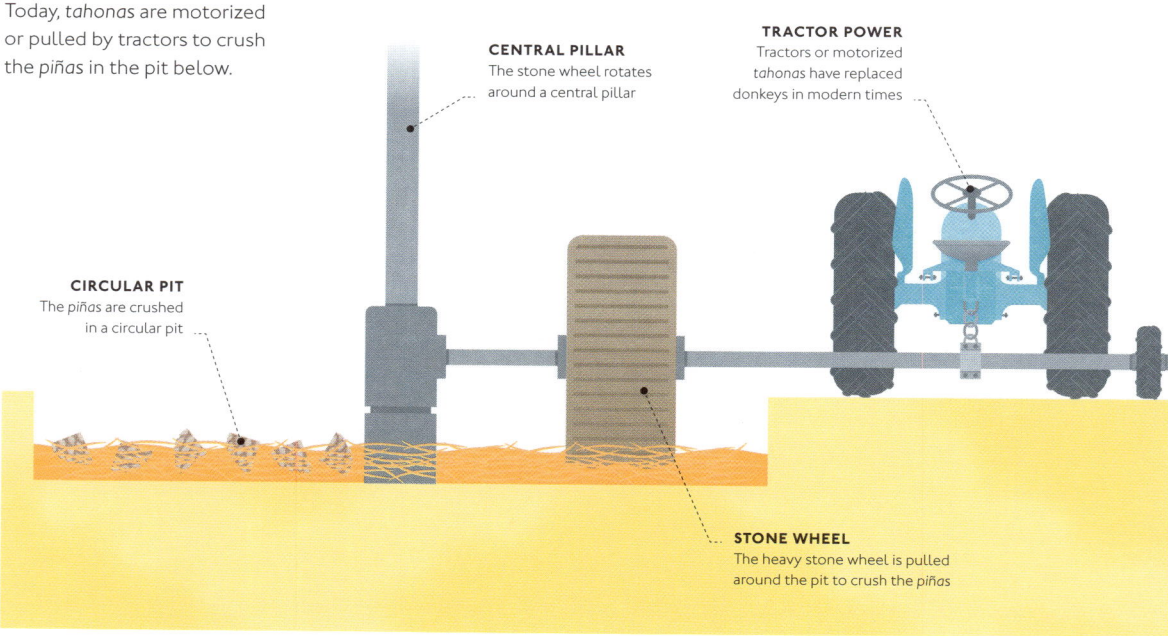

CENTRAL PILLAR
The stone wheel rotates around a central pillar

TRACTOR POWER
Tractors or motorized *tahonas* have replaced donkeys in modern times

CIRCULAR PIT
The *piñas* are crushed in a circular pit

STONE WHEEL
The heavy stone wheel is pulled around the pit to crush the *piñas*

TAHONAS AND ROLLER MILLS HAVE A DIRECT IMPACT ON THE FLAVOUR OF THE FINAL TEQUILA.

Water is also injected to help rinse the fibres and release more sugars.

Distilleries have also adopted their own ways of completing the process. Famously, El Pandillo's Felipe Camarena made a 9,070kg (20,000lb) motorized roller using reclaimed scrap, which is fondly called Felipestein and is quite a sight to behold.

THE PROOF IS IN THE JUICE

Depending on the method used, *tahonas* and roller mills have a direct impact on the flavour of the tequila. *Tahonas* tend to lend more earthy characteristics, as the sugary liquid from the cooked *piñas* (*mosto*) interacts with the fibres (*bagasse*). Roller-milled agave is more fruity and floral, as the fibres are separated from the *mosto*.

Some distilleries release bottles that showcase the flavour achieved by one of these methods, such as Cascahuín Blanco Tahona (see p173). Others use both methods and blend them in the final expression, such as, famously, Patrón Silver (see p152).

ROLLER MILL

The steel blades of a roller mill can crush agaves at great speed.

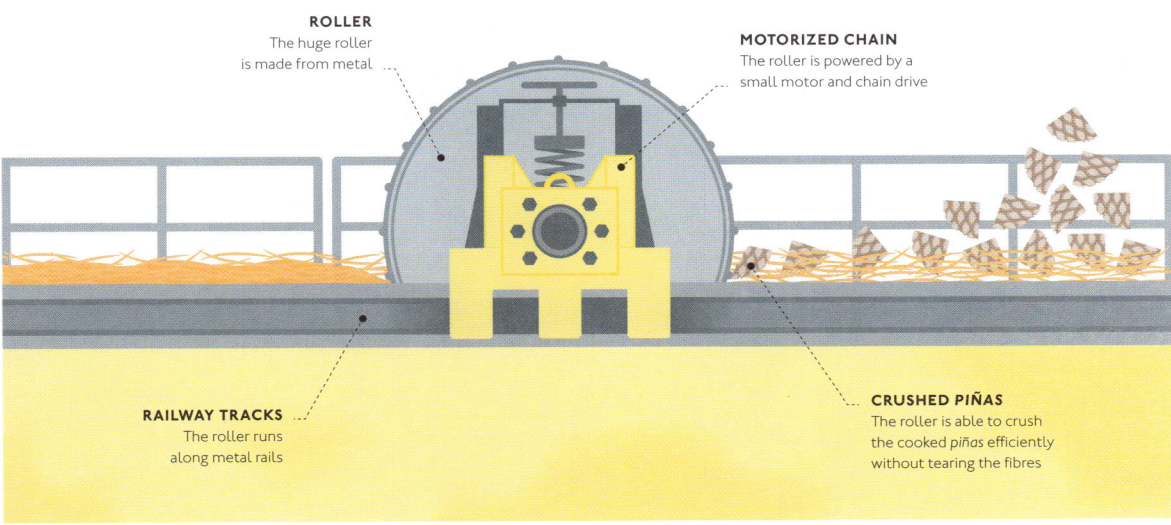

ROLLER
The huge roller is made from metal

MOTORIZED CHAIN
The roller is powered by a small motor and chain drive

RAILWAY TRACKS
The roller runs along metal rails

CRUSHED PIÑAS
The roller is able to crush the cooked *piñas* efficiently without tearing the fibres

THE MAGIC OF FERMENTATION

The flavours we love in our tequilas begin to form here, in the magical chemical reaction of fermentation.

FERMENTATION TANK
Fermentation creates heat and carbon dioxide, which can be visible in fermentation tanks as they fizz, froth, and bubble.

FORMING FLAVOURS

Tiramisu, cappuccino, the moon – these are all words I've used to describe full fermentation tanks. And that's just what they look like. The aromas that engulf you as you approach a tequila distillery can be mainly attributed to the fermentation process that happens post-cooking. Sweet, sour, fruity, earthy – it is really rather magical how the chemical reaction that occurs between sugar and yeast is so fundamentally important in creating the final flavours we find in tequila.

THE SCIENCE BIT

The most important player in fermentation is yeast, a single-celled microorganism. It converts the agave sugars that have been readied for fermentation during cooking into ethanol (alcohol), alongside other compounds or congeners (see p71), creating any given tequila's flavour identity.

FERMENTING WITH YEAST
Understanding fermentation begins with a very simple equation: yeast + sugar = alcohol + flavour.

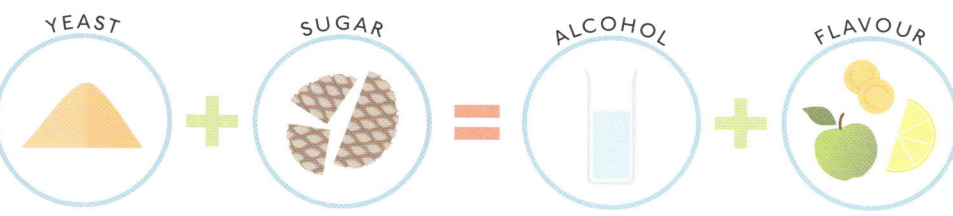

YEAST + SUGAR = ALCOHOL + FLAVOUR

FERMENTATION

The process of fermentation can take several days or weeks, depending on the method distillers use.

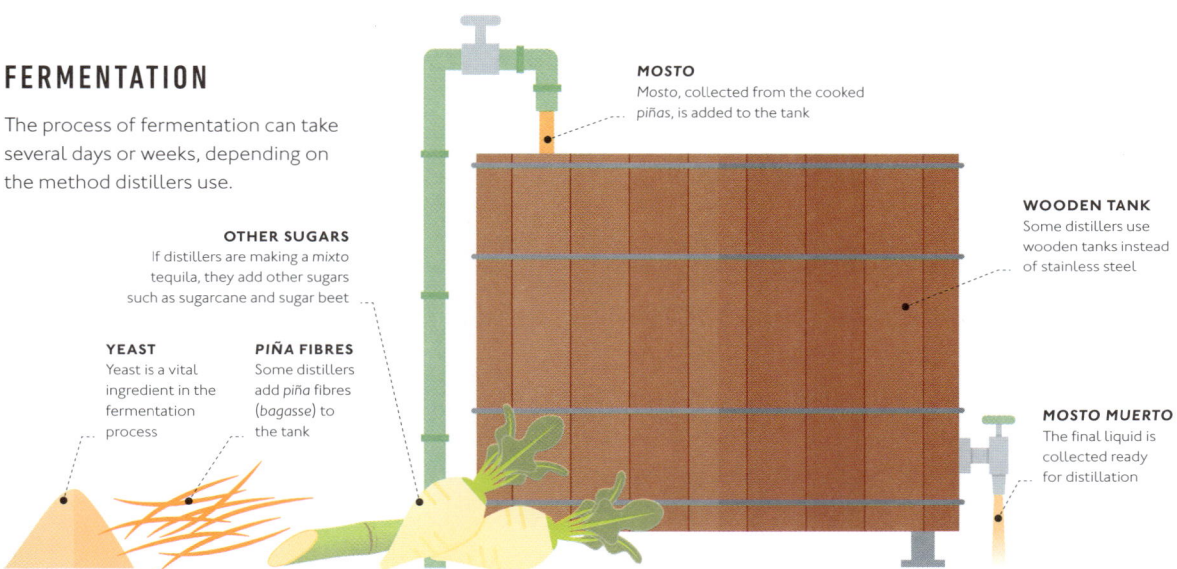

MOSTO
Mosto, collected from the cooked piñas, is added to the tank

OTHER SUGARS
If distillers are making a mixto tequila, they add other sugars such as sugarcane and sugar beet

WOODEN TANK
Some distillers use wooden tanks instead of stainless steel

YEAST
Yeast is a vital ingredient in the fermentation process

PIÑA FIBRES
Some distillers add piña fibres (bagasse) to the tank

MOSTO MUERTO
The final liquid is collected ready for distillation

Many distilleries use commercial yeast, especially the larger, industrial ones, or will have cultivated their own. Fewer distilleries use wild or airborne yeasts, which arguably give their tequila more of a sense of terroir (see p16).

THE PROCESS

The first step is to add the sugary liquid from the cooked piñas (called mosto) to fermentation tanks. The tanks are often open (uncovered) and made of stainless steel, but some distilleries use wooden or concrete vats too and closed (covered) fermentation.

If the distillery is making a mixto tequila (see p12), this is when it can add other sugars, but if a 100 per cent agave tequila is the end goal, it will only add the juice from the cooked piñas.

Distillers sometimes add the leftover piña fibres, called bagasse, to the process too, usually if the piñas have been milled with a tahona (see p66).

Distillers either add yeast to the mosto or allow natural fermentation to occur, and this process can take days or weeks, depending on the process. All of these variables will have some impact on the final flavour of the tequila.

At this stage, the liquid can be anything from 4% to 8% ABV. Once the process is finished, the sugars consumed, and the yeast defunct, the final liquid, called mosto muerto, is ready for distilling.

SECOND FERMENTATION

Distillers might also perform a second fermentation, called malolactic fermentation, which is used in winemaking. In this process, bacteria in the air is left to convert malic acid into lactic acid, creating other flavours and aromas that may or may not be desirable for individual distillers.

HOW DISTILLATION WORKS

Now you have your fermented liquid, or *aguamiel*, it is time to concentrate all that flavour into a clear liquid that will go to make the final tequila.

THE BASICS

Distillation is a practice that has evolved over thousands of years. Its origins are hazy, with China, Egypt, and Mesopotamia all being credited with its beginnings. But the fundamentals of distilling are, at its most practical level, universal.

The aims of distillation are to separate and concentrate elements through the use of heat. Distillers boil their wash, or fermented liquid, in stills (see pp72–75). This separates the ethanol, which boils at a lower temperature (78.4°C/173°F) than water (100°C/212°F), and creates vapours that travel up the still. The vapours are then sent to a condenser, which condenses them back into a liquid before collecting for the final spirit, the heart (*corazón*).

TEQUILA SPECIFICS

Every distiller will do this process slightly differently – such as how long they run their stills, when

MAKING TEQUILA

There are a number of steps in the tequila-making process, from the harvested agave to the bottled tequila.

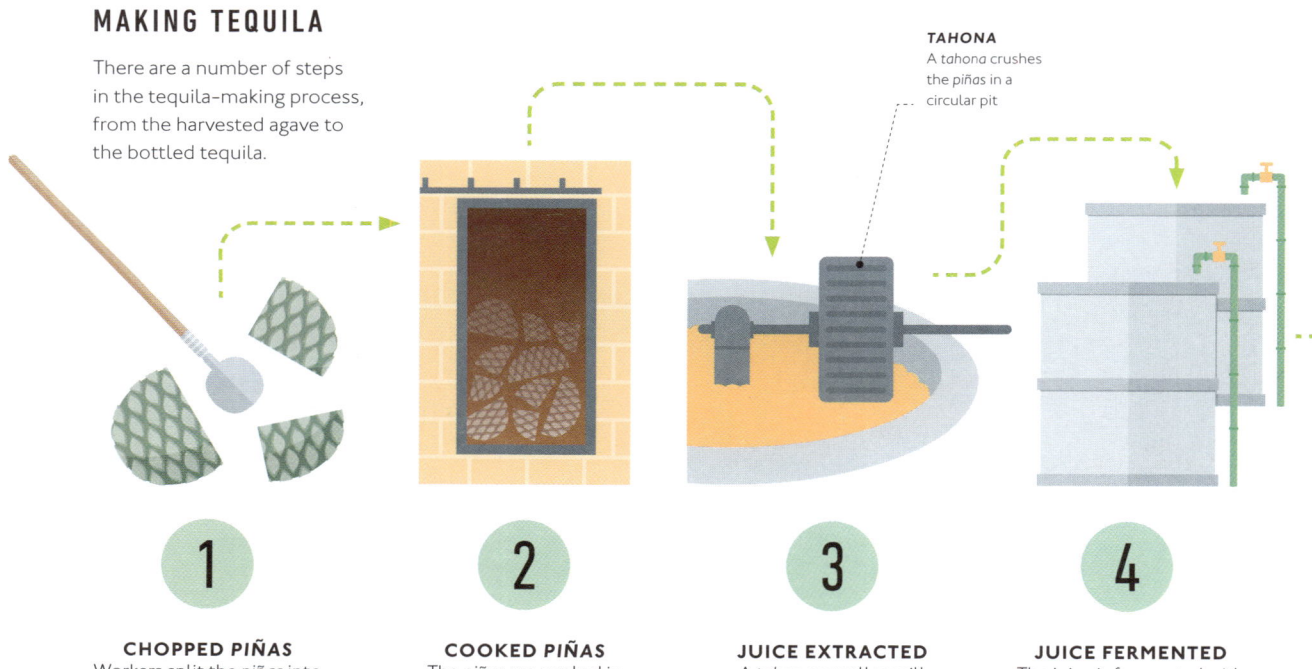

TAHONA
A *tahona* crushes the *piñas* in a circular pit

1

CHOPPED *PIÑAS*
Workers split the *piñas* into halves or quarters, ready for cooking.

2

COOKED *PIÑAS*
The *piñas* are cooked in *hornos*, as here, or in autoclaves.

3

JUICE EXTRACTED
A *tahona* or roller mill extracts fermentable juices from the *piña* fibres.

4

JUICE FERMENTED
The juice is fermented with yeast in large tanks, which can take days or weeks.

they cut their spirit, the still size and type – but there are some common steps. Most tequilas are distilled twice. Distillers use either pot or column stills to make tequila, or a combination of the two, using stainless steel or copper stills. The first distillation produces the *ordinario*, which comes off the still at around 20–25% ABV. It is cut for heads and tails (see box right), which can be redistilled. The second distillation then produces what can be called tequila and comes off the still at 40% to 50% ABV.

DISTILLING TERMS

ALEMBIC Another name for the traditional pot stills used in tequila distillation.

CONDENSER This cools down the vapours coming up the still and turns them back into liquid ready to collect.

CONGENERS Chemical compounds that create flavour as a result of fermentation and distillation.

HEADS, HEARTS, AND TAILS Known as "cuts", heads (*cabezas*) are volatile alcohols, hearts (*corazónes*) are the ethanol and flavour-rich congeners, while tails (*colas*) are undesirable alcohols and other substances. Distillers collect the hearts for the final spirit.

ORDINARIO The resulting liquid of the first distillation. The second liquid is called tequila.

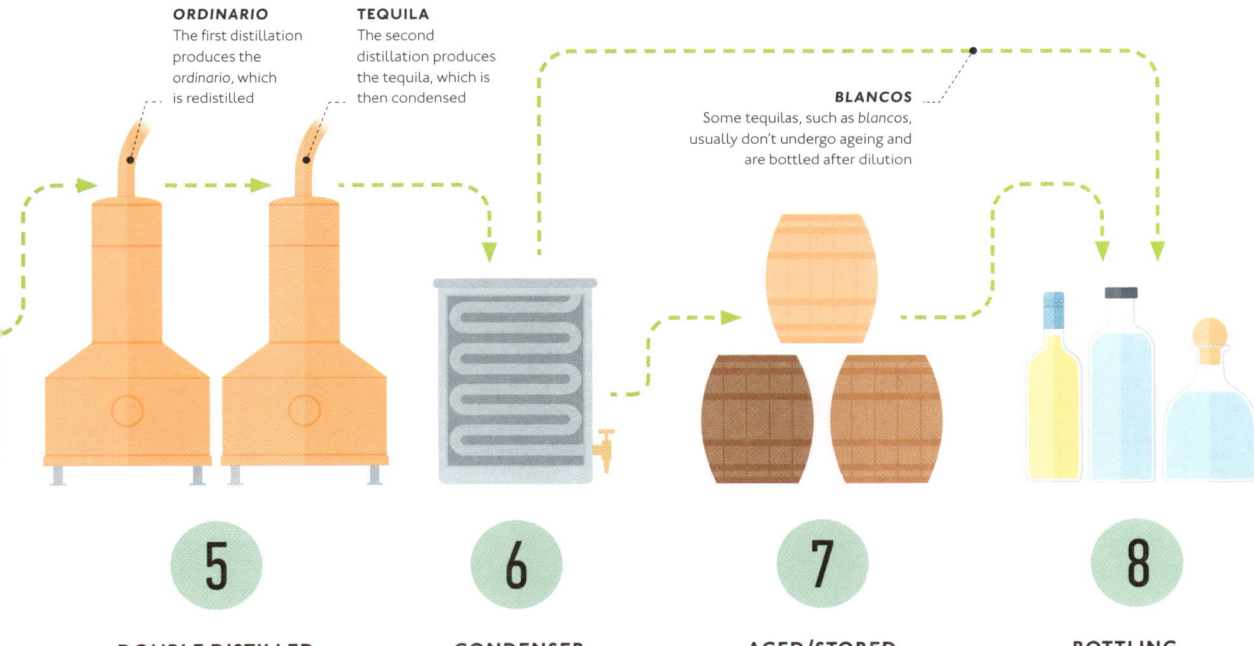

ORDINARIO
The first distillation produces the *ordinario*, which is redistilled

TEQUILA
The second distillation produces the tequila, which is then condensed

BLANCOS
Some tequilas, such as *blancos*, usually don't undergo ageing and are bottled after dilution

5

DOUBLE DISTILLED
Most tequila is double distilled, usually in pot stills. A column still may also be used.

6

CONDENSER
The vapours collected from the stills are condensed to form a liquid.

7

AGED/STORED
Some tequilas are aged in barrels, from months to years, before they are bottled.

8

BOTTLING
After dilution and filtering, tequila is bottled. Mixtos can be bottled outside Mexico.

THE POT STILL

The alembic or pot still is the most traditional still when it comes to distillation in tequila production. How does it work?

TRADITIONAL METHOD

Alembic stills are said to have been invented by an Arab alchemist, Abu Musa Jabir ibn Hayyan (c. 721–815), as far back as 800. While the alembic pot still was not originally invented to make tequila, of course, it was adopted in Mexico when the Spanish brought these stills over to distil agave spirits.

Gourd-shaped, squat containers, made of copper or stainless steel, and sitting unassumingly in rows, pot stills are used by most tequila distilleries to turn the fermented wash into what will eventually become tequila in your bottle.

HOW IT WORKS

Known as batch distillation, distillers charge the pot still with wash, and heat the wide base of the still either with an internal steam coil or a steam jacket. As ethanol starts to boil, vapour rises in the body of the still, leaving water behind.

These vapours pass through the still head and enter the condenser, where they are cooled using an external water cooler system and turned back into liquid.

Distillers take the cuts, or collect the liquid, as either *cabezas* (heads), *corazónes* (hearts), or *colas* (tails) – the *cabezas* and *colas* can be redistilled in the next batch (see p71). The *corazónes* from the first distillation, known as *ordinario*, are distilled again to become tequila.

DISTILLING KNOW-HOW

How much wash is distilled, for how long, and where the cuts are made are all down to the prowess of the distiller and the type of spirit they want to produce.

Tequila is also distilled to a slightly lower ABV than many other spirits to maintain the flavours of the agave that has matured over many years.

Cuts are often based on ABV and time, but the nose and palate of the distiller are also important.

POT AND COLUMN STILLS

A number of tequila brands use column stills (see pp74–75) alongside pot stills in their tequila-making process.

Pot stills are more associated with artisanal tequilas, while larger industrial operations use column stills.

TEQUILEÑA uses both types of still, and blends its column-still tequila with tequila from its pot still.

JOSE CUERVO The largest tequila company in the world, it uses both column stills and copper pot stills.

SAUZA The Sauza distillery uses copper pots as well as diffusers. Owned by Japanese company Suntory Global Spirits, Sauza is often associated with the use of more modern techniques.

HERRADURA has been responsible for some of the category's biggest changes in recent years. It uses column stills alongside stainless steel pot stills.

INSIDE A POT STILL

The fermented wash is heated inside the still. The vapours rise up the still and enter the condenser, where they are cooled and turned back into liquid.

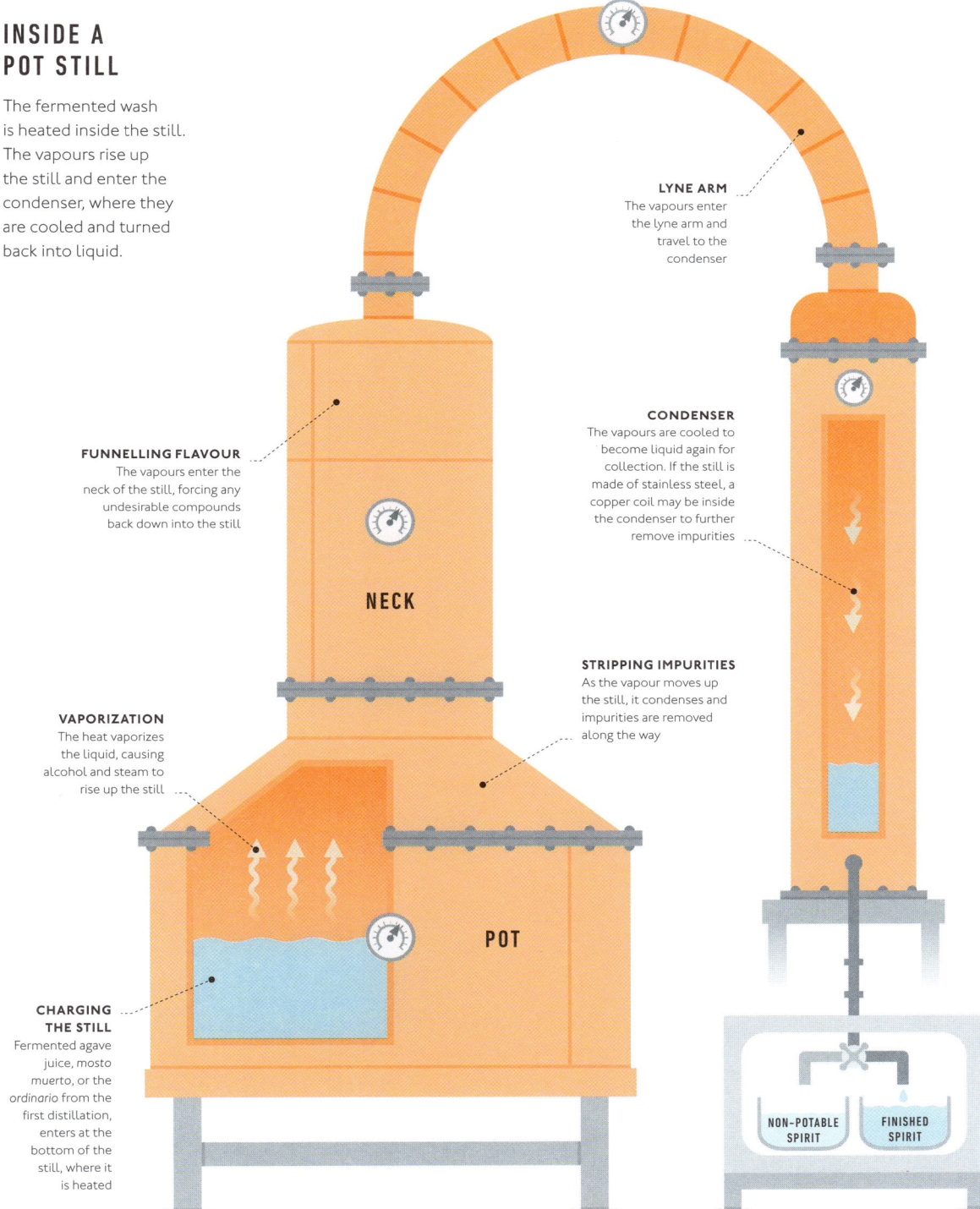

LYNE ARM
The vapours enter the lyne arm and travel to the condenser

FUNNELLING FLAVOUR
The vapours enter the neck of the still, forcing any undesirable compounds back down into the still

NECK

CONDENSER
The vapours are cooled to become liquid again for collection. If the still is made of stainless steel, a copper coil may be inside the condenser to further remove impurities

VAPORIZATION
The heat vaporizes the liquid, causing alcohol and steam to rise up the still

STRIPPING IMPURITIES
As the vapour moves up the still, it condenses and impurities are removed along the way

POT

CHARGING THE STILL
Fermented agave juice, *mosto muerto*, or the *ordinario* from the first distillation, enters at the bottom of the still, where it is heated

NON-POTABLE SPIRIT

FINISHED SPIRIT

THE COLUMN STILL

Column stills can operate continuously, and are a way of making a lot of tequila more quickly and efficiently than pot stills.

EFFICIENT AND ECONOMICAL

Column stills are a modern version of the original Coffey still, invented by Irish inventor and distiller Aeneas Coffey (1780–1839) in 1831. They are used across the spirits industry, including in the making of tequila, and are more often found in larger industrial distilleries.

It's thought that the column still removes more of the congeners (see p71) than pot stills during the distillation process, creating a more neutral tequila as a result. Nevertheless, column stills are used across both *mixtos* and 100 per cent tequilas (see p12), and when making tequila in large volumes, they are much more economical than pot stills.

HOW IT WORKS

The preheated wash enters the column towards the top of the still and begins to make its way down the column, hitting the numerous perforated copper plates inside. These help to purify the vapours that come into contact with them. As steam is injected into the bottom of the still, any ethanol and flavour compounds start to vaporize and rise back up through the still, and are further purified by the plates.

The tendency of a substance to vaporize is called its volatility. The less volatile liquids fall to the bottom of the still, where they are reheated, while the more volatile liquids vaporize and rise to the plates above. At each of the plates, the vapour condenses back into a liquid that is heated by other vapours rising from below, as well as by the still's heat source.

The vapours go through a constant process of heating and cooling. By the time they get to the top of the still, they are free of heavy compounds and are much lighter and purer.

COOLING THE VAPOURS

The vapours are cooled again in a spirit cooler, and the cooled spirit is collected to form the tequila. Note that the traditional system of taking cuts from the distillate (see p71) is not part of the column-still process.

If the still is stainless steel, copper can be used in the spirit cooler to remove undesirable sulphuric compounds.

WHEN MAKING TEQUILA IN LARGE VOLUMES, COLUMN STILLS ARE MUCH MORE ECONOMICAL THAN POT STILLS.

INSIDE THE COLUMN STILL

Tequila makers often use stainless steel stills. The perforated plates inside the still purify the vapours as they rise to the top of the still.

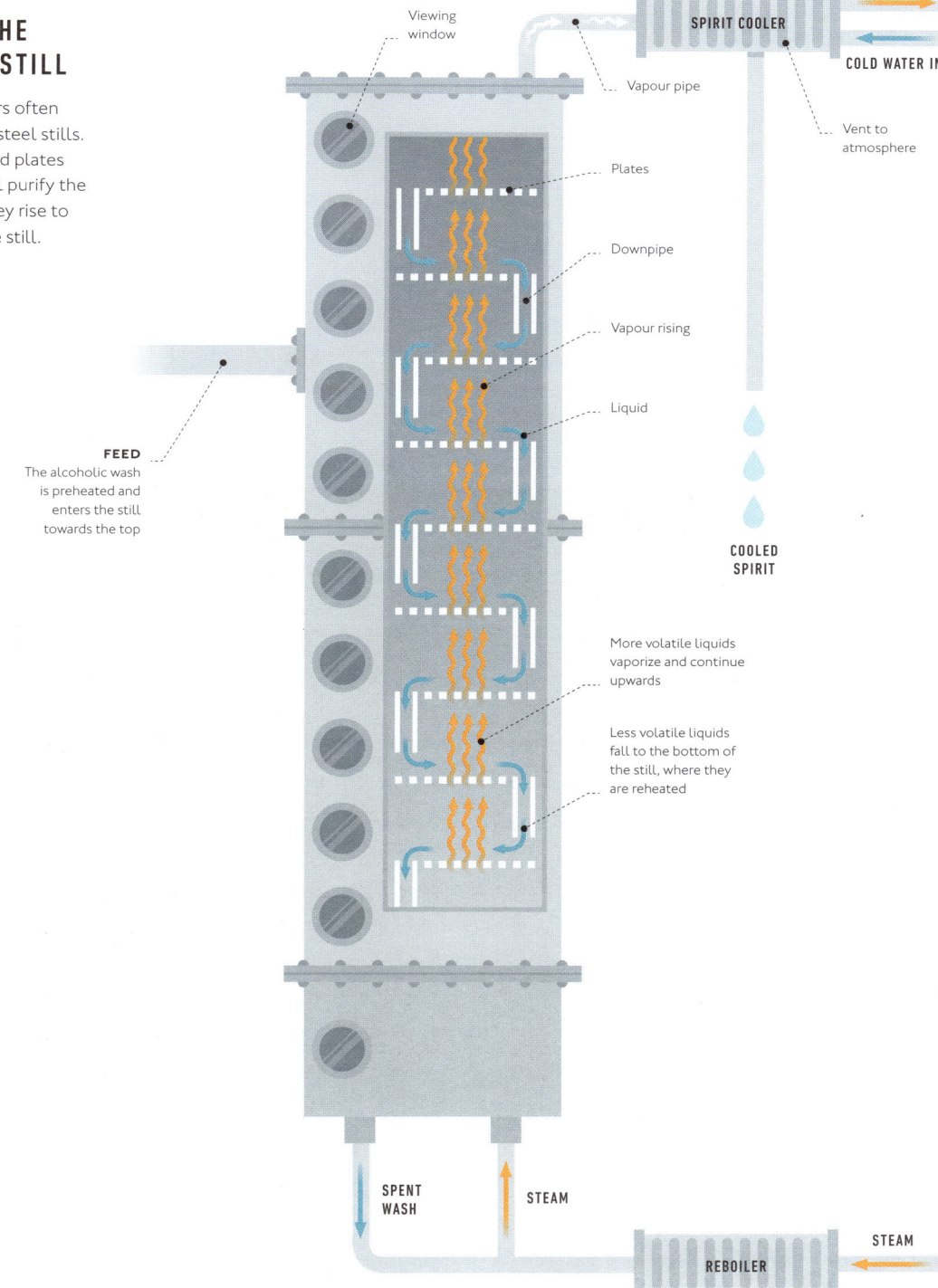

Viewing window

Vapour pipe

SPIRIT COOLER

HOT WATER OUT

COLD WATER IN

Vent to atmosphere

Plates

Downpipe

Vapour rising

Liquid

COOLED SPIRIT

FEED
The alcoholic wash is preheated and enters the still towards the top

More volatile liquids vaporize and continue upwards

Less volatile liquids fall to the bottom of the still, where they are reheated

SPENT WASH

STEAM

REBOILER

STEAM

AGEING TEQUILA

While unaged, or *blanco*, tequila is a finished product without needing to touch a barrel, aged tequilas are becoming increasingly revered, and are akin to aged spirits from other parts of the world, such as whisky and Cognac.

A COMPLEX PROCESS

Stepping into a warehouse that is storing any ageing spirit is a rather magical, ethereal experience, and tequila is certainly no different.

Row upon row of stacked barrels holding precious tequila sit patiently, waiting for the right time to be blended and bottled to end up in your glass. Tequila makers have to be patient – time will show them when their liquid is ready. All the while, what happens inside that barrel is a nuanced and complex process.

Every aged tequila begins life as a *blanco*. It is pumped into oak

STORING THE BARRELS
The barrels that store ageing tequila are stacked in the distillery's warehouse until the designated time has passed for each category.

WHAT HAPPENS INSIDE THE BARREL IS A NUANCED AND COMPLEX PROCESS.

AGEING IN THE BARREL

All aged tequilas start as *blancos* and remain in the barrels for the designated amount of time for each category (see pp22–29).

OAK BARRELS
Distillers pump *blanco* tequila into oak barrels that have previously been used to age other spirits, usually ex-bourbon barrels.

SEALED AND STORED
The barrels are sealed under CRT supervision and stacked on top of each other for efficient use of space.

PUMPED OUT
Once the tequila has spent the alotted time in the barrel, it's tasted, checked, and pumped out ready for blending, dilution, and bottling.

barrels, which are stacked on top of each other, often in an *estiba*, or pyramid formation, in warehouses. The ABV at which the tequila goes into the barrel can vary – for example, Patrón's tequila goes in at 55% ABV or 110 proof.

Depending on the category the brand wants to make – *reposado*, *añejo*, extra *añejo* – the tequila stays in the vessel for any amount of time up to the legal time limit specified by the CRT (see p13). It is then tasted and checked with CRT permission, and when ready, it's pumped out. If it's not being sold as a single-barrel tequila, it's blended with other tequilas to make the final expression.

THE ANGELS' SHARE

A concept found in all categories of aged spirits, the angels' share refers to the evaporation of water and alcohol from a barrel. It varies depending on the temperature and humidity in a warehouse. Tequila distilleries lose anything from 5 to 10 per cent per year.

While losing a percentage of the liquid is, of course, costly, it is an inevitable and necessary part of the ageing process for creating exceptional spirits. Those lucky angels.

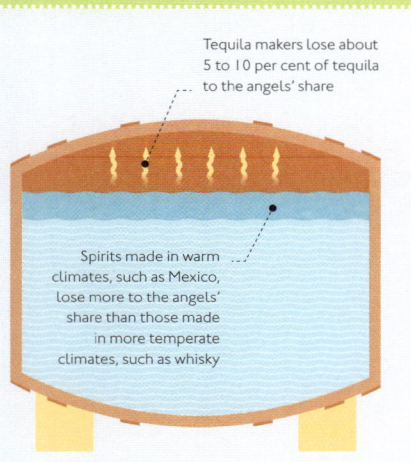

Tequila makers lose about 5 to 10 per cent of tequila to the angels' share

Spirits made in warm climates, such as Mexico, lose more to the angels' share than those made in more temperate climates, such as whisky

THE INTERACTION OF THE LIQUID AND WOOD CHANGES HOW THE LIQUID LOOKS, TASTES, AND FEELS IN THE MOUTH.

INSIDE THE BARREL

Charred American oak previously used for bourbon is used most often to age tequila, while French oak that previously contained wine – a technique pioneered by Casa Noble's *maestro tequilero* Jose "Pepe" Hermosillo – is increasingly being used.

When an alcoholic liquid is in a vessel made of a porous material such as oak, the interaction of the liquid and wood changes how the liquid looks, tastes, and feels in the mouth. As the barrel expands and retracts in reaction to external temperature changes, the liquid moves in and out of the wood's inner surface, and the wood imparts flavour and colour. If the

INTERACTIONS IN THE BARREL

A number of processes occur when the tequila is inside the barrel, including interactions between the wood and the liquid as the wood expands and contracts in response to temperature changes, evaporation of the liquid, and the entry of oxygen into the barrel.

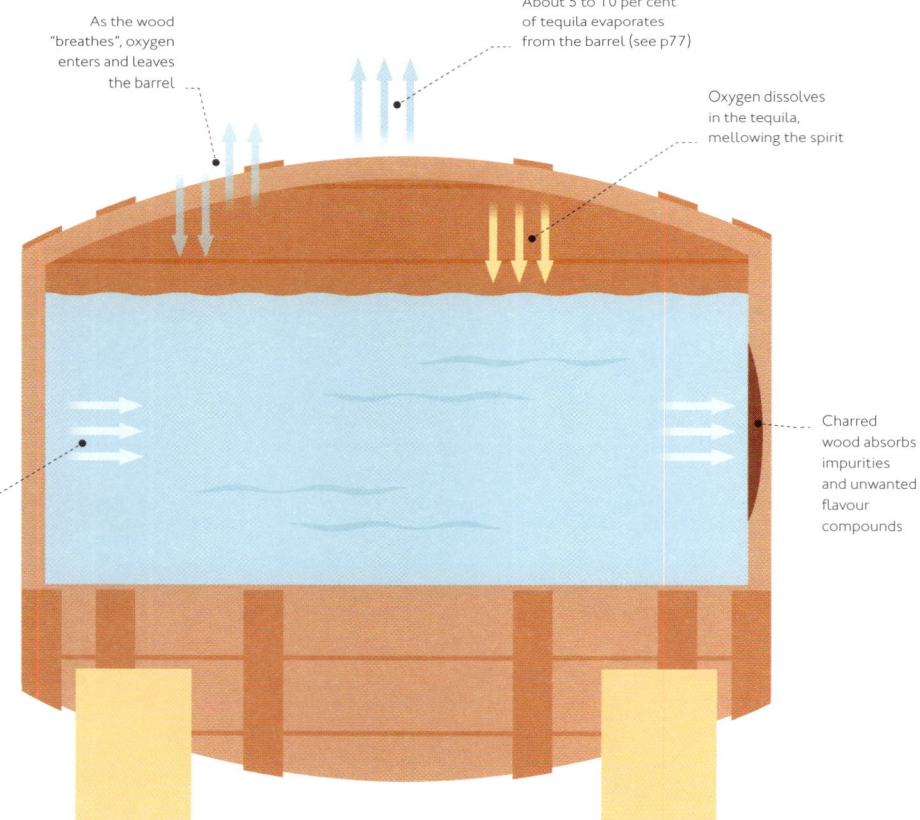

As the wood "breathes", oxygen enters and leaves the barrel

About 5 to 10 per cent of tequila evaporates from the barrel (see p77)

Oxygen dissolves in the tequila, mellowing the spirit

Charred wood absorbs impurities and unwanted flavour compounds

Colour and flavours, such as caramel and vanilla, are extracted from the wood

FLAVOURS FROM THE WOOD

Wood can impart a number of different flavours to the aged tequilas.

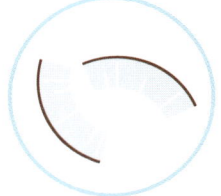

COCONUT FLAVOURS

DILL NOTES

DRIED FRUIT

SPICES, CLOVES, AND SMOKE CHARACTER

SWEETNESS AND LIGHT CARAMEL FLAVOURS

TOASTED OR CHARRED OVERTONES, SUCH AS ALMONDS AND SUGAR

VANILLA AND VANILLA-LIKE FLAVOURS

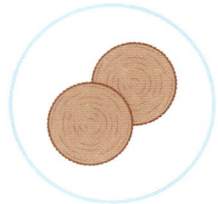

WOODY NOTES

inside of the barrel has been charred, it also removes impurities. Oak also allows oxygen to enter the barrel, which helps to smooth and mellow the spirit.

Factors such as oak variety – American white oak, French Limousin oak, Hungarian white oak – barrel surface area, char level, and external temperatures all have an impact on the final liquid. For example, an ex-bourbon charred American oak barrel imparts more vanilla and caramel notes, while a new French oak barrel has a drying and spiced impact on flavour (see box above). *Rosa* tequilas are aged in ex-red wine barrels, which give them a pink hue and impart fruitier and more floral characteristics.

THE CRT

As with all elements of the CRT's involvement in tequila making, its presence at maturation is felt rather heavily. Every barrel in a warehouse is sealed with a label by a CRT verifier, with the date, quantity, and category. The distillery also needs the permission of the CRT for testing, tasting, or checking the barrels' contents. CRT verifiers change regularly so that they can't form friendships with warehouse staff and thus can remain impartial.

AGEING IN USED TEQUILA BARRELS

Some other spirit categories, such as whisky and rum, finish the ageing process in ex-tequila barrels. Scotch brands such as Deanston, Nc'nean, Chivas Regal, and Lagavulin have all released whiskies that have spent time in used tequila barrels, while rum brand NOËL finishes one of its rums in ex-tequila casks.

NOËL
Rum brand NOËL finishes one of its barrel-aged rums in ex-tequila casks

LAGAVULIN
Lagavulin finishes its 12-year-old whisky in Don Julio Añejo Tequila casks

DEANSTON
Deanston's 15-year-old whisky is finished for two years in ex-tequila casks

BLENDING AND BOTTLING

Once a *blanco* has been distilled, and *reposados*, *añejos*, and extra *añejos* have been aged, it's time to blend, dilute, filter, and bottle the tequila. Blending is especially important in the case of *joven*/gold tequilas.

THE ART OF BLENDING

While every brand has its own recipe for making its tequila, there will always be some inconsistencies in the final liquid for various reasons, including the agave quality, nuances of individual barrels, and warehouse temperature. This is when blending takes place.

Makers monitor the tequila in barrels for taste and aroma, and blend them together to create the final expression. They often use a base of tequila that has been aged in newer barrels and add in some from older ones to create the desired end product.

In the case of *joven* tequila, makers blend *blanco* and aged tequilas together and often use additives to create the desired consistency of colour and taste. Some expressions also blend numerous aged tequilas together, such as Volcán de Mi Tierra X.A, which is a blend of *reposado*, *añejo*, and extra *añejo*.

DILUTION AND FILTRATION

Before bottling, makers dilute tequilas to bottling strength – between 35% and 55% ABV – using distilled or demineralized water. Tequila that is labelled "still strength" is undiluted. Makers often dilute tequila over a period of time because adding water changes the molecular structure of a tequila and so must be done carefully. Some aged tequilas are diluted before spending time in barrel to marry tequila and water together more harmoniously, but

BLENDING TEQUILA

Tequila that has been aged in old barrels is often blended with a base of tequila that has been aged in newer barrels.

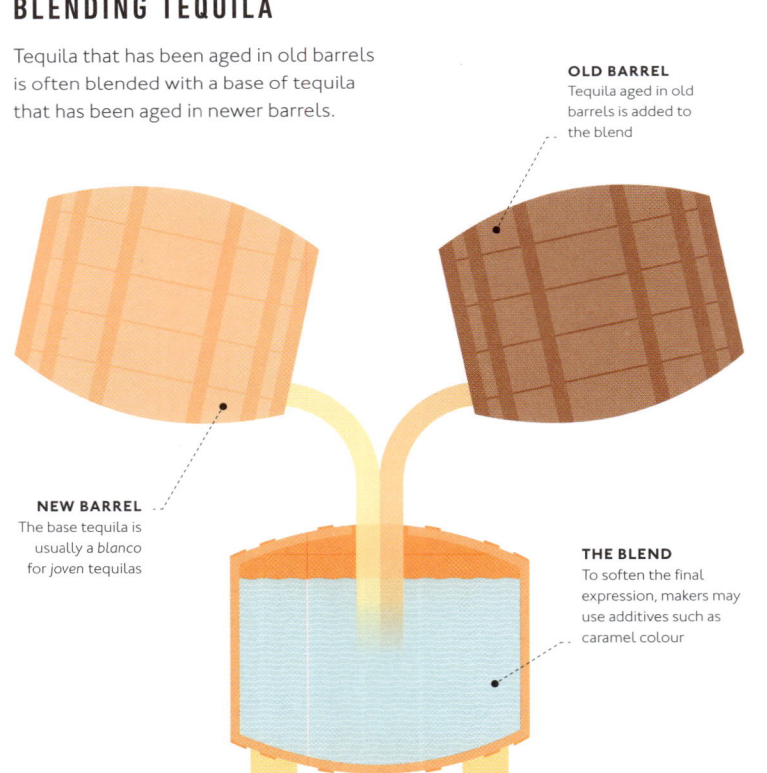

OLD BARREL
Tequila aged in old barrels is added to the blend

NEW BARREL
The base tequila is usually a *blanco* for *joven* tequilas

THE BLEND
To soften the final expression, makers may use additives such as caramel colour

ALL SHAPES AND SIZES
More than most spirits, tequila bottles come in many different shapes and guises.

most are diluted afterwards. Then the tequila is filtered to remove any impurities. The most extreme version of this is in the production of *cristalinos* (see pp30–31).

BOTTLING LINES

Makers bottle tequila either mechanically or by hand, and often use a mixture of the two.

Tequila that is 100 per cent agave must be bottled within the DO, while *mixtos* can be exported in large vats and bottled anywhere. Bottles are rinsed with tequila and filled before being labelled (see pp86–87) and packed for shipping. Bottling by hand is a strenuous task, and the best distilleries move workers around or impose breaks and exercises to avoid injury.

SINGLE-BARREL RELEASES

If a bottle has "single barrel" on the label, it means it has been sourced from one barrel, which has been carefully selected by the master distiller.

BOTTLING LINE
Modern mechanized bottling lines can process up to 26,000 bottles an hour.

A WORD ON ADDITIVES

More than a word, the conversation around additives in tequila is never a short one. And with even more controversy having occurred in 2024, it looks like the subject will continue to garner commentary.

WHAT ARE ADDITIVES?

It's been mooted that around 70 per cent of tequilas on the market contain additives. You might not realize it though, because according to the Consejo Regulador del Tequila (CRT), brands do not have to declare their additives if they fall within the 1 per cent total weight allowance.

The additives used by a brand include *abocantes* (which translates approximately as "smoothers"), while the process is called *abocado* ("mellowing").

There are four types of additives that are widely used: glycerine, which adds mouthfeel; caramel

ADDITIVE FREE

ADDITIVES USED

HOW MANY TEQUILAS CONTAIN ADDITIVES?
The use of additives in tequila is widespread, with as many as 70 per cent, probably more, containing them.

FOUR WIDELY USED ADDITIVES

The main ingredients added to tequila are glycerine, caramel colour, sugar-based syrups, and oak extract, although other additives are also permitted.

GLYCERINE

CARAMEL COLOUR

SUGAR SYRUP

OAK EXTRACT

colour, which darkens the tequila and adds consistency; sugar syrups for sweetness; and oak extract for imparting wood character.

Note that just because a tequila is labelled as "100 per cent agave", it doesn't mean it is additive free – the "100 per cent" refers only to the fermented sugars (see p12).

Since 2005, tequila has also been allowed to contain additives that impart colour, sweetness, or flavour with anything that is fit for human consumption.

ADDITIVE-FREE TEQUILAS

While additives are widely used and accepted, many producers who are passionate about their additive-free credentials have been pushing in recent years for more transparency around the use of additives. In 2020, the Additive Free Alliance (AFA) was launched when online database Tequila Matchmaker published a list of additive-free tequila brands that was available for consumers to search. However, it's worth mentioning this wasn't an exhaustive list and it required involvement from brands themselves. Also important to note is that the AFA has never condemned the use of additives as such, but is motivated by transparency in labelling.

TIDE CHANGE

In 2023, the CRT announced its intention to establish its own additive-free programme, with Patrón endorsed as being additive free. Following opposition from other big tequila brands, the CRT rowed back on this, and in 2024, it made a controversial move by announcing a ban on tequila brands (and third parties) calling or promoting themselves as "additive free". This elicited a huge response from the industry, no more so than from the AFA. It announced via Tequila Matchmaker founder and board president, Grover Sanschagrin, that it had removed all tequila brands from its website, leaving only non-tequila agave-based spirits on the AFA list.

WHAT HAPPENS NEXT?

In a move that has kept additive-free pioneers optimistic, Certificadora Royalty – a new certification body – was accredited in mid-2024. If approved by the Mexican Ministry of Economy, it could be a challenge to the CRT.

IDENTIFYING ADDITIVES IN YOUR TEQUILA

With information on additive-free brands now being more and more limited, here are some tell-tale signs that you might be tasting or seeing additives in your tequila.

ADDITIVES ARE WIDELY USED AND ACCEPTED, BUT THERE IS A DESIRE TO MAKE LABELLING CLEARER.

VANILLA CAKE MIX
Icing, tutti-frutti, synthetic vanilla – if you can detect these on the palate, you're likely tasting additives.

TEQUILA TEARS
Roll the tequila in a glass and look at how it slides down the sides – the tears (or legs). Thick or syrupy tears are tell-tale signs.

NO AGAVE CHARACTER
Get to know what agave tastes like and you'll quickly be able to identify a liquid where that flavour is missing.

COLOUR VS FLAVOUR
Does your tequila look aged but has no flavour characteristics to match? Or vice versa?

THE FUTURE OF THE AFA

In 2024, the AFA relaunched as a non-profit operation and opened up to other agave spirits like mezcal and *raicilla* (see pp84–85), as well as agave products such as syrups. Brands that decide to join the AFA will have their products rigorously tested using liquid chromatography lab analysis and sensory evaluation in order to confirm that they are additive free. In early 2025, the CRT filed a lawsuit against the AFA. The controversy continues.

MEZCAL AND OTHER AGAVE SPIRITS

Tequila may be our hero, but there are numerous other spirits made from the agave plant, even outside Mexico.

MEZCAL

As well known outside of Mexico as tequila – or at least becoming so – mezcal can be made from more than 30 different varieties of agave, although five are recognized as the most common. They are known by their folk names as *espadín*, *tobalá*, *arroqueño*, *tobaziche*, and *tepeztate* (see below).

Mezcal is made from 100 per cent mature agave in nine Mexican states: Oaxaca, Guerrero, Durango, San Luis Potosí, Zacatecas, Tamaulipas, Guanajuato, Michoacán, and Puebla. There are two categories of mezcal, ancestral and artisanal, which are defined by their production methods. Terminology around age is similar to that of tequila.

Pechuga is a style of mezcal made in small batches, often for family celebrations. This mezcal is distilled with nuts, grains, and fruits, with the addition of a raw chicken or turkey breast hanging in the still, which adds flavour and texture to the final mezcal.

Mezcal is a product that truly represents its *terroir* and the character of the agave from which it is made. It is often identified by a smoky characteristic thanks to the slow cooking of the *piñas*, but there is much more to mezcal than smoke alone.

RAICILLA

With more than 300 years of history, *raicilla* cannot be called mezcal but is considered a very close cousin. It follows a similar production method to mezcal, but can be a little bit funkier thanks to the yeast used in its fermentation.

Raicilla has a protected DO and can be made from various agave species, such as *Agave maximiliana* and *A. rhodacantha*. The *piñas* are roasted in stone or brick ovens and crushed, and the juice is fermented with wild yeasts. It can be distilled only once. Flavour wise, expect something herbal, saline, green, and pretty earthy.

BACANORA

By no means easy to acquire, *bacanora* uses an endemic agave, *A. angustifolia*, in its production. It is made in the state of Sonora and has a DO. The *piñas* are cooked

TYPES OF AGAVE USED IN MEZCAL

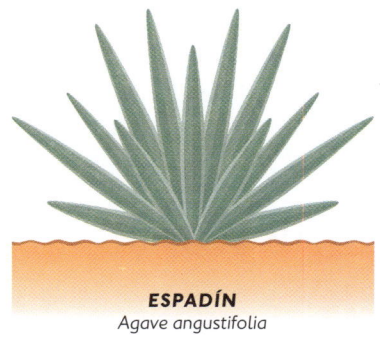

ESPADÍN
Agave angustifolia

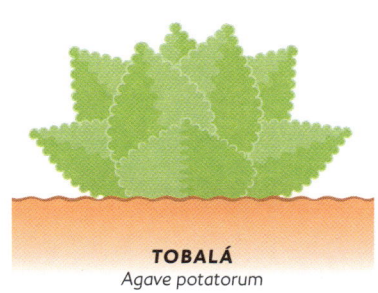

TOBALÁ
Agave potatorum

ARROQUEÑO
Agave americana var. oaxacensis

MEZCAL
Derrumbes San Luis Potosí uses the wild *Agave salmiana* subspecies *crassispina*

RAICILLA
La Venenosa Puntas is named after a specific part of the distillation process

BACANORA
Santo Pecado translates as "holy sin"

AGAVE SPIRITS
Agave spirits can also be referred to as *destilado de agave* when they don't adhere to the rules and regulations of the official categories.

in volcanic-rock-lined earthen ovens, and it is double distilled. The flavour is savoury and earthy and can be influenced by the chips on which the *piñas* are roasted.

ABUNDANT AGAVES

Of the more than 250 species of agave, 75 per cent of them grow in Mexico. As we've seen, only blue Weber agave is used to make tequila, but some of those other agaves are also used to make alcoholic drinks. A few of these are as well known as tequila, but most are relatively unknown or have sadly been lost over the years for various ecological, sociological, and political reasons.

While mezcal, *raicilla*, and *bacanora* are recognizable categories among agave enthusiasts (albeit of varying degrees), there are many others that have been documented. Gary Paul Nabhan (an ethnobotanist and local-food-movement pioneer) and David Suro Piñera (a restaurateur and founder of the Tequila Interchange Project) have compiled a list of more than 20 other agave spirits. Both authors are experts on and champions of agave spirits, and their list includes *bingarrote*, *chichihualco*, *lechuguilla*, *petaquillas*, *sikua*, *tlahuelompa*, *tuxca*, *yocogihua*, and *zotol*.

WORLDWIDE AGAVE SPIRITS

Agave spirits are also produced outside of Mexico. From China and South Africa to Australia, Italy, and India, countries where agaves grow are making distilled drinks from the plant. Some producers also import Mexican agaves and even use agave nectar to make spirits outside Mexico. While these do sit in the agave spirits category, the centuries of history and culture surrounding Mexico's agave-spirit-making prowess will take some beating when it comes to flavour and quality.

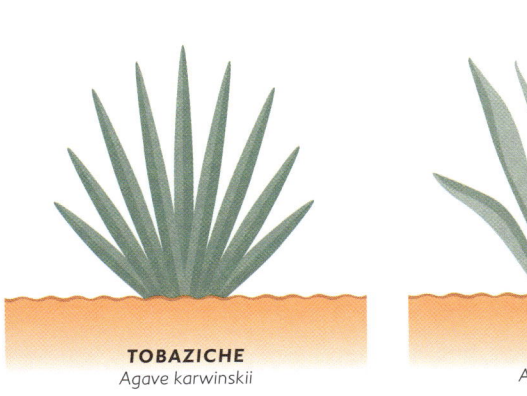

TOBAZICHE
Agave karwinskii

TEPEZTATE
Agave marmorata

A NOTE ON SOTOL

While many people include *sotol* in the category of other agave spirits, it isn't, in fact, made from agave. It's made from a succulent in the *Dasylirion* genus (also known as "desert spoon"), which looks similar to agave. Sotol is made in the states of Chihuahua, Coahuila, and Durango in Mexico.

READING TEQUILA LABELS

Being able to understand what's on the label on a bottle of tequila can go quite a long way in helping you decipher what type or quality of tequila sits inside.

WHAT'S ON A LABEL?

It's worth noting that the amount of information on a bottle of tequila varies wildly. If a bottle has a lack of information, you might need to dig a little deeper to find the answers to your questions. Lots of brands are, however, moving towards much more transparency to let buyers know, pretty much, what they're getting. And remember that a tequila label never tells the whole story.

1. TEQUILA
It sounds obvious, but if a bottle doesn't include the word "tequila" on it, then it doesn't fall within the legal definition of a tequila (see pp12–13).

2. 100% AGAVE
This means that 100 per cent of the sugars in this tequila are derived from agave, but it doesn't mean that there are no additives (see pp82–83). If you don't see this, then the tequila is a *mixto* (see p12), but that doesn't mean it is of worse quality.

3. BRAND NAME
The brand name is not necessarily the same as the name of the distillery that produced it.

4. TEQUILA NAME
Some brands name their releases – this is often for those tequilas outside of the core range.

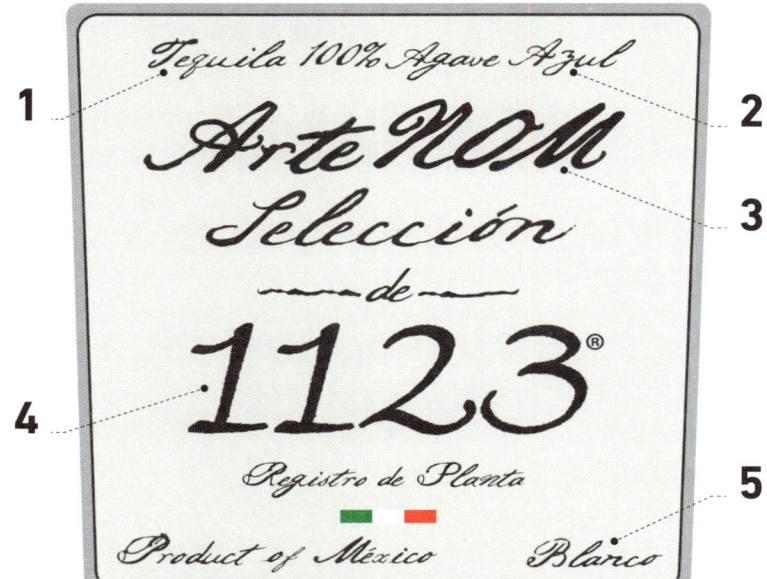

1

2

3

4

5

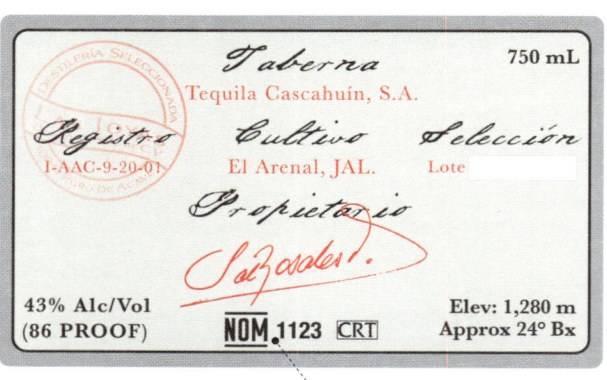

6

LOTS OF BRANDS ARE MOVING TOWARDS MORE TRANSPARENCY ON THEIR LABELS TO LET BUYERS KNOW WHAT THEY'RE GETTING.

5. CATEGORY
Colour (or lack thereof) can be deceiving, so check what category your tequila is: *blanco, joven, reposado, añejo,* or *extra añejo* (see pp20–29). The category will give you an idea of the flavour to expect.

6. NOM NUMBER
Every tequila bottle has a four-digit Norma Oficial Mexicana (NOM) number, which tells you where your tequila actually comes from and the distillery that made it.

7. SINGLE ESTATE/ORIGIN
This refers to the agave being from one traceable location.

8. HECHO EN MEXICO/DESDE MEXICO
Made in Mexico/From Mexico – as you would expect with a tequila. Tequilas that are 100 per cent agave must be bottled in the DO, but *mixtos* (see p12) can be bottled anywhere in the world.

9. ML
The standard bottle contains 700ml (25fl oz) or 750ml (26fl oz), but they can vary in volume.

10. % ALC/VOL
This refers to the amount of alcohol by volume (ABV) of the tequila. Tequilas can range from 35% to 55% ABV.

11. ROASTING
The brand might include how the agaves have been cooked (see pp64–65).

OTHER INFORMATION
Small batch There is no legal definition of what a small batch is, but it normally means a tequila that is made in small quantities at a time. It might also have a bottle number to emphasize its rarity.

Still type The brand might also specify what type of stills it has used to distil the tequila (see pp72–75).

Flavour notes These can be helpful for steering you to your preferences, but remember that taste is subjective.

Serving suggestion It can be helpful to know how to serve a particular tequila, such as in cocktails, with a mixer, or for sipping neat.

PROTECTING
--- TEQUILA'S ---
FUTURE

WE'VE LOOKED AT THE PAST and present of tequila, but what about its future? While tequila may be enjoying a well-deserved boom, there is still more to do to ensure that this very special spirits category is here for the long run. In this section, we will take a look at how tequila can be made more sustainably, who – or what – needs to be protected to maintain the biodiversity of the agave plant, and why the people who make tequila need to be more visible. We also dig deeper into the impact of celebrity tequilas and premiumization on the category's rise, and how demand can impact not only the cost of our tequilas but also the lives of the communities who make them, as well as the cyclical impact on the blue Weber agave.

MAKING TEQUILA SUSTAINABLY

From collecting rainwater to turning agave fibres into compost, brands are working hard to establish tequila's sustainable status.

IT STARTS WITH AGAVE

Like many other spirits, tequila is making some serious moves when it comes to sustainability. As well as working with an agricultural raw material, tequila as an industry also produces plenty of waste, and so is coming up with ways of reducing its impact on the environment. These are becoming more and more formalized.

With rising rates of deforestation in Mexico, the Tequila Regulatory Council (CRT) joined forces with the Jalisco State Government in 2021 to create the Environmentally Responsible Agave (ARA) certification. The aim is to let consumers know they're buying tequila that's made sustainably with agaves that haven't caused deforestation. By 2027, the CRT hopes to have reduced deforestation by 100 per cent. Don Julio was the first brand to get ARA accredited and has also recently launched a programme for farmers to regenerate their land and enhance biodiversity.

SUSTAINABLE TEQUILA

Like many other industries, tequila is on a mission to make its production process and the cultivation of its raw ingredients more sustainable.

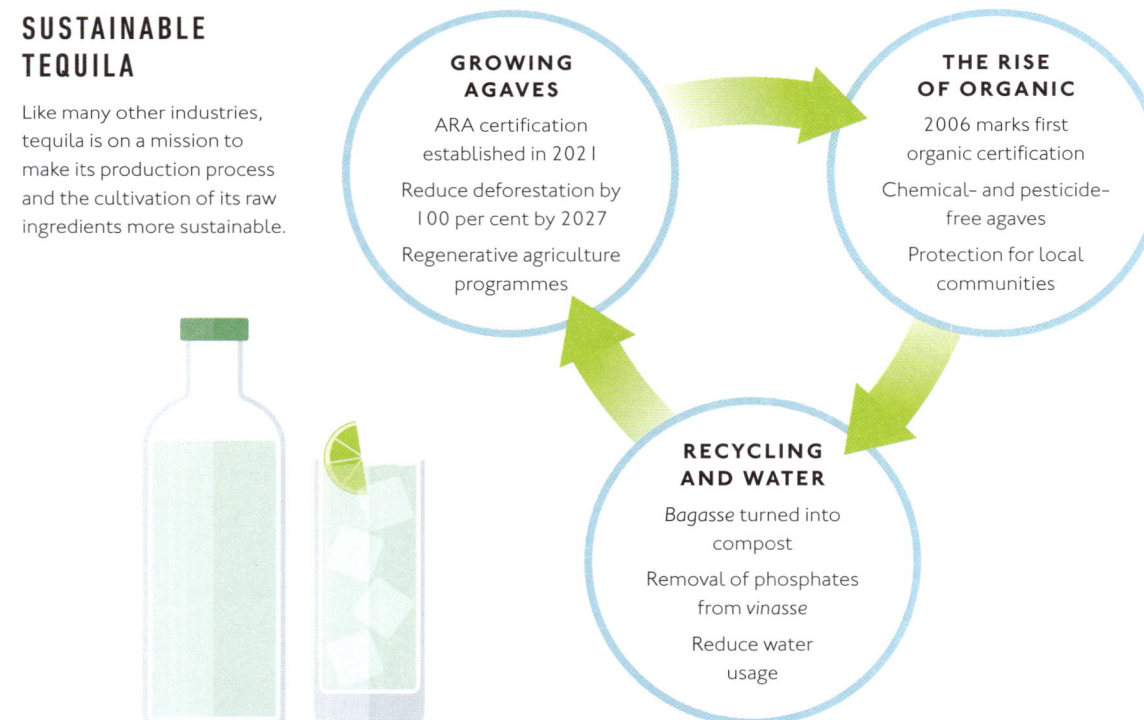

GROWING AGAVES

ARA certification established in 2021

Reduce deforestation by 100 per cent by 2027

Regenerative agriculture programmes

THE RISE OF ORGANIC

2006 marks first organic certification

Chemical- and pesticide-free agaves

Protection for local communities

RECYCLING AND WATER

Bagasse turned into compost

Removal of phosphates from *vinasse*

Reduce water usage

MORE DISTILLERIES ARE DISPOSING OF OR RECYCLING THEIR WASTE BYPRODUCTS RESPONSIBLY.

SUSTAINABLE TEQUILA DISTILLERIES

There are plenty of ways makers can do their bit for the planet. These five distilleries are doing the work.

EL PANDILLO	PATRÓN	AMBHAR TEQUILA	CASA SAUZA	MIJENTA
Proving that new isn't always best when it comes to tequila-making, much of El Pandillo's operations are aided by gravity, meaning it needs less energy to operate.	Patrón has put in place stringent processes to turn leftover agave fibres into compost, reduce its water consumption, fund research to ensure the sustainability of the blue agave, and pay a minimum price to farmers.	Ambhar is utilizing its sustainable expertise to focus on water: it collects rainwater to irrigate its agave fields.	Both the CRT and National Quality Award have recognized Casa Sauza for its sustainability credentials. These include removing 99 per cent of the pollutants in its waste water.	The first tequila brand to gain B Corp status, Mijenta is completely carbon neutral: its bottles are made from recycled glass, and its labels are made with recycled agave fibres.

THE RISE OF ORGANIC

In 2006, 4 Copas became the first certified organic tequila, using chemical- and pesticide-free agaves. Since then, more brands are adopting organic status, such as Casa Noble and 123. The wellbeing and economic stability of farmers are also important factors, and organizations like SACRED are working with the land and communities that look after it to make sure families and agaves are protected from industrialization.

WHAT ABOUT WASTE?

At the end of the production process, distilleries are left with two main waste byproducts: *bagasse* (agave fibres) and *vinasse* (an acidic water left over from distillation). More distilleries are disposing of or recycling these responsibly, such as turning *bagasse* into fertilized compost, and removing hazardous pollutants, such as phosphates, from their *vinasse*.

THE ROLE OF BATS

The unsung heroes of agave pollination, bats are part of the conversation when it comes to biodiversity and the future of agave spirits like tequila.

PROLIFIC POLLINATORS

More than 500 plant species rely on bats to pollinate their flowers, and agave is one of them. Species such as the lesser long-nosed and greater long-nosed bat have evolved over time to carry pollen between agaves, which sustains genetic diversity.

Cultivation of the blue agave for tequila is a monoculture, and with industrial agave farming on the rise and excessive cloning of plants, which bypasses pollination, the genetic diversity of agaves is dwindling. In fact, in the last 10 years, experts have discovered that hundreds of millions of agave plants are descendants of just two individual agaves. Bats, it's believed, could still play a crucial role in maintaining the genetic diversity of agaves.

GENETIC DIVERSITY

Why does the lack of genetic diversity between agave plants matter? The reason is that if all blue agave plants are essentially genetically identical, they are all potentially susceptible to pests and disease. Given that, by law, tequila relies solely on the blue agave for its production, this lack of genetic diversity could be very problematic for the industry.

> BATS COULD PLAY A CRUCIAL ROLE IN MAINTAINING THE GENETIC DIVERSITY OF AGAVES.

THE BAT MAN OF MEXICO

An expert in the field is Rodrigo Medellín, a Mexican ecologist and senior professor of ecology at the University of Mexico. Known affectionately as "the bat man of Mexico", he has worked continuously on discovering groundbreaking information about bats and documenting the role they play in the ecosystem all over Mexico. He has featured in multiple documentaries, including one narrated by British natural historian Sir David Attenborough: *The Bat Man of Mexico* (2014).

RODRIGO MEDELLÍN
Medellín has spent more than 30 years researching and campaigning to save bats in Mexico.

HOW BATS POLLINATE

The pollination of plants by bats is called chiropterophily. Some bats, such as the lesser long-nosed bat, are nectarivorous – they feed on nectar. They find this food source in the flowers of plants like the agave. As they feed at night, they become covered in pollen. When they fly from plant to plant, they disperse the pollen onto other flowering agaves, spreading pollen over vast distances and promoting genetic diversity.

POLLEN PORTERS
The bat's body and wings become coated in pollen as it flies from plant to plant

1 Nectar-feeding bats are attracted to the flowers of the agave plant, which open at night.

2 As they feed on the nectar inside the flowers, their body and wings become covered in pollen.

3 They deposit the pollen on other agave plants as they feed, sometimes over long distances.

THE BAT FRIENDLY PROJECT

With a roll call of tequila and mezcal brands – and industry bigwigs including Rodrigo Medellín (see box opposite) – on its board, Bat Friendly is an organization that works to recognize and preserve sustainable practices in bats' ecosystems where agave is the main crop used for making agave distillates, such as tequila.

The majority of agaves are harvested for tequila before they flower so that sugars are diverted to the *piñas*. In an effort to promote diversity, the project aims to incorporate a number of practices in tequila making, such as allowing 5 per cent of agaves to flower so there is enough food for nectar-feeding bats, resulting in pollination and more genetic diversity in agaves. If implemented in the long term, this could be a big step forward not only for bats but also for the tequila industry.

THE FARMING COMMUNITY

The people at the very beginning of the tequila-making process, the farmers, are arguably the most important. Without dedicated and skilled farmers, quality tequila wouldn't exist, and efforts are being made to ensure they are protected and given the respect they deserve.

WHAT'S AT STAKE?

Farmers plant and tend to the precious agave plants until it is time to harvest them, monitoring soil quality and navigating climate change, and they are often the victims of tequila's ever-fluctuating market. When supply outstrips demand, the price of agaves drops, and the fallout for smaller-scale farmers can be business ending.

During the tequila crisis in the 2000s, when the price of agave dropped from 25 pesos per kilogram (2¼lb) in 2000 to 3 pesos per kilo in 2007, 15,000 farmers in 2000 were reduced to 8,000 by 2007. In 2024, there were 22,000 registered farmers and prices were falling, so it's difficult to predict how many will still be operating by 2030.

When farms close down, farmers often leave their agaves in the ground as they can't afford to pay to have them harvested. Left untended, these plants fall prey to pests and disease, which jeopardize wildlife and nearby agave crops.

In 2025, a slow in demand led to a 500-million-litre (110-million-gallon) tequila surplus, raising further doubts about the industry's future.

THE TEQUILA CRISIS

The tequila crisis in the 2000s saw the price of agaves drop and the number of farmers reduced by almost a half.

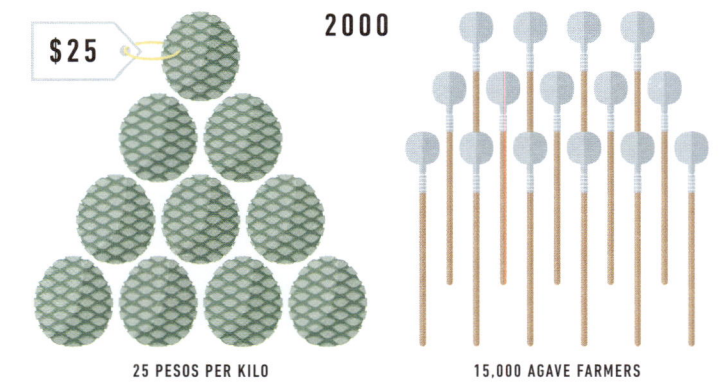

$25

2000

25 PESOS PER KILO   15,000 AGAVE FARMERS

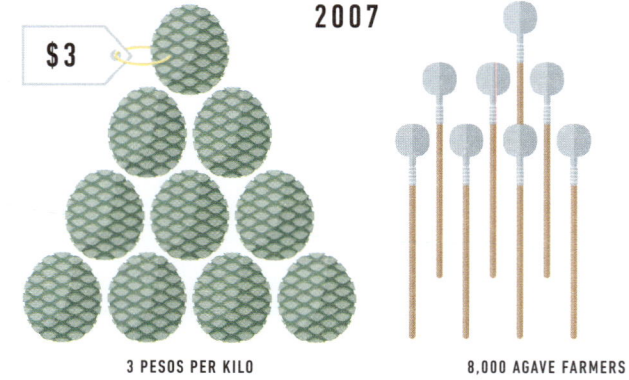

$3

2007

3 PESOS PER KILO   8,000 AGAVE FARMERS

A NUMBER OF TEQUILA BRANDS ARE WORKING ON A FAIR TRADE AGREEMENT WITH THEIR FARMERS.

BRANDS THAT CARE

To reduce the risk for farmers and maintain healthy relationships with suppliers, a number of brands are working on a fair trade agreement with their farmers. The aim is to engender loyalty from suppliers and ensure brands take responsibility for sourcing agaves in an ethical and respectful way. Tequila Ocho, 123, Casa Noble, and Hermosa are all brands that pay a standard minimum price for their agaves, regardless of the market price, and they also ensure their farmers work in safe and sustainable conditions. Mijenta's Community Foundation offers healthcare and education development for local team members and their families.

FARMERS OF NOTE

Agave farmers deserve more credit. Here are five that are worthy of note.

ILIANA PARTIDA	ADOLFO MURILLO	PEDRO CHAVEZ ESQUIVEL	CARLOS PADILLA	LETICIA HERMOSILLO RAVELERO
The daughter of a third-generation farmer and distiller, Partida has continued her family's legacy by farming agave as well as making tequila, and is the CEO of Hacienda de Oro distillery.	Founder, president, and CEO of Alquimia Tequila, Murillo was born in Mexico and raised in the United States. He returned to his birth town of Agua Negra, Jalisco, where he took on the family farm and began planting agave.	A farmer for Don Julio, Esquivel started his career as a mule driver and now manages a group of *jimadores*. Following in the footsteps of his father, he works with his brothers and sons in the agave fields.	The Padilla family has been producing tequila for decades, and Carlos and his family continue that story in San Julian in Los Altos, Jalisco, as an agave farmer as well as *tequilero* for brands like Madre, TCapri, and Tepozán.	Before Ravelero and her husband launched their brand Cava de Oro in 1998, they were agave farmers, and they still are. Ravelero is a pioneer for women working in this part of the industry (see p50).

THE FUTURE OF TEQUILA

Unstable agave costs, growing demand, and lack of biodiversity could all be tequila's undoing. So, what does the future of tequila look like?

CELEBRITY RUSH

When Diageo bought Casamigos from George Clooney for a staggering US$1 billion, the "Clooney Effect" set in motion an influx of celebrity brands, such as Kendall Jenner's 818 and Matthew McConaughey's Pantalones. The celebrity brands have supercharged consumer awareness of the category but have also led to a surge in demand, which, due to the time needed to grow agaves, suppliers sometimes struggle to keep up with.

HIGH POINTS

In 2021, tequila production hit the highest rate ever at 530 million litres (116 million gallons). Then, in 2022, it beat its own record and made 650 million litres (143 million gallons). Although demand is still high, the length of time needed for agaves to mature means the supply chain is often unbalanced. There was a tequila lake in 2025 (see p94) as demand for tequila wasn't sufficient to keep pace with the quantity of agaves planted seven or so years ago.

DANGERS OF DEMAND

Predicting what the market will look like in five or eight years' time from planting the agaves isn't easy. There is often a shortage or surplus of supply, which impacts agave prices and tequila quality, with agaves being harvested earlier to meet demand. People such as Iván Saldaña, an agave expert who has launched more than 60 spirits brands, are leading the discussion about extending the DO to allow agaves to grow in other regions in Mexico.

AGAVE SUPPLY
The price of agaves is higher in shortage and lower in surplus. When prices are low, the economic stability of farmers is at risk.

PROTECTING AGAVE STOCKS

Deforestation is also a growing issue in Mexico (see p90), so looking after the stocks of agave we do have will be important in the years to come. Cross-pollination is attracting more interest through programmes like the Bat Friendly Project (see p93), which aims to protect agave crops from pests and disease and ease pressure on farmers.

PREMIUMIZATION

Although demand for premium tequilas has slowed in key markets like the US, thirst for 100 per cent agave tequilas is growing. While this feeds innovation and often improves sustainability credentials (see p91), it also requires more agaves and puts the huge *mixto* market under threat. But using 100 per cent agave doesn't always equal quality, and the use of additives, diffusers, and column stills for yield and efficiency may impact quality.

    With countries outside Mexico, such as India and Australia, beginning to experiment with making agave-based spirits, tequila is going to have to work hard to maintain its peak status in what feels like its golden age.

AGAVE'S WORTH

This graph shows how the price of agave has flip-flopped over the last few decades, with large fluctuations in price per kilogram (2¼lb). When prices are high, farmers tend to plant more agaves. This can lead to a surplus seven or so years later, driving the price down, which, in turn, can lead to underplanting.

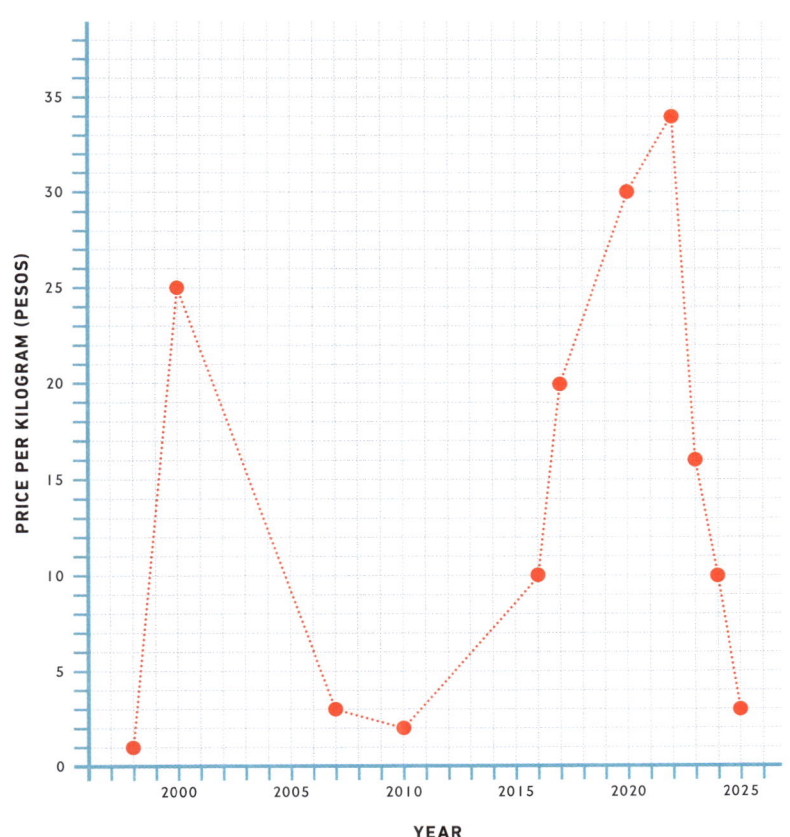

TASTING
----- TEQUILA -----

LEARNING HOW TO TASTE SPIRITS while also having fun is the name of the game for this section. There are multiple factors that can impact our sense of taste and therefore the flavours we experience when drinking tequila. Here we'll explore what happens when we drink it. We start with the dual concepts of taste and flavour, both often misunderstood but key when it comes to observing what we experience when we drink tequila. There's a crash course in tasting terms and common descriptors of tequila to help you start your tasting journey. Then it's on to the cool stuff: choosing your glassware, food pairing, and nifty ways of serving tequila. Don't forget – tasting is meant to be fun!

LET'S TALK FLAVOUR

While the perception of flavour is a physiological process, it can also be highly subjective, based on our memories and expectations of flavour and aroma. Here we look at how this impacts the flavours we experience in tequila.

TASTE AND FLAVOUR

Although taste and flavour are two different things, they are intrinsically linked. Taste is the identification of five main characteristics in the mouth – sweet, salty, umami, bitter, and sour (see pp104–05). Flavour is a more subjective process in which we sense volatile molecules, and our brain translates them into what we know to be flavour. The perception of flavour can also involve the other senses, such as smell, texture and mouthfeel, visual clues, temperature, and even sound (see p105).

COMPOUNDS

Compounds can relate to a certain set of aromas and flavours.

ETHYL ACETATE	Glue-like aroma
ISOAMYL ACETATE	An important aroma of fruits such as banana and flowers
2-PHENYLETHANOL	Rose, jasmine, and honey aromas
ISOBUTYL ACETATE	Sweet-fruits aromas
ETHYL CAPROATE/ CAPRYLATE	Sour-apple aroma
DIACETYL	Buttery, popcorn aromas and flavours
LINALOOL	Citrus, spicy, and tropical aromas and flavours
VANILLINS	Often absorbed from wood and present as vanilla, nuts, and sweetness
ISOVALERALDEHYDE	In small amounts, it adds characterful sour, cheese, and damp aromas
BETA-DAMASCENONE	Associated with fruits and spices like strawberry, apple, and tobacco

IT'S JUST CHEMISTRY

What we smell (aromas) and taste when we're drinking tequila are the volatile compounds that have been created during fermentation and concentrated during distillation. Compounds can relate to a certain set of flavours (see box left). The receptors in our mouth and nose detect these chemicals and signal them to the brain, which then translates them into known aromas and flavours it can recognize.

PERSONAL EXPERIENCE

How we experience flavours is different for everyone, depending on the foods we are sensitive to, know best, or have a connection to through memories. While this can make it difficult to find a common ground for describing flavours in tequila, understanding the usual flavours associated with tequila is a good place to start when we want to describe it (refer to the "Tequila Flavour Wheel" on pp106–07).

THE OLFACTORY SYSTEM

Our sense of smell is intrinsically linked with how we experience flavours. If you hold your nose while tasting tequila, you'll notice that you might be able to identify sweet or sour tastes but not individual flavours (see p104). This illustration shows the movement of molecules through the olfactory system, which are detected by our brain as certain aromas and flavours.

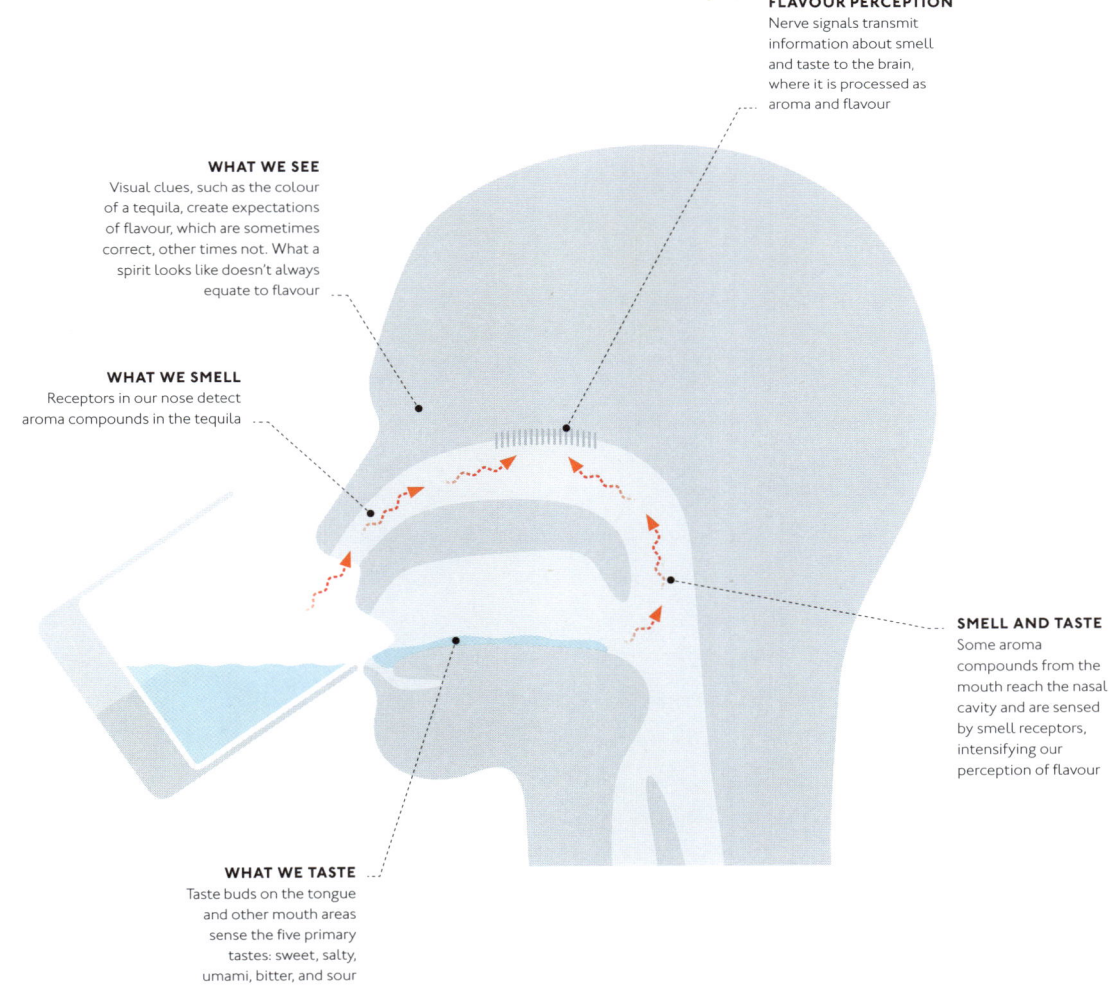

FLAVOUR PERCEPTION
Nerve signals transmit information about smell and taste to the brain, where it is processed as aroma and flavour

WHAT WE SEE
Visual clues, such as the colour of a tequila, create expectations of flavour, which are sometimes correct, other times not. What a spirit looks like doesn't always equate to flavour

WHAT WE SMELL
Receptors in our nose detect aroma compounds in the tequila

SMELL AND TASTE
Some aroma compounds from the mouth reach the nasal cavity and are sensed by smell receptors, intensifying our perception of flavour

WHAT WE TASTE
Taste buds on the tongue and other mouth areas sense the five primary tastes: sweet, salty, umami, bitter, and sour

FLAVOUR PROFILES AND DESCRIPTORS

Understanding the various styles of tequila and why they taste the way they do can be an intimidating task. But luckily, there is some common ground to help you talk about taste like a pro.

TEQUILA FLAVOUR PROFILES

From *blanco* and *joven* to *reposado*, *añejo*, and extra *añejo*, tequila's flavour profiles can sometimes be best understood as twin or juxtaposed characteristics.

SWEET AND RICH Sweetness doesn't equate to saccharine – far from it. Here, we're mainly referring to bright, well-rounded tequilas that showcase a honeyed note coming from the agave. Richness in tequila can come from myriad sources, such as how long a tequila has been aged or the quality of the agave. It can also apply to the mouthfeel.

GRASSY AND HERBAL Herbal and grassy are two of the most common, and combined, profiles, and while they might both conjure similar characteristics, herbal can run the gamut from mint and dill to thyme and coriander (fresh to dried), while grassy often refers to freshly cut grass or even the smell after a rainstorm. Both are derived from that precious agave.

CITRUS AND FLORAL Citrus can come in many forms, such as lime, lemon, orange, or grapefruit, and can be detected in numerous guises, from zest to peel. Floral notes are often present as white or lightly coloured flowers, like elderflower and orange blossom, as well as bringing a distinct freshness to tequilas.

FRUIT AND SPICE Fruit characteristics are often varied, ranging from green apple, pear, and pineapple to citrus oils and peels, and they are derived either from fermentation or ageing, or both. Spice can come in many forms, from white pepper all the way to baking spices like cinnamon and nutmeg, the latter two of which are synonymous with the agave and ageing.

EARTHY AND MINERAL Earthy and mineral notes fall into similar but not identical camps. "Earthy" may refer to the texture as well as to some seemingly undesirable but actually very pleasant notes, like clay or earth. These likely can be attributed to the agave, its *terroir*, and the distillation process. Mineral tequilas are often in earthy territory and are a result of the agave's *terroir*.

SAVOURY AND VEGETAL Savoury tequilas can fall into the green vegetable and earthy descriptors, and the term can sometimes be attributed to younger tequilas. Vegetal qualities are in the form of green veggies, like cucumber or green peppers. These are volatiles drawn out from fermentation and distillation. Both descriptors are indicative of agave character and distillation.

TEQUILA DESCRIPTORS

Keep some of the below descriptors in your back pocket to help you identify some of tequila's key flavour profiles.

AGAVE
Akin to sweet potato (vegetal, caramelized sugar, sweet, and earthy), a common flavour descriptor, usually referenced as "cooked" or "agave".

BANANA
Both green and ripe, works beautifully with coconut.

BUTTERSCOTCH
Creamy and caramel flavour that brings roundness.

CARAMEL
Of the crème or runny variety and associated with sweetness.

CLOVES
A spice that brings some woody and deeper nuance.

COCOA
Often expressed as dark chocolate; can verge into a milkier character.

CUCUMBER
Fresh and crunchy, normally accompanied by other green notes.

EARTH
Clay or soil notes that add complexity and depth.

EUCALYPTUS
A slight medicinal but cleansing aroma that adds freshness.

GRAPEFRUIT
A defined citrus note that bring zip and tartness.

GRASS
Freshly cut, green, wet aroma that brings cleanliness.

GREEN APPLE
Sits with other green notes and adds some floral aromatics too.

HERBS
Mint, dill, tarragon, and thyme all bring a vegetal element.

HONEY
Manuka, blossom, or runny; may have floral characteristics.

JALAPEÑO
Associated with greenness, heat, and brine-like qualities.

LEATHER
Can come with smoke or sometimes a richer, tannic texture.

LIME
Citrus-forward notes with a bit more bite and not too sweet.

LIQUORICE
Can be among general spice notes or a specific aniseed quality.

NUTMEG
Heady and earthy spice that can also bring warmth.

OAK
Found in perhaps young aged tequilas, bringing some texture.

OLIVES
Relating to green olives and brings pleasant drying and bitter notes.

ORANGE
Peel or candied with a perfumed aroma.

PEAR
Orchard fruit notes that aren't particularly apple like.

PEPPER
A salad-like note that combines nicely with white pepper.

PINEAPPLE
Cooked or fresh, found in more tropical-leaning tequilas.

SMOKE
Anything that contains struck-match or smoky aromas and finishes.

VANILLA
Essence or pod, often found in aged tequilas and are a sign of oak.

WHITE/BLACK PEPPER
Usually comes through late on the palate.

WILDFLOWERS
Less common but very distinctive in more ethereal tequilas.

HOW WE TASTE

We taste food and drink every day, and yet *how* we actually taste isn't something we often think about. When we're tasting spirits, it's important to understand exactly what's happening.

TASTE RECEPTORS

Humans have anything from 2,000 to 10,000 taste buds on our tongue. Each taste bud can contain up to 150 receptor cells, which are responsible for identifying the five main taste characteristics: sweet, salty, umami, bitter, and sour. These five can be helpful places to start when we begin trying to identify flavours in our tequila.

All areas of the tongue can detect these tastes, although some may be more sensitive to some tastes than others. There are also taste buds on the roof of the mouth and in the throat. Perceived sweetness

TASTES AND TEQUILA FLAVOURS

The five main tastes can be a useful area to start when identifying flavours in tequila. Let's identify what flavours in tequila belong to each taste category.

SWEET

VANILLA

CARAMEL

HONEY

SOUR

CITRUS

LACTIC

GOOSEBERRY

BITTER

DARK CHOCOLATE

ARTICHOKE

COFFEE

UMAMI

TOBACCO

SEAWEED

TOMATOES

SALTY

CAPERS

JALAPEÑOS

BRINE

DID YOU KNOW?

MUCH OF WHAT WE KNOW
ABOUT TASTE HAS COME TO
LIGHT AS RECENTLY AS THE
LATE 20TH CENTURY.

is often impacted by genetics, which account for up to 30 per cent of the variation between people.

EXTERNAL FACTORS

While we might be focusing on what is in our glass, there are external factors like texture, colour, and sound that impact how we taste. Professor Charles Spence at the University of Oxford has done extensive research on the topic, and his findings include that angular glasses make people more likely to taste sour, bitter, or salty flavours, roundness is associated with sweetness, and that high-pitched music accentuates sweet flavours, as does the colour pink.

TASTING TEQUILA

These external factors all play a role when we are tasting tequila, including what glass we use (see pp114–15), where we taste, and when we taste. The time of day we taste can change our experience – most professional tasters taste in the morning before they've eaten anything. And let's not forget that part of tasting is informed by our memories. Tasting a tequila at a bar in Tequila town will no doubt be a different experience from sipping it in your living room. But as long as you're enjoying it, that's all that really matters.

EXTERNAL FACTORS
The shape of our glass, colours, music, and the time of day we taste can all affect our perception of the flavours in our tequila.

ROUND GLASSES
People often associate round glasses with sweet tastes.

ANGULAR GLASSES
People are more likely to taste sour, bitter, or salty flavours in angular glasses.

THE FIVE MAIN TASTES CAN BE HELPFUL PLACES TO START WHEN IDENTIFYING FLAVOURS IN OUR TEQUILA.

TEQUILA FLAVOUR WHEEL

Identifying flavours in tequila isn't always easy. A flavour wheel can help you to categorize some of the spirit's most common characteristics, which are rated for each tequila in the tasting section (see pp122–79). Use it as a handy reference.

AGAVE FLAVOURS
Agave flavours are hard to identify if you haven't tasted them, but usually they have a caramelized note

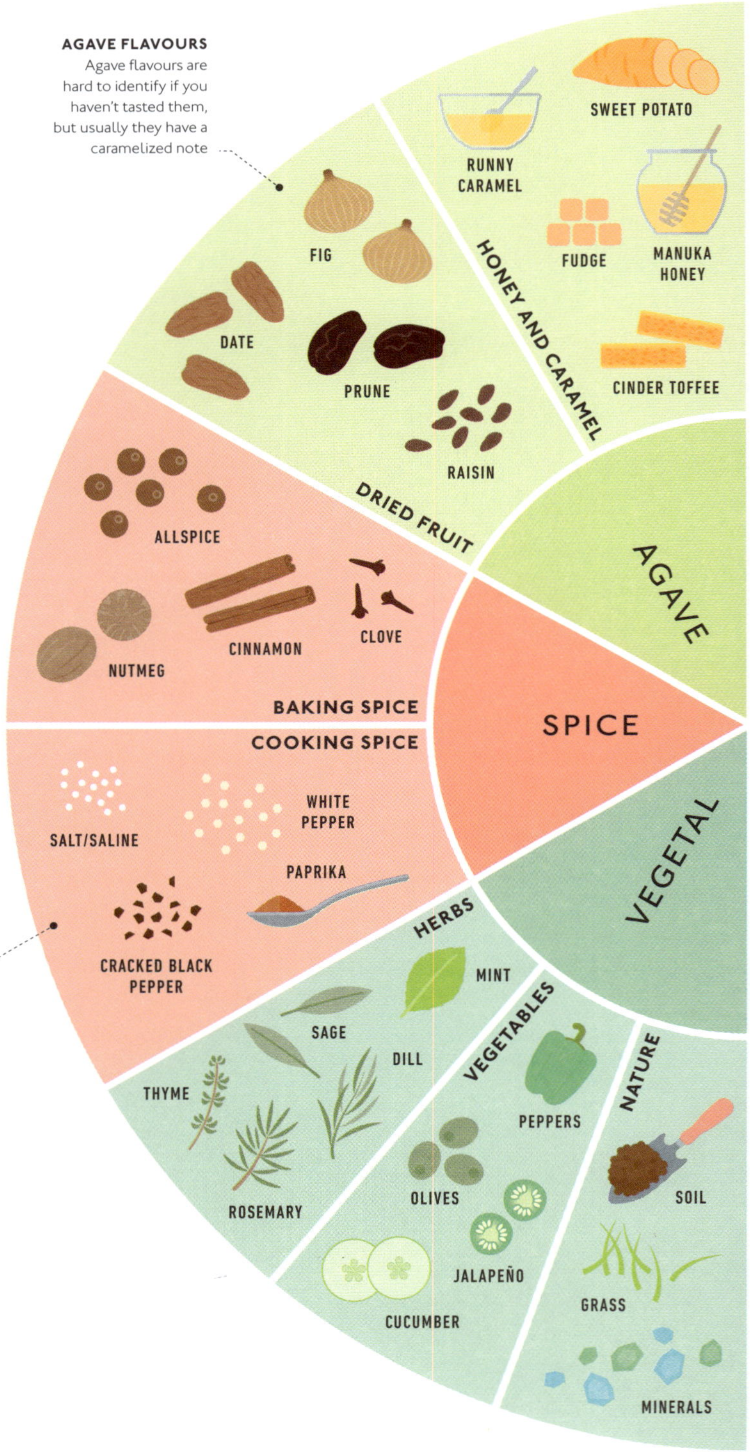

SPICED FLAVOURS
Spiced flavours can translate as a pleasant heat on the palate as well as through flavour

THE FLAVOURS OF TEQUILA

Flavours in tequila can range from the fresh taste of citrus and orchard fruits and the vegetal notes of herbs and jalapeños, to the rich, textural flavours of toasted oak that ageing in wood can impart.

SWEET POTATO
RUNNY CARAMEL
FUDGE
MANUKA HONEY
CINDER TOFFEE
HONEY AND CARAMEL
FIG
DATE
PRUNE
RAISIN
DRIED FRUIT
AGAVE
ALLSPICE
CINNAMON
CLOVE
NUTMEG
BAKING SPICE
COOKING SPICE
SPICE
SALT/SALINE
WHITE PEPPER
PAPRIKA
CRACKED BLACK PEPPER
VEGETAL
HERBS
MINT
SAGE
DILL
VEGETABLES
THYME
PEPPERS
NATURE
ROSEMARY
OLIVES
JALAPEÑO
SOIL
CUCUMBER
GRASS
MINERALS

PINEAPPLE

MANGO

GUAVA

STAR FRUIT

EXOTIC FRUIT

APPLE

APRICOT

CHERRY

PEAR

PEACH

ORCHARD FRUIT

FRUIT

CITRUS

RICH

GRAPEFRUIT

ORANGE

LEMON

LIME

FRUITS

PEEL, JUICE, AND OIL

JUICE

ZEST

PITH

OIL

PEEL

BLOSSOM

NUTS

WOODY

BRAZIL NUTS

ALMONDS

PINE NUTS

HAZELNUTS

TOASTED OAK

BUTTER

COCONUT

VANILLA

CITRUS FLAVOURS
Whether as fruit, peel,
juice, or oil, citrus flavours
can bring a brightness and
zip to tequilas

RICH FLAVOURS
Rich flavours often
translate to texture,
such as mouth coating

A FLAVOUR WHEEL
CAN HELP YOU TO
CATEGORIZE SOME
OF THE SPIRIT'S
MOST COMMON
CHARACTERISTICS.

A SYSTEMATIC APPROACH TO TASTING TEQUILA

While swilling glasses and looking profoundly into the distance are well-worn tropes when it comes to tasting drinks, there are numerous ways in which most spirits professionals approach the task at hand. While everyone has their own way of tasting, there are some common and helpful questions to ask yourself as you work through your tequilas. And remember – have fun!

WHAT DOES IT LOOK LIKE?

Make sure your glass is clean before you start. While the visuals of a spirit, and especially tequila, don't necessarily give accurate information on flavour or age, having a good look at the liquid in your glass can help to determine a number of things. If there is a colour to the liquid, the chances are it has either been aged or has had colouring added to it to give the illusion of age. The clarity of the liquid is important too. You should be able to see a clear (but not necessarily colourless) liquid. If it's murky or has residue or sediment present, this might indicate a fault in the liquid.

WHAT DOES IT SMELL LIKE?

What professionals or tasting notes might refer to as the "nose" is what a spirit smells like. It's a good indicator of what this spirit is and what to expect from it. A tip: avoid swilling spirits in the glass too vigorously, as this usually just releases the alcohol and will give you a big blast of ethanol when you go in for a sniff. When you're ready to smell, hold your glass near your chest and slowly bring it to your nose until you begin to detect certain aromas. Then try to identify what those aromas are. Whatever category your tequila is, it will have some tell-tale notes: aged tequilas might give off some vanilla notes, while a *blanco* could be more vegetal or herbal.

WHATEVER CATEGORY YOUR TEQUILA IS, IT WILL HAVE SOME TELL-TALE NOTES, SUCH AS VANILLA, VEGETAL, OR HERBAL.

WHAT DOES IT TASTE LIKE?

The next step is to identify what you can taste on the palate. As with anything, practice makes perfect, so try to get used to holding the tequila in your mouth and allowing it to coat the surface. Think about the aromas you identified on the nose and see if you can expand them: for example, what was apple on the nose might now be green apple on the palate. Think about texture too: is it mouth coating, thin, hot with alcohol, or pleasantly warming? Finally, have a think about the lasting impression or finish once you've either swallowed or spat your tequila into a spittoon. Do the pleasant flavours linger or do they dissipate? Are you left with an unpleasant taste in your mouth?

WHAT DO YOU THINK OF IT?

When it comes to professional judging, personal preferences shouldn't impact what you believe to be the quality of a tequila. If you're tasting for pleasure, though, then of course start to build an idea of what you like and don't like. Either way, it's helpful to have an idea of what you consider to be the quality or success of the tequila you tasted, and have some kind of scoring system that you find helpful. Numerous bodies such as the Wine & Spirit Education Trust (WSET) have tasting criteria checklists that can be useful to follow. See "Writing Tasting Notes" on pp112–13 for some ideas on how to review and rate your tequila.

THE A–Z OF TASTING

The words used in tequila tasting notes can sometimes be elusive and confusing for a beginner to the game. Here is a helpful A–Z to help you become more familiar with the lingo.

ACIDIC

A sharp or sour taste, normally associated with citric acid or citrus fruits in cocktails.

BALANCED

A group of flavours or aromas working in harmony, not overpowered by one distinct characteristic.

CRISP

Clearly defined and vivid flavours, which usually leave the palate feeling fresh and clean.

DRY

Makes the lips smack or cheeks pucker slightly and is dependent on a lack of sugars.

EARTH

Evokes the flavours of soil or unwashed vegetables and is often a rich undertone. It may sound unpleasant but can be delicious.

FINISH

The lasting impact of flavours in the mouth, often described as short, medium, or long.

GREEN

Refers to a herbaceous, green fruit, such as lime, or vegetal characteristic.

HOT

Can refer to alcohol that is too strong and overpowering on the palate.

INSIPID

Lacking any clear flavours or lingering notes of any description.

JUICY

Elicits a mouthwatering effect on the palate, or is reminiscent of sweet fruit juice rather than fruit oils or peels.

KUMQUAT

Fruits are common flavour descriptors. Fruit flavours can come from the agave, or from the fermentation and/or ageing process.

LACTIC

Referring to lactic acid, this might present itself as slightly milky or sour on the palate, and is not necessarily unpleasant.

MOUTHFEEL

Refers to how the spirit feels in the mouth, such as thick, thin, mouth coating, silky, or creamy.

NOSE

Refers to what we smell, which can often give us an inkling as to what flavours to expect.

OILY

An oil-like consistency or texture to the liquid, normally detected on the palate.

PHENOLIC

A distinctive compound that might give off medicinal or sticking plaster (Band Aid) aromas that are a result of the ageing process.

QUALITY

Judging a tequila's quality is a skill learnt over time. Practice and tasting a large range of tequilas help to decipher the best of the best and understand production techniques.

RICH

A combination of flavour and texture, this often refers to tequilas that exhibit notes of chocolate and caramel and have a full-bodied or viscous mouthfeel.

SULPHUROUS

Copper is used in distillation to reduce sulphur compounds that occur during fermentation. They present as a rotten-eggs smell – not good.

THIN

Refers to a thin and insipid mouthfeel, almost like water.

UMAMI

When used correctly, this taste is often associated with savoury flavours like mushroom, seaweed, yeast extract, and soy sauce.

VISCOUS

A thick, almost sticky mouthfeel and texture. Too viscous, and it can tip into being sickly and cloying.

WARMING

Refers to alcohol levels that are well judged and create a pleasant, warming effect in the mouth and throat. Can also refer to any spiced notes.

(E)XPRESSIVE

Bursting with clear flavours associated with a particular tequila, such as caramel for aged or citrus for *blanco*.

YELLOW

Some people taste in colours (called synesthesia), and describing spirits as colours can help them discern certain flavours.

ZIPPY

Lively on the palate, dancing with flavours, and usually rather exciting and enlivening for the taster.

WRITING TASTING NOTES

Putting your thoughts about a spirit down on paper can be daunting, but it's a brilliant way of recalling patterns and also developing your vocabulary around tequila.

WHY DO WE WRITE TASTING NOTES?

Getting into the practice of writing tasting notes is helpful in a number of ways. First, it forces you to verbalize and identify key aroma and flavour characteristics by writing something down. Second, as you build up a database of your own tasting notes, you begin to notice patterns and common notes that are distinctive to you. This can be a good way of realizing what you are good at identifying, but it also highlights areas in aroma and flavour detection that you may need to expand.

HOW DO WE RECORD TASTING NOTES?

I'd be lying if I said I had a fool-proof way of recording tasting notes. My desk is littered with notebooks full of sticky notes. But having a specific tasting notebook for when you are on the move, either on a tablet or laptop or a hard copy, is something that – if you're serious about building up this skill – would be a good idea.

Whichever method (paper or online) you prefer, you can break it down into tequila categories, alphabetize your entries, or section them into brand groups to keep track of your notes.

HOW DO WE USE TASTING NOTES?

Think how you want to use these notes in the future – as a record, a resource, or an inventory? While professionals might use tasting notes to write an article or a review or judge a competition, the enthusiast can use their tasting notes in any way they want.

If you're recording electronically, you could use helpful filters to find your favourites quickly, or add handy common flavour columns – like vanilla, chocolate, or grassy – so you can select tequilas for your friends based on their favourite tasting notes.

If price is important to you, include that too – value doesn't impact flavour, but you should bear it in mind when considering quality and how the product has been made. And once you've built your confidence, honing your rating system will be valuable too.

HONING YOUR NOTES

As you begin to build your tasting notes, see if you can refine some of the most common words. For example, is pepper white, black, or pink? Is vanilla fresh or essence? This will help you develop as a taster.

WRITING TASTING NOTES CAN BE A GOOD WAY OF HIGHLIGHTING AREAS OF AROMA AND FLAVOUR DETECTION YOU MAY NEED TO EXPAND.

TASTING SHEET

Use your tasting sheet to note down details of the tequila you're tasting, such as category and age, as well as your observations on its aroma, palate, and finish.

TEQUILA NAME

CATEGORY ☐ *BLANCO* ☐ *JOVEN* ☐ *REPOSADO* ☐ *AÑEJO* ☐ *EXTRA AÑEJO*

INFORMATION (AGE, PRODUCTION, ADDITIVES)

NOSE
SUCH AS GRASS, CITRUS, CARAMEL, SPICE

PALATE
SUCH AS WHITE PEPPER, THYME, GRAPEFRUIT, CACAO

FINISH
SHORT, MEDIUM, OR LONG

OTHER OBSERVATIONS
SUCH AS TEXTURE, LOOK, MOUTHFEEL

USP
SUCH AS PRICE POINT, BOTTLE DESIGN, PACKAGING

RATING
★ VERY POOR ★ POOR ★ GOOD ★ VERY GOOD ★ OUTSTANDING

DOES THE GLASS MATTER?

When we're tasting or sipping a drink, the receptacle we use – its shape, texture, weight, temperature, and material – can change our experience of what we're drinking.

THE SENSORY EFFECTS

Much research has gone into how human perception as well as a liquid's density and aroma change depending on the vessel it is served in. Professor Charles Spence of Oxford University was commissioned by Maestro Dobel Tequila to produce "The Perfect Serve" report, which showed, among other things, that the heavier the glass, the greater a person's perception of aromas.

As we've seen, how we taste has a lot to do with our olfactory system and what we smell. So how can different glasses influence our sensory system? Shape is probably the most important factor for tasting, as it changes the movement of molecules and how we perceive them as aromas. Wide-rimmed glasses let aromas out of the glass, while narrower ones concentrate them. Roundness is also said to be more likely to highlight sweeter flavours, while angular receptacles might be better suited to more bitter tastes (see p105).

Traditional Mexican materials like ceramics or clay can add a pleasant point of difference. Clay can round or soften a liquid. And an opaque vessel removes any visual cues that might affect our perception of aroma or flavour.

WHICH GLASS WHEN?

Having done many tastings over the years, I've been served tequila in everything from stemmed glassware to *barro negro* (black clay) cups. For me, the glass you use depends on the occasion when you're enjoying your tequila.

FOR TASTING
These glasses should be reserved for professional settings or tastings.

RIEDEL BAR TEQUILA
The official tequila tasting glass as approved by the CRT, designed in 2001.

TULIP TASTING GLASS
These generic tasting glasses are often used for tasting all kinds of spirits.

FOR COCKTAILS
Different tequila cocktails call for different glasses.

STEMMED GLASS
Serve cocktails without ice in a stemmed glass to avoid heat from the drinker's hands warming up the glass.

ROCKS GLASS
Serve short cocktails with ice in a rocks glass.

FOR SIPPING

These are suitable for less formal tastings when you're casually exploring tequila.

VELADORA GLASS
This small, ridged shot glass is beautifully tactile and not too serious, but allows tequilas to open up.

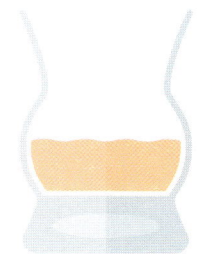

DENVER & LIELY AGAVE GLASS
This glass can be used across the agave spirit category and concentrates aromas before opening them up.

GLASS SHAPE IS PROBABLY THE MOST IMPORTANT FACTOR FOR TASTING.

FOR SOCIALIZING

Treat yourself and your friends to something a little different or special with these receptacles.

BARRO NEGRO CUP
This style of pottery from Oaxaca is often associated with mezcal, and it brings a beautiful and traditional feel to a tasting.

SMALL CERAMIC BOWLS
A series of sipping bowls can be a lovely way of presenting tequila and sharing it with friends.

CLAY CUP
Traditional clay cups for serving the Cantarito cocktail (see pp192–93) impart flavour and texture.

HIGHBALL
Serve long cocktails with more dilution in a highball or Collins glass.

NICK & NORA
This is a more modern style that is useful for multipurpose cocktails and riffs like Martinis.

COUPE OR MARGARITA
These are more versatile and can be used for multiple cocktails like Margaritas and Matadors (see pp196–201).

THE C WORD: CITRUS

Lime, lemon, grapefruit, orange, yuzu – you name it, citrus and tequila are the perfect bedfellows. Taste the fruits side by side to see how different they can be.

COCKTAIL CHUM

Oil, peel, juice – however you use them, citrus fruits are a staple when it comes to drinking and mixing agave spirits, including, of course, tequila. Citric acid is the friend of many a cocktail for balance and zip, and – shocker – citrus fruits are the perfect, although not only, way to introduce it into cocktails.

Some of tequila's best-known serves – the Margarita (see pp196–97) and Paloma (see pp202–03), for instance – use citrus fruits as key ingredients or garnishes, while a squeeze of lemon or lime might lift the less citrus-forward ones to new heights. We're not talking a wedge of lime with salt – more like a triangle of grapefruit or orange to have between sips. Use leftover peel to make citrus syrup (see p186) to add to cocktails.

Not all citrus fruits are created equal though, so understanding their profiles, acid, sugar levels, and capabilities is important if you want to experiment with them.

Here are some of the key citrus fruits and varieties to add to your flavour wheelhouse.

LIME

Most likely originating in the Indonesian Archipelago or mainland Asia, limes have been traded for centuries from India to Africa, the Mediterranean, and, in the mid-15th century, to Mexico, Florida, and the West Indies. Limes often surpass lemons in their acid and sugar content, which are key in cocktails.

KEY
Also known as the Mexican lime, this is most likely what you'll find being used in cocktails across Mexico.

PERSIAN
A hybrid of a Key lime and a lemon, Persian lime is what most people associate with this citrus fruit family.

MAKRUT
Native to Southeast Asia, the makrut is a dappled and distinctive lime and errs on the tart side, more like a lemon.

LEMON

The lemon's origins are believed to be in India and Southeast Asia, later spreading to Egypt and Iran. Since then, it has become one of the world's most recognizable citrus fruits. Its juice is often added to cocktails, but usually the peel is most used for its abundance of oil cells that can boost aroma.

EUREKA
The most common lemon around the world, it has a distinctive "nipple" on one end. Its juice is sweet, acidic, and tart.

MEYER
A cross between a lemon and a mandarin, this is a much less acidic lemon, and it can be played with cleverly in tequila cocktails.

SICILIAN
Known primarily for the incredible oiliness of its peel, the Sicilian lemon is the ideal variety for peel garnishes or for expressing over cocktails.

SOME OF TEQUILA'S BEST-KNOWN SERVES USE CITRUS FRUITS AS KEY INGREDIENTS OR GARNISHES.

GRAPEFRUIT/ POMELO

With origins in Barbados, the grapefruit is a hybrid of the pomelo and sweet orange. It became popular in the West Indies, before spreading to the Americas and other citrus-growing countries. Distinctive in flavour, it varies in its tartness and bitterness depending on the variety.

PINK
Subtly sweet and sour, the pink grapefruit is often actually not that pink in colour. It is the base for one of tequila's most popular cocktails, the Paloma.

POMELO
The largest of the citrus fruits, and ancestor of the grapefruit, pomelos are native to Southeast Asia and are more sweet than acidic in taste.

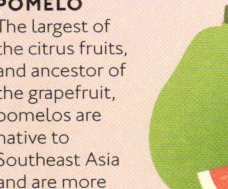

RUBY RED
If it's colour and acidity you want to add to cocktails, then the fresh, vibrant, red juice of the Ruby Red grapefruit is the way to go.

ORANGE

Believed to be native to the tropical regions of Asia, especially the Malay Archipelago, oranges were primarily consumed as food before their acidic and sweet juice started to be drunk. High in sugar, it is an interesting citrus to work with, and its peel is full of oils and complex floral aromas.

BLOOD
With its crimson flesh, the blood orange, also known as the raspberry orange, is sweet in flavour and less acidic than other oranges and has a floral edge.

SEVILLE
Sitting on the bitter and sour scale of the orange varieties, the Seville orange is super high in acidity.

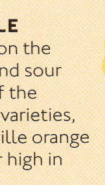

NAVEL
Probably the most shop-bought variety of orange, the navel is a good option for garnishing or adding a wedge.

BEST OF THE REST

The options are endless, and seasonality and availability will, of course, be factors to consider. Feel free to experiment with the three citrus fruits below, or grab something curious at the market and have a play around.

YUZU
A cross between a mandarin and an Ichang papeda, yuzus are super tart, sour, and strong in aroma too – excellent for cocktail making.

BERGAMOT
A hybrid of bitter orange and lemon, the bergamot adds a slightly woodier and earthier element than other citrus fruits.

TANGELO
A mix between a tangerine and a pomelo, the tangelo is tart, tangy, and seriously juicy.

WAYS TO SERVE TEQUILA

Incorporating tequila into your next dinner party or gathering? There are numerous ways to serve it, whether with food, for sharing, or throughout the evening.

SERVING OPTIONS

While you may be a tequila evangelist, introducing tequila to potential converts takes more than just handing them a glass and telling them to try it. It's better to give people options that might already be familiar to them. Offering tequila with a small bucket of ice, some sliced citrus, tonic water, and flavoured sodas

means they can create their own format to enjoy their tequila. If you need some inspiration for vessels in which to serve tequila, refer to pp114–15.

TEMPERATURE MATTERS

When it comes to temperature, it's most commonly accepted that neat tequila should be enjoyed at room temperature (21°C/70°F).

Adding a large cube of ice will allow for some dilution and chilling (see p187), while tequila also works just as well in things like granita as it does in hot cocktails like toddies.

COMMUNAL COCKTAIL

Ceremonially delivering a *cazuela voladora* ("flying casserole" or Guadalajara punch) to the table

CAZUELA VOLADORA

Also known as a Guadalajara punch, a *cazuela voladora* is a way to serve tequila that is sure to impress.

METHOD

1. Mix blanco tequila with equal parts orange, lemon, and grapefruit juice, and a half part of lime juice.

2. Top with grapefruit soda and a large pinch of salt.

3. Add ice and fruit slices, such as orange and grapefruit, and stir.

4. Serve in single small *cazuelas* (earthenware dishes) or punch-style glasses.

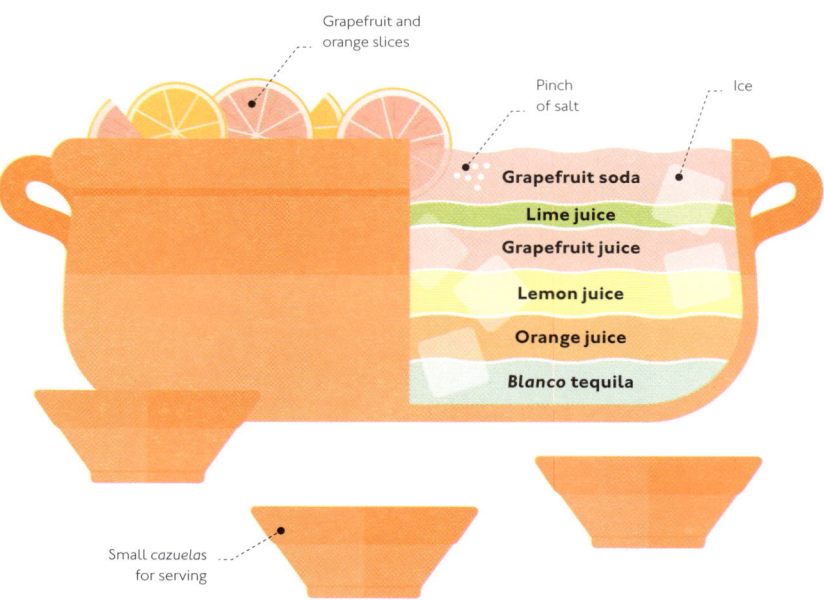

Grapefruit and orange slices

Pinch of salt

Ice

Grapefruit soda
Lime juice
Grapefruit juice
Lemon juice
Orange juice
Blanco tequila

Small *cazuelas* for serving

IF YOU'RE INCORPORATING TEQUILA INTO YOUR DINNER PARTY MENU, START WITH *BLANCOS* AND WORK THROUGH TO AGED TEQUILAS.

THE VIAJANTE WAY

London's Viajante87, a Latin American–inspired bar, has a fun way of serving tequila with its sharing and savouring Agave Serve, which is designed to last through the evening.

A 250ml (9fl oz) or 500ml (18fl oz) carafe of tequila is served with sliced fruit, chilli salt, Verdita (see p214), Sangrita (see p215), guacamole, and tortilla chips.

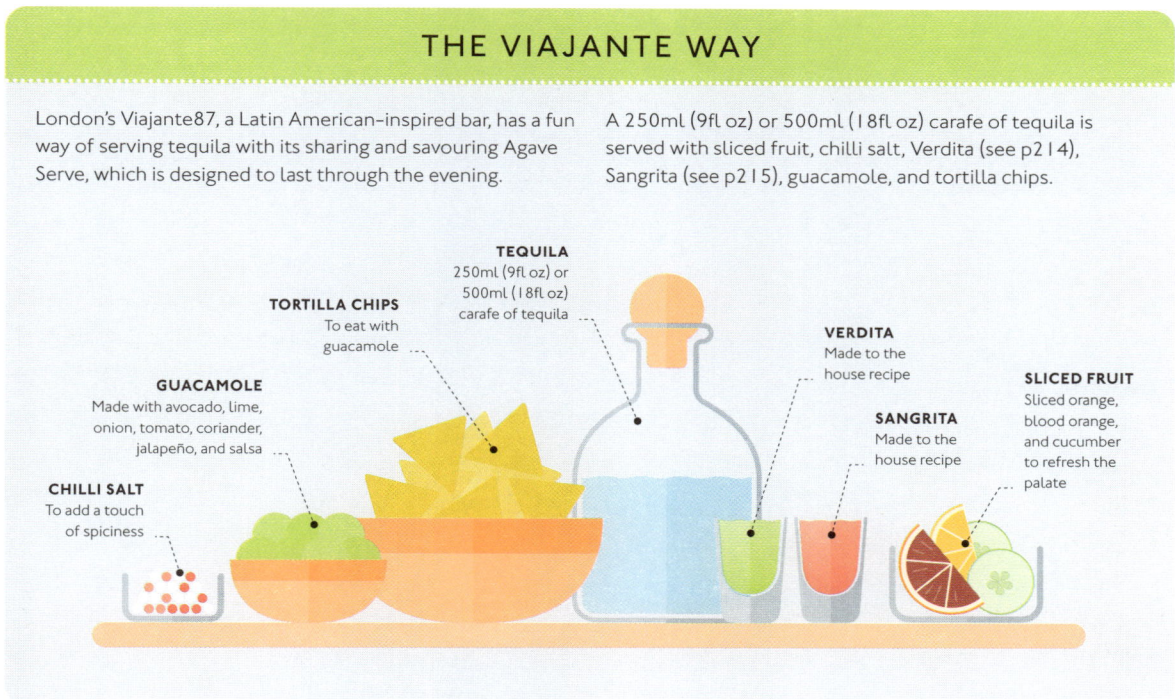

TEQUILA
250ml (9fl oz) or 500ml (18fl oz) carafe of tequila

TORTILLA CHIPS
To eat with guacamole

VERDITA
Made to the house recipe

GUACAMOLE
Made with avocado, lime, onion, tomato, coriander, jalapeño, and salsa

SANGRITA
Made to the house recipe

SLICED FRUIT
Sliced orange, blood orange, and cucumber to refresh the palate

CHILLI SALT
To add a touch of spiciness

is always a showstopper. Made with *blanco* tequila and fruit juices (see left), you can serve it in single small *cazuelas* (earthenware dishes) or punch-style glasses. It is said to have been created in the 1990s at La Barca, a city in Jalisco 100km (60 miles) southeast of Guadalajara, and is now a popular serve in Tlaquepaque.

TEQUILA'S NOT JUST FOR COCKTAILS

Tequila in all its styles pairs beautifully with food (see pp120–21). If you're looking to incorporate tequila into your dinner party menu, consider beginning with a Verdita (see p214) to prepare your guests'

palate, before moving into the matching tequila for your starter, main course, and dessert.

A general rule of thumb is to start with *blancos* through to aged tequilas via *reposados*. *Blancos* work beautifully with fish and salads; *reposados* with some spice, sauces, and red meats; and *añejos* with sweet dishes.

PAIRING TEQUILA AND FOOD

Tacos; chocolate; fruit; cheese; smoked, charred, and grilled meat; fish; and vegetables – the possibilities are endless for pairing your tequilas with food.

FIND YOUR METHOD

The two main principles of pairing food and drink are either matching the flavours of your drink with your food or contrasting them. For example, you could either pair a super-umami and savoury drink with a mushroom dish, or contrast it with a fresh, light food such as fruit or fish.

When it comes to tequila, the principles remain the same, but there are certain foods that really make tequila sing and vice versa. In most instances, the food will dictate the tequila you pair with it, but if you want to start small with your tequila collection, finding foods to match what you have is often more cost effective.

FOODS TO PAIR WITH TEQUILA

You can match food and tequilas neat or in cocktails, depending on what your favourite format is. The best way to find your perfect pair is to experiment, but here are some ideas to get you started.

FISH
Serve with grassy, floral, and citrus-forward *blancos*.

Grilled octopus

Ceviche

Fresh oysters

MEAT
Serve with savoury, earthy *reposados*.

Carnitas tacos

Birria taquitos

Fried chicken

VEGETABLES
Serve with herbal, savoury, and spicy *blancos*.

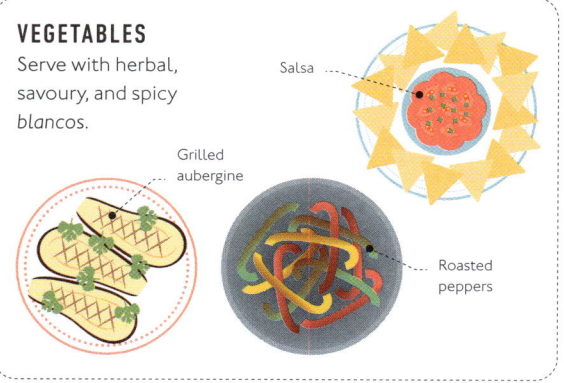

Salsa

Grilled aubergine

Roasted peppers

COOKING WITH TEQUILA

Tequila isn't just for drinking – it can bring another dimension to cooking too.

- **SALSA** Add a splash of tequila to your favourite salsa recipe to bring extra bite to the sweeter flavours of tomato, lime, and garlic.
- **CEVICHE** Mix tequila with some lime to cure raw fish in a classic ceviche recipe with avocado, coriander, and jalapeño. It's particularly good with shrimp ceviche, which is often meatier and can stand up to some alcohol.
- **FLAMBÉ** Nothing says drama like flambé, and using aged tequila to take your dessert, especially tropical fruit, to the next level is a fun way of incorporating it into the menu.

SNACKS

Serve with sweet, herbal, and citrus-forward *blancos*.

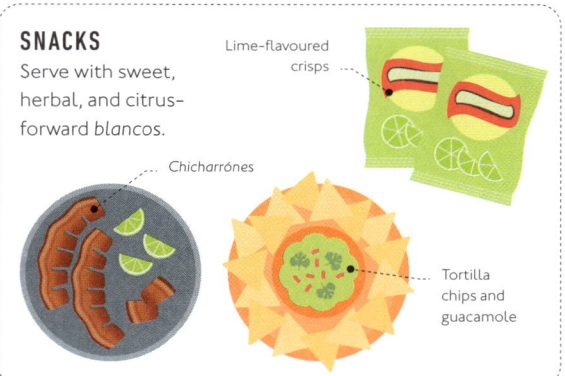

Lime-flavoured crisps

Chicharrónes

Tortilla chips and guacamole

CHOCOLATE

Serve with spicy, rich, and sweet *añejos*.

Dark chocolate with sea salt

Cherry chocolate

Candied citrus dipped in dark chocolate

CHEESE

Serve with earthy, spicy, and fruity extra *añejos*.

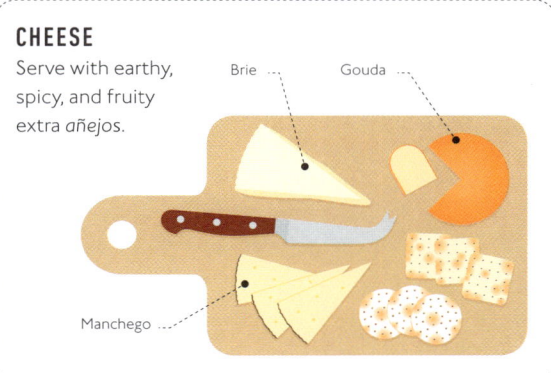

Brie

Gouda

Manchego

FRUIT AND COFFEE

Serve with fruity and savoury *reposados*.

Strawberries

Coffee

Caramelized bananas

NAVIGATING
TEQUILA
----- BY -----
FLAVOUR

WHEN IT COMES TO BUYING TEQUILA or building a collection, it can often feel like a daunting exercise. How do you know what it tastes like before you buy it? Is it good for sipping or better for cocktails? How or where has it been made? In the following pages, you'll find 100 tequilas organized into six dual categories to help you find the perfect style: sweet/rich, grassy/herbal, citrus/floral, fruit/spice, earthy/mineral, and savoury/vegetal. The entries include information about the dominant flavour characteristics, where and how the tequila was made, and the percentage of agave used, as well as tips on how to drink it or standout USPs. Use this section as a nifty database to make choosing your tequilas that bit simpler.

SWEET/RICH TEQUILAS

When we use terms like "sweet" and "rich" in tequila, we aren't talking about tequilas being sickly or confected, but rather showcasing the more unctuous flavours that can be expressed from agaves. Not all of the tequilas in this section have spent a considerable time in wood, which just shows how versatile all the categories of tequila can be.

FLAVOUR NOTES

Dessert sweetness is the name of the game here, with caramel, dried dark fruits, cooked sugar, and baking spices all being present among these styles of tequilas. Richness can also apply to the texture of the tequila, which might have a mouth-coating character or a tannic nature.

SPICES · VANILLA · CARAMEL · DRIED FRUIT · CHOCOLATE · COOKED AGAVE

MIXERS	COCKTAILS
ARTISAN DRINKS COMPANY Fiery Ginger Beer	**SHORT** Honey Trap, Siesta
BIG TOM Spiced Tomato Juice	**LONG** El Diablo, Paloma Negra
KARMA DRINKS Organic Karma Cola	**RIFF** Negroni, Old Fashioned

ARTENOM SELECCIÓN DE 1579

40.7% ABV	*BLANCO*	AGAVE: 100%	EL PANDILLO, JALISCO

FLAVOUR

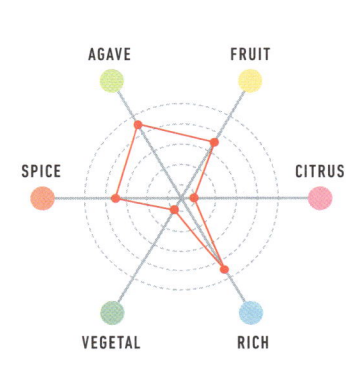

The ArteNOM brand showcases the skill of *maestros tequileros* at some of tequila's NOMs (see p13). This one, made by master distiller Felipe Camarena, is an absolute revelation.

Its aromatic profile begins with vanilla and croissant flakes, followed by buttered popcorn, crème brûlée, tinned pears, and lychees in syrup. When the nose opens up, there is more herbaceousness too. There is florality on the palate, with sticky vanilla pods and elderflower, striped mint sweets, and saltwater toffee. It's an absolutely charming tequila!

AVIÓN RESERVA 44

40% ABV	EXTRA *AÑEJO*	AGAVE: 100%	PRODUCTOS FINOS DE AGAVE, JALISCO

FLAVOUR

Aged for 44 months in American oak (hence the name), this extra *añejo* manages to preserve its agave character alongside classic notes of ageing.

The nose is full of vanilla essence and oak, with some florality and a touch of citrus. For an older tequila, it is surprisingly bright on the palate, not too viscous or syrupy, and is sweet with dried fruit and soft and buttery with a trail-mix quality. The finish is nutty and textured, with some lingering cigar-box smoke and oiliness too. It is an impressive sipper and would work well in whisky cocktail switches.

CASA NOBLE REPOSADO

40% ABV	*REPOSADO*	AGAVE: 100%	LA COFRADÍA, JALISCO

FLAVOUR

AGAVE · FRUIT · CITRUS · RICH · VEGETAL · SPICE

Founded by *maestro tequilero* Jose "Pepe" Hermosillo, Casa Noble grows its organic agave in the mountains of western Jalisco. It triple distils its tequila, and Hermosillo is known for making tequila aged in French oak more popular. This *reposado* has been aged in oak for 364 days.

A vibrant orange-gold colour, it is rich with coconut, vanilla fudge, sweet oak, and toasted almonds on the nose, while the palate is nutty with hints of butter, a slight smokiness, desiccated coconut, muscovado sugar, orchard fruits, and charred peaches too.

CENOTE REPOSADO

40% ABV	*REPOSADO*	AGAVE: 100%	FABRICA DE TEQUILAS FINOS, JALISCO

FLAVOUR

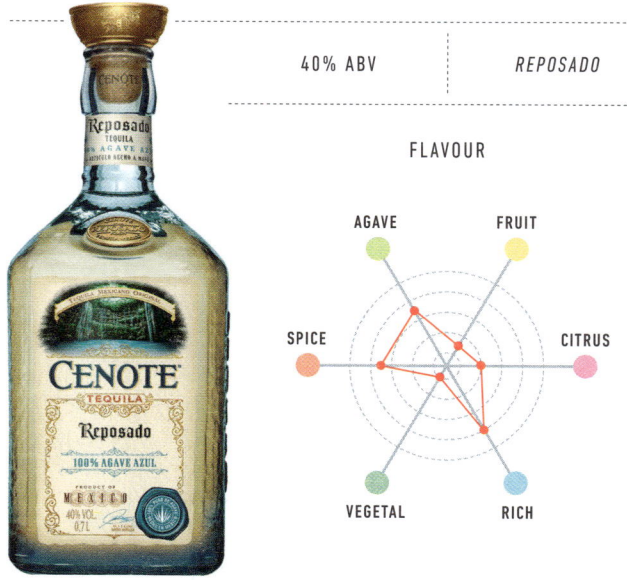

AGAVE · FRUIT · CITRUS · RICH · VEGETAL · SPICE

Formulated by the skilled hand of master distiller Arturo Fuentes Cortes, and using lowland-grown agaves, this *reposado* has spent three months in American oak before being bottled. Beautifully light gold in colour, this tequila really amplifies the impact of wood on Cenote's citrussy, woody *blanco*.

You'll find lightly dusted Turkish delight, pink rose petal, manuka honey, and that tell-tale vanilla on the nose, followed by milk chocolate truffle, baking spices, and hazelnuts on a dryish palate.

CINCORO TEQUILA REPOSADO

40% ABV	*REPOSADO*	AGAVE: 100%	DESTILADORA DEL VALLE DE TEQUILA, JALISCO

FLAVOUR

AGAVE · FRUIT · CITRUS · RICH · VEGETAL · SPICE

Cincoro is owned by National Basketball Association (NBA) legend Michael Jordan and four of his contemporaries. This *reposado* comes at a higher price point than many others on the market, and it's a warming and rich tequila.

Aged underground in Tennessee whiskey barrels for up to 10 months, it is all clotted cream, tonka bean, and a touch vegetal on the nose, while the palate is reminiscent of frangipani, custard doughnuts, brown sugar, and warm baking spices. It's thick, creamy, and mouth coating.

CÓDIGO 1530 REPOSADO

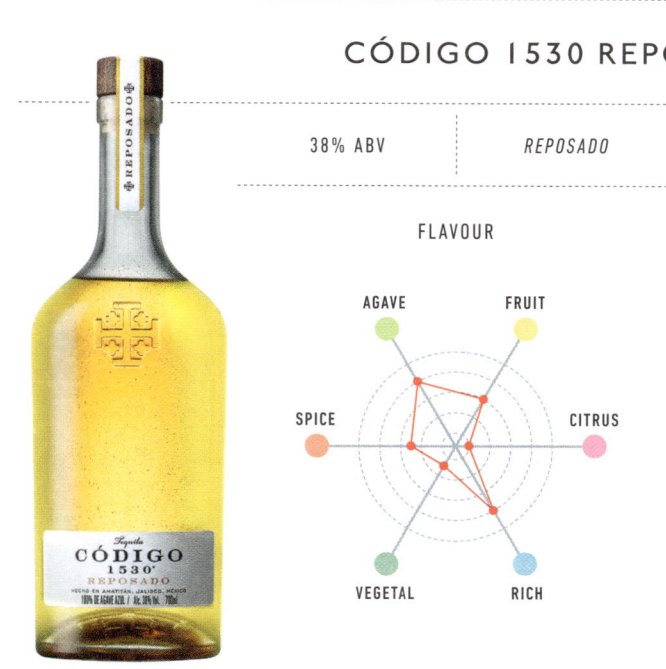

38% ABV	*REPOSADO*	AGAVE: 100%	VARO DESTILERÍA, JALISCO

FLAVOUR

AGAVE · FRUIT · CITRUS · RICH · VEGETAL · SPICE

With a history stretching over generations, but only a decade or so of commercialization, Código 1530 shows its ability to make beautifully balanced tequilas with its *reposado*. Bright and glinting, it is aged for six months in French oak ex-red wine barrels from the Napa Valley.

It's surprisingly light and gentle on the nose, with a lovely florality, vanilla custard, cocoa powder, and a back note of green pepper. On the palate, there's desiccated coconut and fresh vanilla, with a creamy texture. A really elegant sip, this.

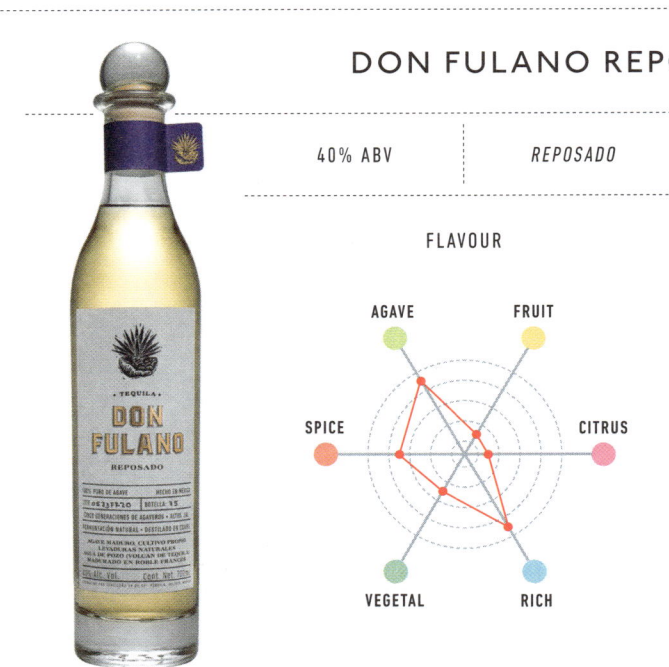

DON FULANO REPOSADO

40% ABV	*REPOSADO*	AGAVE: 100%	TEQUILEÑA, JALISCO

FLAVOUR

This *reposado* tells you it has serious character as soon as you smell it, and it is rich not only in flavour but texture too. While it seems to exert a slightly funky and grassy nature at first, it morphs into sweeter and richer characters.

There are bags of cooked agave with fresh vanilla and milk-bottle sweet notes on the nose. This moves into dark chocolate and chilli on the palate, with a slight smoked element on the finish. This tequila really develops over time, so give it a moment to unfold in the glass.

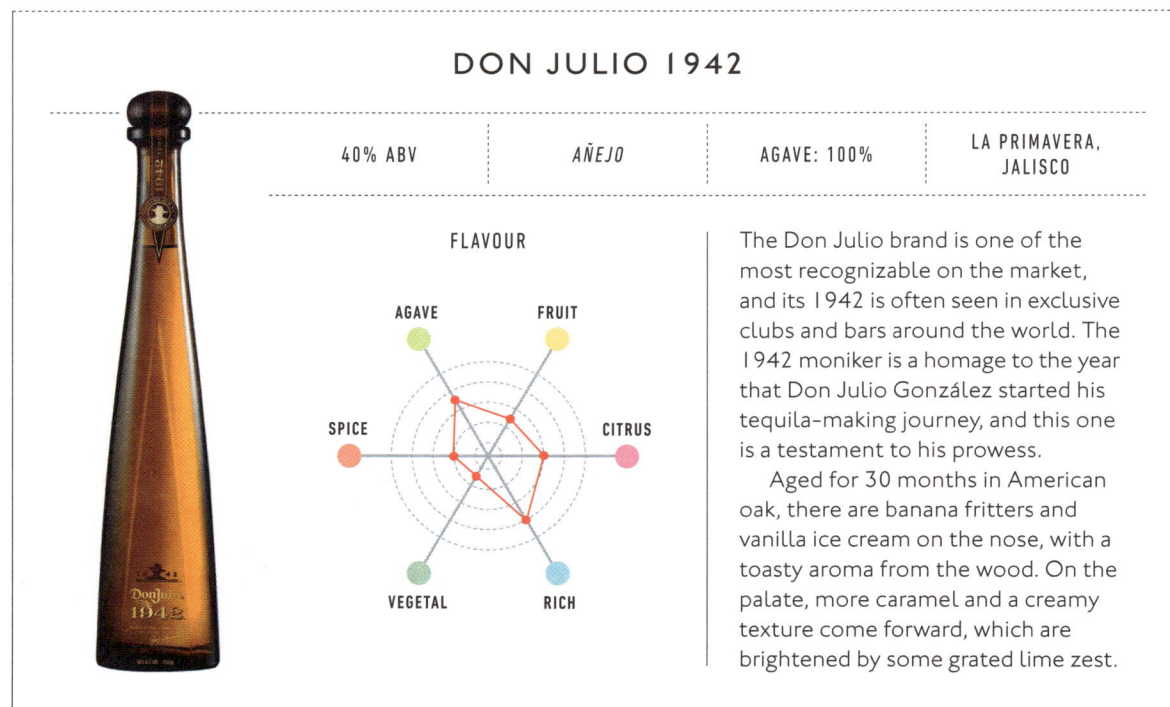

DON JULIO 1942

40% ABV	*AÑEJO*	AGAVE: 100%	LA PRIMAVERA, JALISCO

FLAVOUR

The Don Julio brand is one of the most recognizable on the market, and its 1942 is often seen in exclusive clubs and bars around the world. The 1942 moniker is a homage to the year that Don Julio González started his tequila-making journey, and this one is a testament to his prowess.

Aged for 30 months in American oak, there are banana fritters and vanilla ice cream on the nose, with a toasty aroma from the wood. On the palate, more caramel and a creamy texture come forward, which are brightened by some grated lime zest.

EL MAYOR REPOSADO

40% ABV	*REPOSADO*	AGAVE: 100%	DGL DESTILADORES, JALISCO

FLAVOUR

Behind the El Mayor brand is a fourth-generation family, the Gonzalezes, with *maestro tequilero* Rodolfo Gonzalez at the helm. This *reposado* has been aged in white oak barrels for nine months and is a dessert tequila through and through.

Patisserie cream, toasted coconut, coconut ice cream, chocolate, and cooked agave on the nose are followed by a slightly salty, flaky, butter pastry and sweet spice on the palate, rather like chai tea. It has a creamy texture and a clean but characterful finish. It would work well over vanilla ice cream.

EL TEQUILEÑO REPOSADO

38% ABV	*REPOSADO*	AGAVE: 100%	LA GUARREÑA, JALISCO

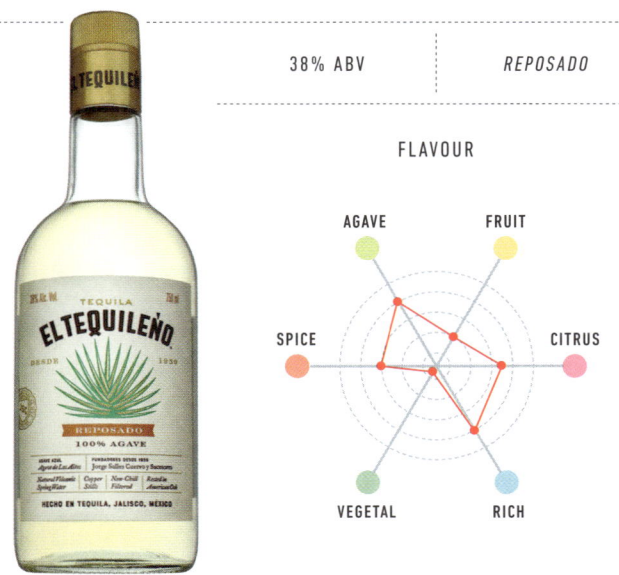

FLAVOUR

Founded in 1959 by Don Jorge Salles Cuervo, El Tequileño is still one of the most recognizable brands in Tequila decades later. While its *blanco* might be the hero expression at home, its *reposado* is much loved too, and its lightness of touch means it retains all that agave character while layering in delicate sweet notes.

There are some orange peel and lime zest briefly on the nose. On the palate, expect more salted caramel and vanilla, along with a whisper of spice and a touch of smoke too.

EL TEQUILEÑO REPOSADO RARE

40% ABV	*REPOSADO*	AGAVE: 100%	LA GUARREÑA, JALISCO

FLAVOUR

Made at La Guarreña distillery and aged in *pipones* (large American oak casks) for six years, this expression from the historic El Tequileño brand was the first of its kind when it launched in 2018, and, to date, it remains the only *reposado* rare.

Fans of marzipan will love this tequila, as it is joined by sweet agave, vanilla, and a fudge-like nose. On the palate, the texture is mouth coating and rich, with a whisper of spice coming through on the finish and a caramelization that lingers beautifully.

KAH REPOSADO

40% ABV	*REPOSADO*	AGAVE: 100%	FABRICA DE TEQUILAS FINOS, JALISCO

FLAVOUR

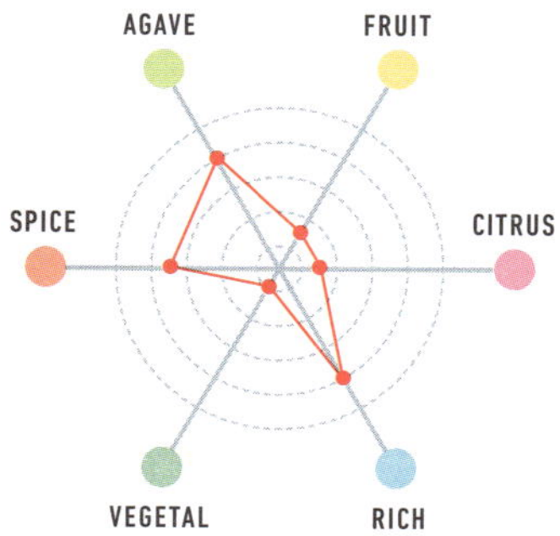

Kah, which means "life" in Mayan, celebrates the Mexican tradition of the Day of the Dead with its skull-format bottles. What's inside the bottle is made by master distiller Arturo Fuentes Cortes, who has half a century of making alcoholic drinks behind him.

This is a sweet and moreish dessert *reposado*, with buttered popcorn, cinder toffee, fudge, and vanilla ice cream on the nose. It moves into a drier palate, which is warming with allspice and cinnamon, with a finish of chocolate nibs.

LA DAMA

40% ABV	BLANCO	AGAVE: 100%	INTEGRADORA SAN AGUSTIN, JALISCO

FLAVOUR

Said to be the biggest grower of organic blue Weber agave in the world, La Dama makes tequila with biodynamic practices in mind. Its *blanco* is green, fresh, and singing with lots of sweet and sour flavours, which makes this a distinctly different tequila, perhaps down to that agave.

On the nose, there is a burst of green apple – almost a bubblegum apple – freshly cut grass, and bright, sweet agave. The texture is chalky, with the sweetness intensified, and it finishes with a white pepper dusting.

MAESTRO DOBEL SILVER

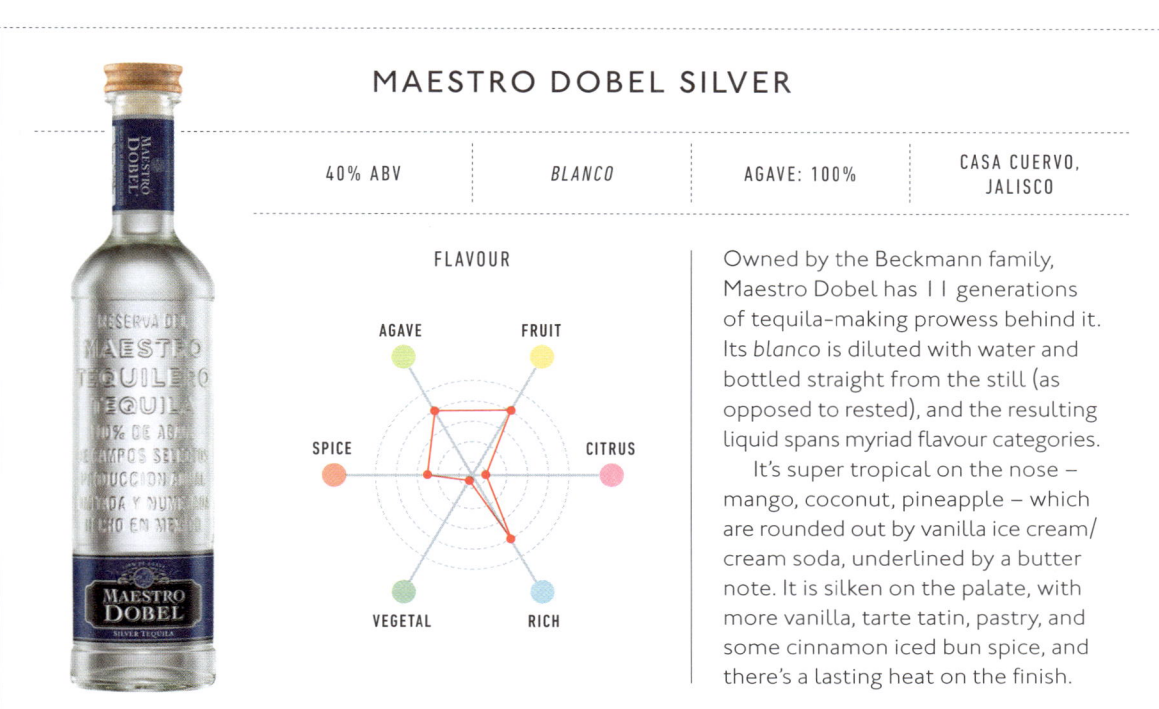

40% ABV	BLANCO	AGAVE: 100%	CASA CUERVO, JALISCO

FLAVOUR

Owned by the Beckmann family, Maestro Dobel has 11 generations of tequila-making prowess behind it. Its *blanco* is diluted with water and bottled straight from the still (as opposed to rested), and the resulting liquid spans myriad flavour categories.

It's super tropical on the nose – mango, coconut, pineapple – which are rounded out by vanilla ice cream/cream soda, underlined by a butter note. It is silken on the palate, with more vanilla, tarte tatin, pastry, and some cinnamon iced bun spice, and there's a lasting heat on the finish.

PATRÓN EL CIELO

40% ABV	BLANCO	AGAVE: 100%	HACIENDA PATRÓN, JALISCO

FLAVOUR

It only takes a glimpse at the statuesque bottle of this *blanco* to know that there is more than meets the eye. The departure from Patrón's usual bottlings means this one might be just a bit special. Indeed, El Cielo has been quadruple distilled to result in an incredibly creamy *blanco*.

On the nose, there is sweet agave and butterscotch. Both notes only become richer on the palate, and a cracked-black-pepper finish follows. The brand suggests serving over ice with a slice of orange, but I'd add a square of dark chocolate too.

ROOSTER ROJO AÑEJO

38% ABV	AÑEJO	AGAVE: 100%	FABRICA DE TEQUILAS FINOS, JALISCO

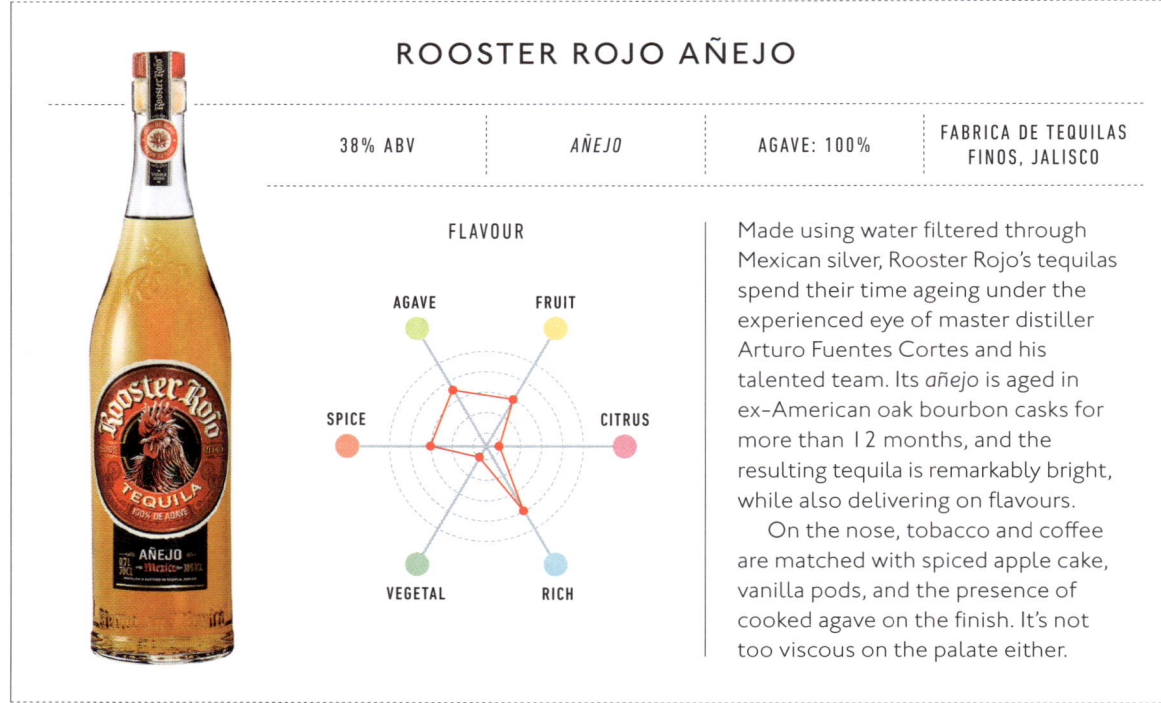

FLAVOUR

Made using water filtered through Mexican silver, Rooster Rojo's tequilas spend their time ageing under the experienced eye of master distiller Arturo Fuentes Cortes and his talented team. Its *añejo* is aged in ex-American oak bourbon casks for more than 12 months, and the resulting tequila is remarkably bright, while also delivering on flavours.

On the nose, tobacco and coffee are matched with spiced apple cake, vanilla pods, and the presence of cooked agave on the finish. It's not too viscous on the palate either.

TEQUILA OCHO REPOSADO 2018
"LAS PRESAS"

40% ABV	REPOSADO	AGAVE: 100%	DESTILERÍA LA ALTEÑA, JALISCO

FLAVOUR

AGAVE · FRUIT · CITRUS · RICH · VEGETAL · SPICE

The single-ranch-focused brand has a lovely connection with this expression, as the agaves are grown on Las Presas (The Dams) ranch, which once belonged to Tequila Ocho master distiller Carlos Camarena's great-grandfather.

This *reposado*, which has been aged in ex-bourbon barrels for two months, has a distinct dessert quality, with notes of sugar-dusted doughnuts, allspice, and toasted almonds, alongside brighter, earthier notes. It's a very surprising drop indeed and certainly one to savour.

TEQUILA OCHO REPOSADO 2021
"LA LADERA"

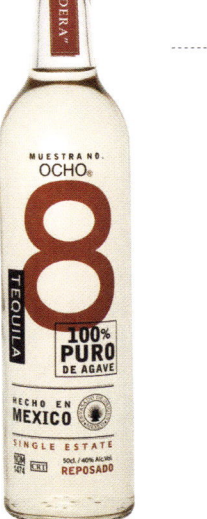

40% ABV	REPOSADO	AGAVE: 100%	DESTILERÍA LA ALTEÑA, JALISCO

FLAVOUR

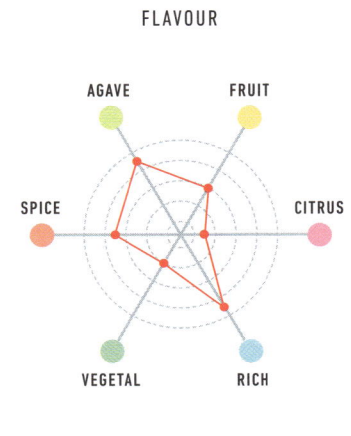

AGAVE · FRUIT · CITRUS · RICH · VEGETAL · SPICE

The brainchild of Tomas Estes and Carlos Camarena, Tequila Ocho's focus on making single-ranch tequilas has put the concept of *terroir* in tequila on the map. The agaves grown for this expression at La Ladera (The Hillside) are the perfect example. They don't grow large but contain a serious percentage of sugar.

This *reposado* punches way above its weight, considering the short time spent in the barrel. Think tanned leather, cacao nibs, and salted caramel, with a whisper of peppermint and black pepper on the finish.

GRASSY/HERBAL TEQUILAS

Grassy as a flavour profile is something that is hard to grasp until you experience it. It is often more present in the aroma of a tequila and gives it an incredible green note. Herbal tequilas are similar but come with a larger range, which is why these two characteristics fit so well together.

FLAVOUR NOTES

Grassy notes usually present themselves in numerous forms: wet, freshly cut, and dried. Herbal notes are more singular, and refer to individual herbs like thyme, rosemary, basil, sage, or mint, which is normally menthol or peppermint.

WET GRASS

FRESHLY CUT GRASS

DRIED GRASS

THYME

BASIL

MINT

MIXERS	COCKTAILS
BIG TOM Spiced Tomato Juice	**SHORT** Spicy Margarita, Tequila Matador
FANTA Pineapple & Grapefruit	**LONG** Batanga, Ranch Water
FEVER-TREE Classic Margarita Mixer	**RIFF** Daiquiri, Mojito

ARETTE BLANCO

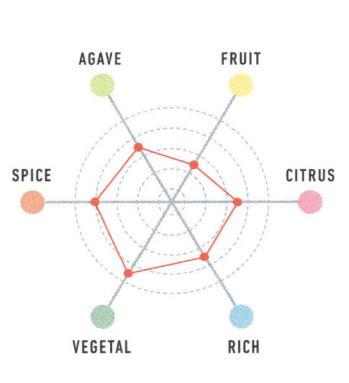

| 38% ABV | BLANCO | AGAVE: 100% | EL LLANO, JALISCO |

FLAVOUR

AGAVE   FRUIT

SPICE   CITRUS

VEGETAL   RICH

Made at the historic El Llano distillery and launched in 2007, Arette tequila is named after a one-eyed horse that won three medals at London's 1948 Olympics. It's produced by one of the most respected families in tequila making, the Orendain family, and this *blanco* is testament to their heritage.

On the nose, lemon balm, thyme, and lemongrass are all followed by notes of crunchy salad, a slightly bitter rocket note, and a warming spice on the palate. It would work beautifully served long with tonic water.

ARTENOM SELECCIÓN DE 1123

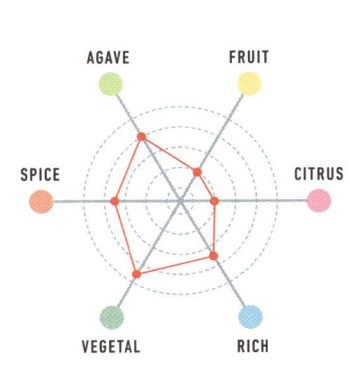

| 43% ABV | BLANCO | AGAVE: 100% | TEQUILA CASCAHUÍN, JALISCO |

FLAVOUR

AGAVE   FRUIT

SPICE   CITRUS

VEGETAL   RICH

Part of the ArteNOM brand, this *blanco* was made by master distiller Salvador Rosales Torres. It has spent 21 to 28 days in ex-brandy casks that previously held Oaxacan mezcal, and the result is fascinating.

You'll find petrichor, lots of wet grass, and fresh rain on the nose, alongside agave sweetness, spearmint, flat-leaf parsley, red pepper flakes, and white flower petals. The texture is surprisingly creamy, and there is a big burst of hot mint, followed by crunchy herbs and a touch of nuttiness too. It's a seriously cool tequila.

ATANASIO ORÍGENES
ESPÍRITU FUERTE BLANCO

46% ABV	BLANCO	AGAVE: 100%	FAMILIA LANDEROS, JALISCO

FLAVOUR

Founded by the Landeros brothers in 1995, this small but mighty distillery in Tequila now turns out artisanal tequilas made by its *maestro tequilero*, René Carranza. This *blanco* has a higher ABV than most, and the result is a complex and lusciously textured tequila.

There are bags of cooked agave and a pronounced thyme and pine note on the nose. On the palate, it's waxy with a resinous character and a medley of thyme, mint, and green pepper.

CALLE 23 BLANCO

40% ABV	BLANCO	AGAVE: 100%	HACIENDA CAPELLANÍA, JALISCO

FLAVOUR

Founded, owned, and made by French-born biochemist and engineer Sophie Decobecq, Calle 23 is made from agaves grown in Jalisco's highlands. Its *blanco* is brimming with herbs and makes a brilliant sipping tequila or for pairing with bright and fresh foods.

Spearmint is complemented by pear-skin texture, cooked agave, and green elements like sage, jalapeño, and apple skin on the nose. On the palate, the herbaceousness ramps up, which is grounded by olive brine, oregano, and sweetheart lettuce.

CASAMIGOS TEQUILA BLANCO

40% ABV	BLANCO	AGAVE: 100%	PRODUCTOS FINOS DE AGAVE, JALISCO

FLAVOUR

Arguably the celebrity brand that started them all, Casamigos was founded in 2013 by George Clooney, Rande Gerber, and Mike Meldman, before selling it to Diageo in 2017. The fermentation uses a unique yeast blend, giving a refined flavour.

On the nose, vanilla, wet grass, lemon verbena, pine needles, thyme, coriander, and romaine lettuce are matched with an oily texture and more crunchy, forest floor, samphire, and citrus pith on the palate. It's surprisingly round and balanced with a menthol peppermint note right on the finish.

CASCAHUÍN BLANCO

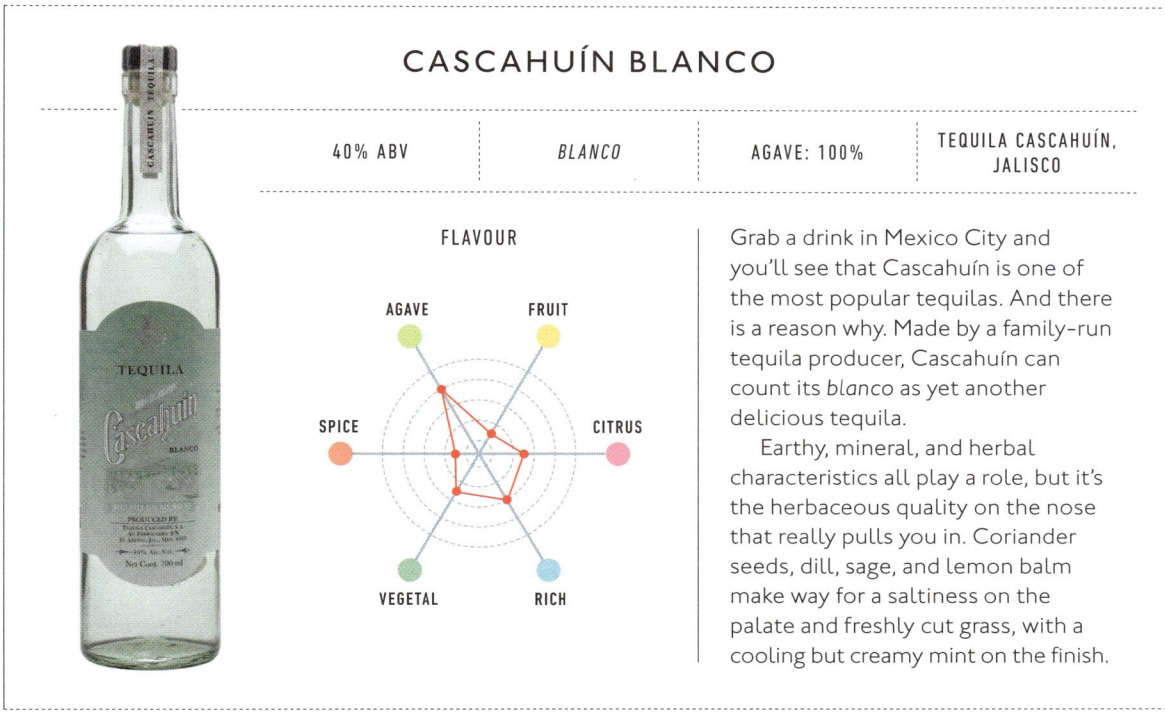

40% ABV	BLANCO	AGAVE: 100%	TEQUILA CASCAHUÍN, JALISCO

FLAVOUR

Grab a drink in Mexico City and you'll see that Cascahuín is one of the most popular tequilas. And there is a reason why. Made by a family-run tequila producer, Cascahuín can count its *blanco* as yet another delicious tequila.

Earthy, mineral, and herbal characteristics all play a role, but it's the herbaceous quality on the nose that really pulls you in. Coriander seeds, dill, sage, and lemon balm make way for a saltiness on the palate and freshly cut grass, with a cooling but creamy mint on the finish.

DEFRENTE

35% ABV	BLANCO	AGAVE: 100%	TEQUILA EMBAJADOR, JALISCO

FLAVOUR

Founded by Mexican singer/actor Diego Boneta, Defrente *blanco* brings with it bags of herbaceousness that make this a seriously characterful and striking tequila. It would work well in many guises – sipping, Martinis, Margaritas, you name it.

There is an explosion of herbs on the nose – coriander seed, parsley stalks, and marjoram, followed by grapefruit peel and pith, with cooked agave. On the palate, there's dried oregano, chimichurri, and a menthol heat, with white pepper on the finish and a pleasant bitterness too.

DON FULANO BLANCO

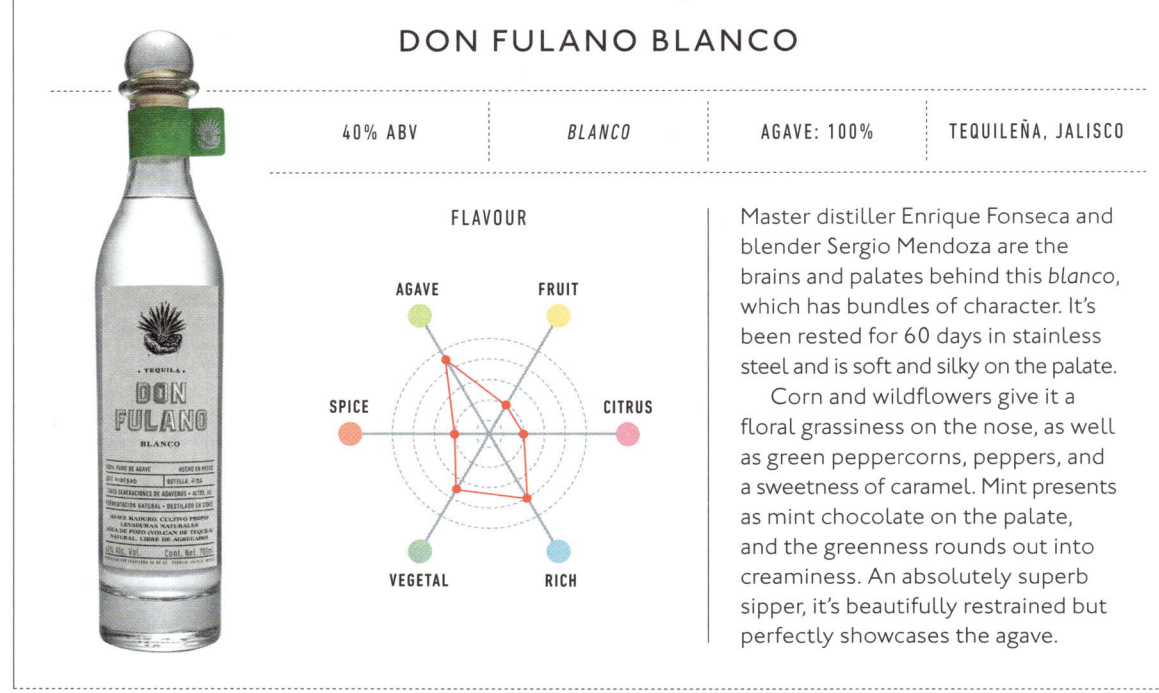

40% ABV	BLANCO	AGAVE: 100%	TEQUILEÑA, JALISCO

FLAVOUR

Master distiller Enrique Fonseca and blender Sergio Mendoza are the brains and palates behind this *blanco*, which has bundles of character. It's been rested for 60 days in stainless steel and is soft and silky on the palate.

Corn and wildflowers give it a floral grassiness on the nose, as well as green peppercorns, peppers, and a sweetness of caramel. Mint presents as mint chocolate on the palate, and the greenness rounds out into creaminess. An absolutely superb sipper, it's beautifully restrained but perfectly showcases the agave.

EL JIMADOR BLANCO

| 38% ABV | BLANCO | AGAVE: 100% | CASA HERRADURA, JALISCO |

FLAVOUR

Named in honour of the *jimadores* (farmers) who tend to the agave used to make tequila, El Jimador was founded in 1994 at the Herradura distillery in Amatitán.

There are heaps of caraway seeds on the nose, with wild garlic, curry leaf, and bright citrus peel quick on their heels. On the palate, think more citrus pith with dried oregano, rocket leaves, and cooked agave, with an aftertaste of preserved lemons and green chilli heat. It would pair brilliantly with snacks such as pickles, olives, and cured meats.

EL TEQUILEÑO BLANCO

| 38% ABV | BLANCO | AGAVE: 70% | LA GUARREÑA, JALISCO |

FLAVOUR

Proving that 100 per cent agave tequilas aren't always the best, this *mixto* from El Tequileño is a local favourite and has been since the 1970s. You'll find it in the Batanga cocktail at La Capilla bar and all around Tequila. It's lauded outside its home too, and for good reason.

There are white flowers, sweet agave, citrus pith, and green salad on the nose. On the palate, herbs are met with a trademark white pepper note. Versatile but complex in equal measure, this is a true expression of just how good a *mixto* can really be.

JOSE CUERVO ESPECIAL SILVER

35% ABV	*BLANCO*	AGAVE: 51%	CASA CUERVO, JALISCO

FLAVOUR

This unaged *mixto* from the world's best-selling tequila brand, Jose Cuervo, is a popular house pour and mixing tequila. It's sweetly herbaceous and delivers a lot of the key components of a versatile tequila.

There is a touch of caramel, agave sweetness, and green pepper underpinned with a green herbal note on the nose, with shiso leaves, coriander, and green apple. On the palate, there is plenty of pepper and some spice, such as cloves and aniseed, and bitter grapefruit, with a menthol cooling quality on the finish.

KAH EXTRA AÑEJO

40% ABV	EXTRA *AÑEJO*	AGAVE: 100%	FABRICA DE TEQUILAS FINOS, JALISCO

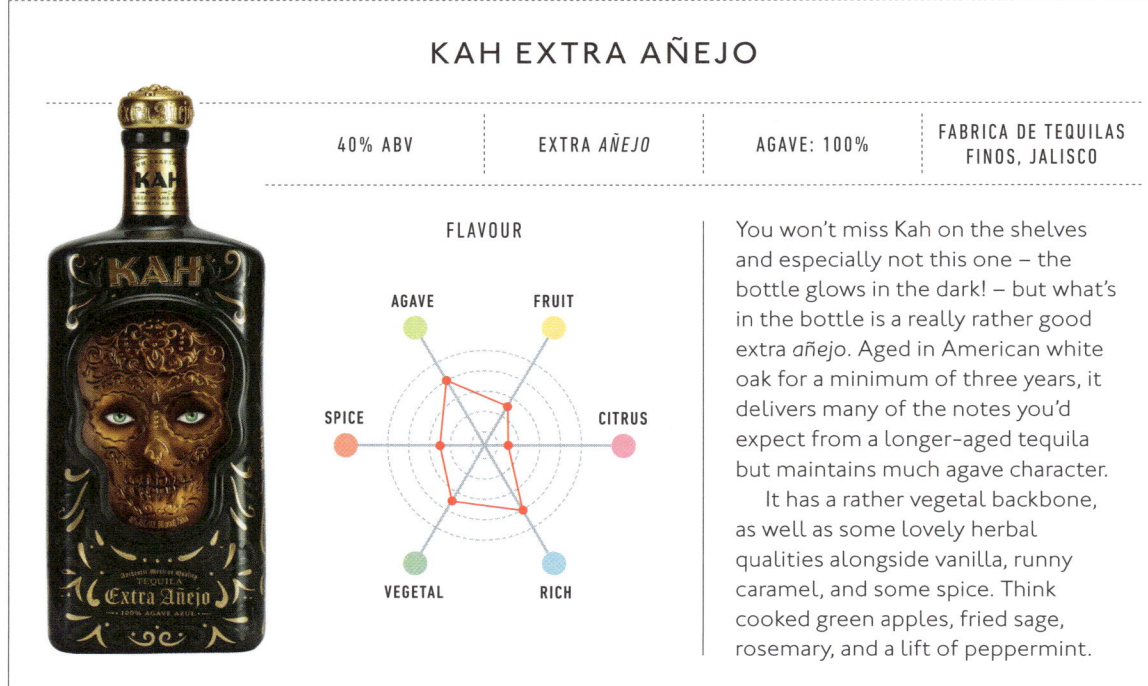

FLAVOUR

You won't miss Kah on the shelves and especially not this one – the bottle glows in the dark! – but what's in the bottle is a really rather good extra *añejo*. Aged in American white oak for a minimum of three years, it delivers many of the notes you'd expect from a longer-aged tequila but maintains much agave character.

It has a rather vegetal backbone, as well as some lovely herbal qualities alongside vanilla, runny caramel, and some spice. Think cooked green apples, fried sage, rosemary, and a lift of peppermint.

PARTIDA BLANCO

40% ABV	BLANCO	AGAVE: 100%	AUTENTICA TEQUILERA, JALISCO

FLAVOUR

Partida tequila is named in honour of Enrique Partida, a master agave farmer. It's made by *maestro tequilero* Jose Valdez, whose background in industrial engineering makes this *blanco* laser sharp. A beautiful expression of the agave, it is bursting with creamy, herbal, and grassy notes.

On the nose, there is wheatgrass, dry grass, dried flowers, and cooked green fruits like apple, prickly pear, and kiwi. On the palate, you'll find bags of herbaceousness from soft sage to thyme, and a minerality that moves into pink grapefruit right on the finish.

TEQUILA OCHO BLANCO 2021 "EL TIGRE"

40% ABV	BLANCO	AGAVE: 100%	TEQUILERA LOS ALAMBIQUES, JALISCO

FLAVOUR

Located in Atotonilco el Alto, the agaves on El Tigre (The Tiger) ranch grow at 1,900m (6,230ft) above sea level. When harvested, they showed staggeringly high sugar levels of 33 per cent, and it shows in this *blanco*.

The nose is bursting with greenness and brightness, with parsley, freshly cut grass, and pineapple, before moving into jalapeño savouriness, green pepper, and a slight smokiness on the palate. It's a brilliant *blanco* to pair with spicy Mexican food like salsa or guacamole, or simply sipped over ice on a hot summer's day.

TEREMANA TEQUILA BLANCO

40% ABV	BLANCO	AGAVE: 100%	DESTILERÍA TEREMANA DE AGAVE, JALISCO

FLAVOUR

Founded by American actor and wrestler Dwayne "The Rock" Johnson, Teremana is one of the most recognizable celebrity tequilas on the market. Made in the town of Jesús María, it is crafted at a family-owned distillery in small batches.

The *blanco* expression is fresh and herbal, with lime zest, lemon peel, and coriander on the nose, alongside peppermint, sage, and that sweet agave character. On the palate, there is a touch of smokiness and cut grass, with a hint of white pepper on the finish.

THE LOST EXPLORER BLANCO

40% ABV	BLANCO	AGAVE: 100%	DESTILERÍA EL MAGNIFICO, JALISCO

FLAVOUR

Mezcal producer The Lost Explorer recently introduced its first tequila, made by *maestro tequilero* Enrique de Colsa. It's produced in small batches using agaves from local farmers, and is sold in bottles made with more than 55 per cent recycled glass.

This is a lush, herbaceous tequila that begins with cacao nibs, green coffee beans, and pistachio on the nose, before a swathe of hay and grass. On the palate, this moves into the herbal qualities of coriander, dill, and thyme, as well as a spot of sweet cinnamon and a creamy texture.

TRES GENERACIONES TEQUILA PLATA

| 38% ABV | BLANCO | AGAVE: 100% | TEQUILA SAUZA, JALISCO |

FLAVOUR

Made by the historic Sauza family, Tres Generaciones is a brand that produces a triple-distilled *blanco*, *reposado*, and *añejo*. The *blanco* is a cracking example of how to retain flavour after the extra distillation, and it's a silky and characterful number.

Sweet mint and anise come through on the nose, alongside agave character, while some lemon balm freshens the palate. A pine-resin texture and flavour note bring a lasting greenness to the finish.

VOLCAN DE MI TIERRA BLANCO

| 40% ABV | BLANCO | AGAVE: 100% | AGROTEQUILERA DE JALISCO, JALISCO |

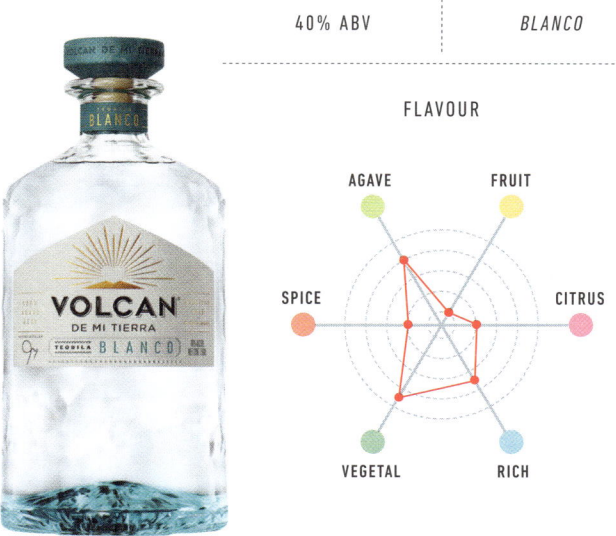

FLAVOUR

Volcan de Mi Tierra was founded by Don Juan Gallardo, whose tequila heritage speaks volumes in the expressions that come out of the Agrotequilera de Jalisco. Its *blanco* is brimming with grassy herbaceousness.

Freshly cut grass, oregano, cucumber, parsley stalks, and sweet agave all come together beautifully on the nose, while the palate brings some bitter pink grapefruit, wet autumn leaves, and a salinity on the finish too. A slight sweetness and a crack of black pepper right on the end lifts this *blanco* nicely.

CITRUS/FLORAL TEQUILAS

Citrus is a common characteristic in tequila. Whether as peel, juice, or oil, it brings brightness and zip. It is often a characteristic originating from the agave, which is accentuated through the distillation process. Floral notes are also common, creating freshness, and can be in the form of white or light flowers. They are often more dominant on the nose than the palate.

CITRUS   FLORAL

FLAVOUR NOTES

The most common citrus notes are grapefruit, lemon, lime, and orange, and they can appear in numerous forms: oil, peel, and zest being the primary trio. Floral characteristics sit on the lighter scale, like elderflower and pink roses, or have a citrus lilt like orange blossom.

GRAPEFRUIT

LEMON

LIME

ORANGE

ELDERFLOWER

ORANGE BLOSSOM

MIXERS	COCKTAILS
KARMA DRINKS Organic Karma Cola	**SHORT** Cantarito, Margarita
THE LONDON ESSENCE Original Indian Tonic Water	**LONG** Paloma, Ranch Water
THREE CENTS Pink Grapefruit Soda	**RIFF** Bloody Mary, Martini

1800 SILVER

40% ABV	BLANCO	AGAVE: 100%	CASA CUERVO, JALISCO

FLAVOUR

Owned by the Beckmann family, who also own Jose Cuervo, 1800 is one of the most recognizable tequilas on the international market. The *piñas* are cooked in autoclaves and distilled in column stills, and the resulting tequila is a staple *blanco* that is perfect to have at your disposal for mixing in cocktails.

The nose is classic citrus with lemon and more tropical fruits like guava and pineapple. Spice such as cinnamon comes through on the palate with a lovely creamy texture. It's a great all-rounder and good value.

CASA DRAGONES BLANCO

40% ABV	BLANCO	AGAVE: 100%	DESTILERÍA LEYROS, JALISCO

FLAVOUR

This tequila often knocks first-timers and jaded sceptics alike off their feet. It's a small-batch tequila from Casa Dragones, which was launched in 2008 by the "First Lady of Tequila", Bertha González Nieves. Made using agaves grown in the rich volcanic soil of the Trans-Mexican Volcanic Belt, it's incredibly crisp and fresh, and sings of handcraft and attention to detail.

On the nose, green apple and flowering herbs like thyme jump out, before moving into grapefruit oil and orange on the palate. Warming white pepper and soft spice linger on the finish.

CASA DRAGONES REPOSADO

40% ABV	*REPOSADO*	AGAVE: 100%	DESTILERÍA LEYROS, JALISCO

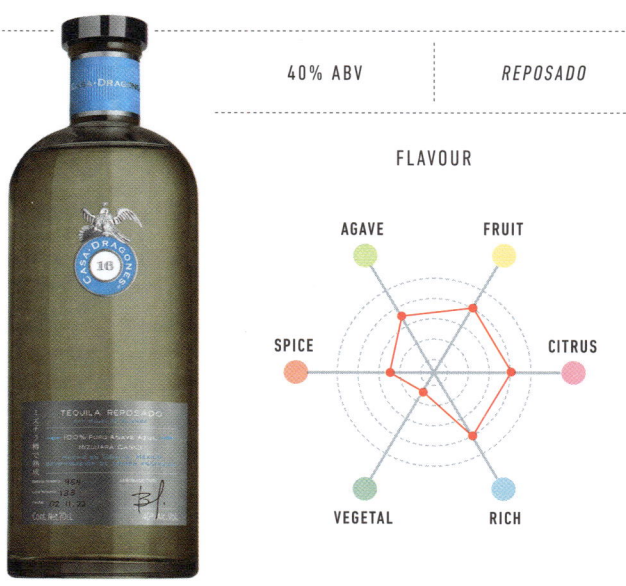

FLAVOUR

When it comes to a tequila's USP, this *reposado* has a rather special one: it's the first tequila to be rested exclusively in new *mizunara* casks. This rather rare Japanese oak (*Quercus crispula*), which is seen much more in whisky ageing, imparts some serious character to this tequila.

On the nose, orange-blossom water and heady honey give a delicate but bright sweetness, before moving into butterscotch and richer fruit flesh on the palate. The finish is long but light, with a touch of nuttiness right at the end.

CENOTE TEQUILA BLANCO

40% ABV	*BLANCO*	AGAVE: 100%	FABRICA DE TEQUILAS FINOS, JALISCO

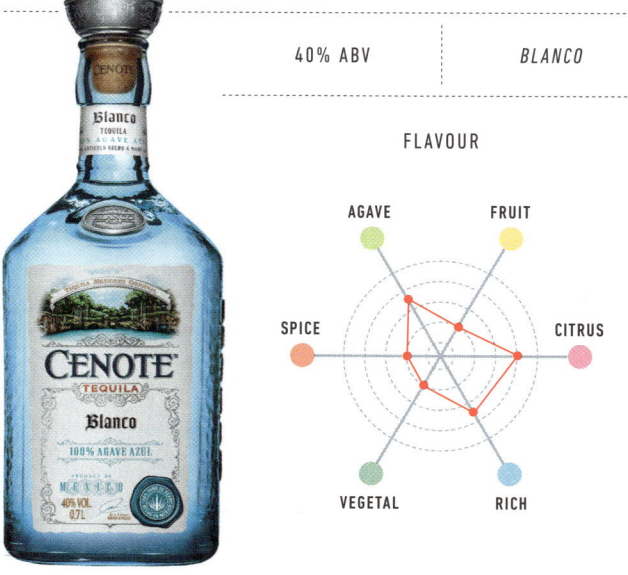

FLAVOUR

Named after the natural sinkholes found in the Yucatán Peninsula, Cenote Tequila is made by master distiller Arturo Fuentes at the base of the Tequila Volcano.

This *blanco* is a heady mix of citrus and florality with notes of honeysuckle, sweet vanilla, lemon peel, and lime on the nose, while notes of chamomile and more of that citrus freshness follow on the palate. The texture is beautifully viscous, with a long, bright finish and a whisper of black pepper for a little welcome bite. It's the perfect sipper.

CIMARRÓN TEQUILA BLANCO

40% ABV	BLANCO	AGAVE: 100%	TEQUILEÑA, JALISCO

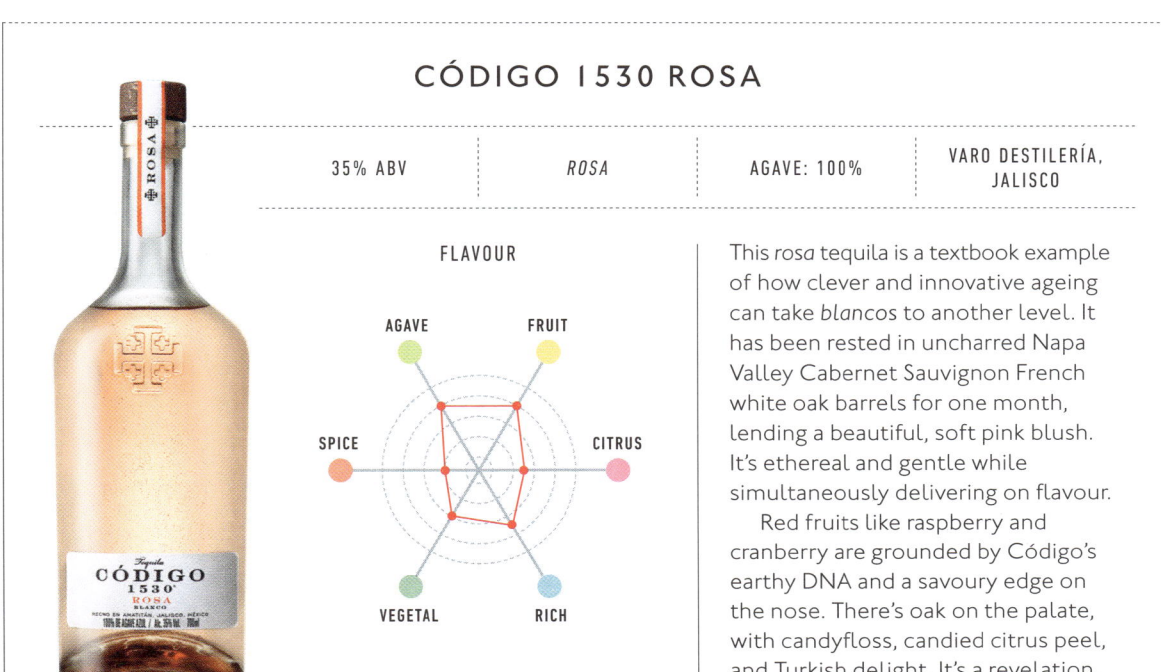

FLAVOUR

AGAVE · FRUIT · CITRUS · RICH · VEGETAL · SPICE

Cimarrón is produced under the expert eye of *maestro tequilero* Enrique Fonseca. Citrus is the hero here, and there are some other earthier, herbal players that bring this *blanco* to life too.

Aromas such as pomelo oil, lime zest, lemon sherbert, and agave are matched with freshly cut mint, dried lavender, and sugared almonds. On the palate, there is a sweet honey note, juxtaposed with bitter grapefruit peel, pink peppercorns, menthol, and a waxy texture. It's cracking in a Paloma (see pp202–03).

CÓDIGO 1530 ROSA

35% ABV	ROSA	AGAVE: 100%	VARO DESTILERÍA, JALISCO

FLAVOUR

AGAVE · FRUIT · CITRUS · RICH · VEGETAL · SPICE

This *rosa* tequila is a textbook example of how clever and innovative ageing can take *blancos* to another level. It has been rested in uncharred Napa Valley Cabernet Sauvignon French white oak barrels for one month, lending a beautiful, soft pink blush. It's ethereal and gentle while simultaneously delivering on flavour.

Red fruits like raspberry and cranberry are grounded by Código's earthy DNA and a savoury edge on the nose. There's oak on the palate, with candyfloss, candied citrus peel, and Turkish delight. It's a revelation.

CORAZÓN BLANCO

40% ABV	BLANCO	AGAVE: 100%	TEQUILA SAN MATÍAS DE JALISCO

FLAVOUR

Corazón infuses this single-estate *blanco* tequila with oxygen before bottling, which it believes enhances the agave flavours. It shows beautiful cooked fruits alongside bright citrus and herbs. A lovely silken texture is matched with some heat of jalapeños and green peppercorns on the palate, alongside spearmint, Thai basil, and a creamy, lactic cheese note that is really pleasant and rounding.

The nose has vegetal and bitter notes, but this *blanco* has a powerful bite that works well in a Margarita and with a Verdita (see pp196–97, 214).

DON JULIO BLANCO

38% ABV	BLANCO	AGAVE: 100%	LA PRIMAVERA, JALISCO

FLAVOUR

In 1942, Don Julio González established his own distillery at the age of 17. Now, the brand Don Julio is one of the tequila category's most recognized names, and its tequilas are pure quality. This *blanco* is the perfect expression of the citrus note you often find in this style of tequila.

On the nose, agave character is matched with lemon and orange peel, lime zest, pink rosebuds, and white flowers. It is sweet and fresh on the palate with green pepper and herbal notes, like sage and coriander seeds, and it has a resinous mouthfeel.

EL MAYOR BLANCO

| 40% ABV | *BLANCO* | AGAVE: 100% | DGL DESTILADORES, JALISCO |

FLAVOUR

Made by a fourth-generation tequila family, the Gonzalezes, with Rodolfo Gonzalez as master distiller, El Mayor's *blanco* is made using lowlands agaves grown in mineral-rich, sandy soil. This is a sumptuous and elegant *blanco* with a marked floral character offset by fruits and spices.

Coffee and milk chocolate are the undertones to white flowers and vanilla on the nose, before moving into crème caramel, lemon balm, ginger, and clementines. It's a lovely tequila that showcases how delicate *blancos* can be while also remaining flavourful.

EL SUEÑO SILVER

| 38% ABV | *BLANCO* | AGAVE: 70% | DESTILADORA DEL VALLE DE TEQUILA, JALISCO |

FLAVOUR

El Sueño was founded in 2021 by Paul Hayes and Nav Grewal, who had worked with agave for 16 years in Mexico. Five generations of farmers and tequila makers lie behind this *mixto*, which deftly combines florality and sweetness and is one of the best *mixtos* to emerge in recent years.

On the nose, there is buttered popcorn, candyfloss, white petals, and a hint of almond-blossom tea, with citrus notes on the palate, such as grapefruit, lemon pith, and zest, and an intense peppery hit, and more buttery, creamy notes on the finish.

FUENTESECA COSECHA 2018
HUERTA "LAS ANTENAS"

44.8% ABV	BLANCO	AGAVE: 100%	TEQUILEÑA, JALISCO

FLAVOUR

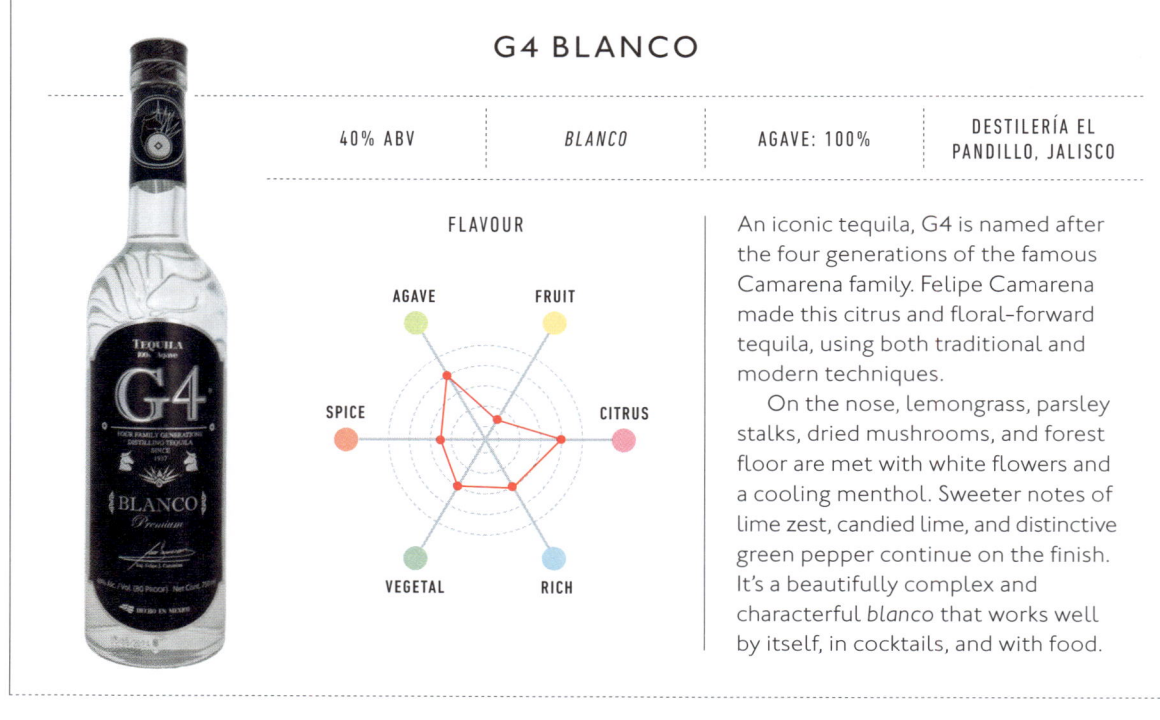

Maestro tequilero Enrique Fonseca may be well known for his love of aged tequilas, but this *blanco* is truly intriguing. Why? Because while it is made in Jalisco, its blue Weber agave was grown in the mineral-rich soils of Michoacán at an altitude of 1,525m (5,000ft). The result is something rather unique.

White flowers and milk-bottle sweets on the nose move into hot chocolate, which turns to chai spices and a herbal and mineral finish. It's a flavour rollercoaster of a tequila and it's absolutely delicious.

G4 BLANCO

40% ABV	BLANCO	AGAVE: 100%	DESTILERÍA EL PANDILLO, JALISCO

FLAVOUR

An iconic tequila, G4 is named after the four generations of the famous Camarena family. Felipe Camarena made this citrus and floral-forward tequila, using both traditional and modern techniques.

On the nose, lemongrass, parsley stalks, dried mushrooms, and forest floor are met with white flowers and a cooling menthol. Sweeter notes of lime zest, candied lime, and distinctive green pepper continue on the finish. It's a beautifully complex and characterful *blanco* that works well by itself, in cocktails, and with food.

GRAN CENTENARIO PLATA

38% ABV	BLANCO	AGAVE: 100%	CASA CUERVO, JALISCO

FLAVOUR

AGAVE · FRUIT · CITRUS · RICH · VEGETAL · SPICE

Gran Centenario follows the traditions of its 1857 founding, when Lázaro Gallardo blended newly rested tequilas with aged reserves to craft his final tequilas. Following suit, the brand's *blanco* has been blended in oak, which adds a certain roundness and wood quality to this expression.

Aromas of lemon peel and pith and blood-orange peel are matched with pollen and rose petals and sweet agave. On the palate, there is yellow grapefruit and mint with a nasturtium note. It's a different take on a *blanco* that works well with food.

MUNDO BLANCO TEQUILA

35% ABV	BLANCO	AGAVE: 70%	LA COFRADÍA, JALISCO

FLAVOUR

AGAVE · FRUIT · CITRUS · RICH · VEGETAL · SPICE

Made at the third-generation distillery by La Cofradía family, Mundo is a *mixto* using 70 per cent blue agave and 30 per cent *piloncillo* (raw cane sugar) with spring water from the highlands of Jalisco. Its packaging is a brilliant way of telling some of tequila's stories, from how it's made to who makes it.

It's well rounded and comes with a freshness from grapefruit and lime zest on the nose, which is matched with some cooling menthol and white pepper on the palate and notes of pencil shavings too.

PATRÓN SILVER

40% ABV	BLANCO	AGAVE: 100%	HACIENDA PATRÓN, JALISCO

FLAVOUR

AGAVE · FRUIT · CITRUS · RICH · VEGETAL · SPICE

Patrón has a reputation for making excellent tequilas of varying styles. Its *blanco* is one of the best on the market and is distilled three times at the Hacienda Patrón. It's crisp and fresh, and works wonders in a Margarita (see pp196–97).

There are citrus and earthy undertones on the nose, with a resinous pine note and crunchy green pepper on the palate. It finishes with white pepper warmth and refreshing grapefruit peel. The freshness of the agave really stands out. It's a reliable tool in the bar cart.

TEQUILA ENEMIGO 55 BLANCO

38% ABV	BLANCO	AGAVE: 100%	DESTILERÍA LEYROS, JALISCO

FLAVOUR

AGAVE · FRUIT · CITRUS · RICH · VEGETAL · SPICE

Enemigo is made using a diffuser and column still. The result is a tequila that is still characteristic of the lowland agaves used to make it. The number 55 refers to the amount of times it is said it took the founders to get to the final tequila recipe.

The nose is full of green pepper, sweet key limes, green-apple-skin florality, and some earthy herbal notes too. On the palate, it is cooling and fresh – almost like fresh laundry – with citrus-pith bitterness, orange oil, and stevia plant (candyleaf) rounding it out beautifully.

TEQUILA KOMOS AÑEJO RESERVA

40% ABV	AÑEJO	AGAVE: 100%	DESTILERÍA ORENDAIN, JALISCO

FLAVOUR

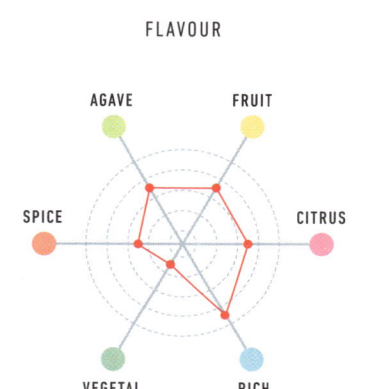

This Añejo Reserva from the Orendain distillery has been aged for a minimum of 12 months in French oak wine barrels, ex-bourbon barrels, and sherry casks, and then blended to create a seriously characterful result.

Coffee and caramel are immediate on the nose, before moving into crème caramel, latte, and brighter jammy orange and citrus zest on the palate. The finish is warming with allspice and hazelnuts, and there is a lingering sweet florality that saves it from being cloying.

TIERRA-NOBLE CRISTALINO REPOSADO

40% ABV	CRISTALINO REPOSADO	AGAVE: 100%	LA ESTACADA, JALISCO

FLAVOUR

Located at 2,195m (7,200ft) above sea level, La Estacada is one of the highest distilleries in the world. Tierra-Noble uses agaves from the Tequila Valley and Los Altos de Jalisco, an eight-day fermentation process, and small stills to craft its tequilas. Its *cristalino* is made from a *reposado* blend.

It is perfumed on the nose with bergamot, lime zest, lemon peel, yuzu, and wildflowers. The palate is characterful, with lots of that citrus coming through with herbal notes, green banana, and candied oranges.

FRUIT/SPICE TEQUILAS

Fruit notes in tequila can conjure a huge range of varieties. Stone, tropical, and seed fruits often present themselves well on the nose, while berries and dried and caramelized fruits usually come with age. Spices can be found in both aged and unaged tequilas, and they are usually more dominant on the palate, especially on the finish.

FLAVOUR NOTES

Fruits can range from apple, apricot, and pineapple all the way to dates, green banana, and dried fig. When it comes to spice, we're talking baking spices like cinnamon and nutmeg in aged tequilas, and white and black pepper in *blancos*.

APPLE   DATES   PINEAPPLE

PEPPER   CINNAMON   CLOVE

MIXERS	COCKTAILS
BUNDABERG Root Beer	**SHORT** Margarita, Toreador
FENTIMANS Curiosity Cola	**LONG** Batanga, Tequila Sunrise
RAPSCALLION SODA Strawberry	**RIFF** Negroni, Old Fashioned

ARETTE ARTESANAL SUAVE AÑEJO

| 38% ABV | *AÑEJO* | AGAVE: 100% | EL LLANO, JALISCO |

FLAVOUR

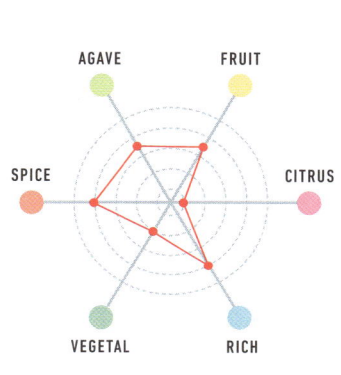

Founded in the 1900s by the famous Orendain family, Arette makes some of the most delicious tequilas on the market. Its Suave range is the premium side of the brand, and its *añejo* is worth every penny and delivers something rather unexpected.

Mouth-filling and moreish, it brings the expected notes of caramel and vanilla on the nose. These are joined by peppers, coconut, walnuts, and a lasting spice warmth – cinnamon, nutmeg, cardamom – on the palate, which last long into the finish. It's a very special drop indeed.

ARTENOM SELECCIÓN DE 1146

| 40% ABV | *AÑEJO* | AGAVE: 100% | TEQUILEÑA, JALISCO |

FLAVOUR

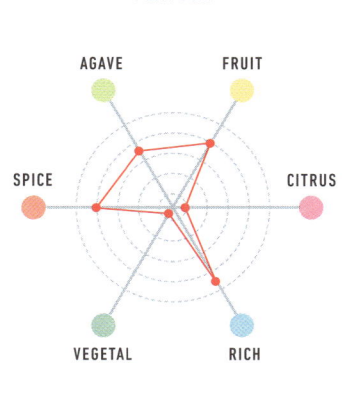

The ArteNOM brand was founded by master distiller Enrique Fonseca to showcase the skill of *maestros tequileros* at some of tequila's NOMs (see pp13). This *añejo* celebrates the 1146 NOM and was first matured in Cabernet Franc wine barrels, before moving into ex-Canadian and Tennessee rye whiskey casks.

It has a moody, dark amber colour, with notes of cherry, almond, Black Forest gateau, cloves, and cinnamon, as well as some tannins on the palate and a serious, smoky finish. It's a big, bold, complex tequila.

ATANASIO AÑEJO

40% ABV	AÑEJO	AGAVE: 100%	FAMILIA LANDEROS, JALISCO

FLAVOUR

This characterful and artisanal tequila producer punches above its weight when it comes to the quality of its tequilas. *Maestro tequilero* René Carranza and his team, including daughter Sheccid, who is the brand's global ambassador, produce some beautifully made expressions, such as this *añejo*.

Aged for 13 months, it's buttery on the nose with lots of spice like cinnamon and nutmeg, before moving into caramelized pineapple and peach on the palate with an oily mouthfeel.

CASCAHUÍN REPOSADO

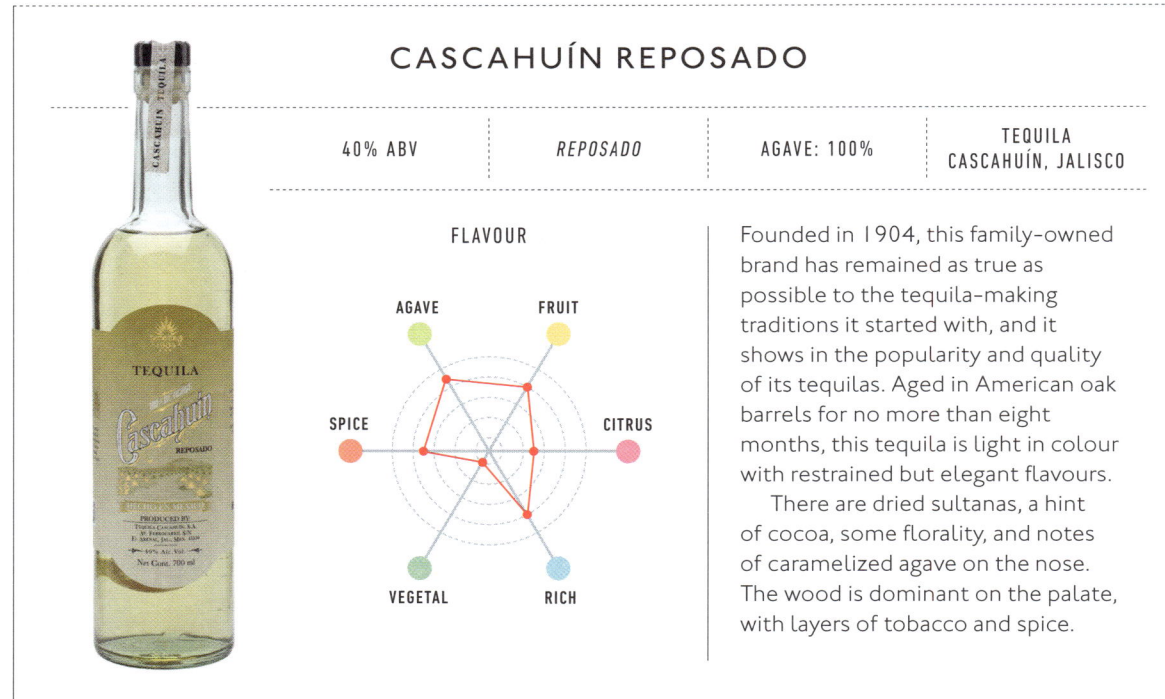

40% ABV	REPOSADO	AGAVE: 100%	TEQUILA CASCAHUÍN, JALISCO

FLAVOUR

Founded in 1904, this family-owned brand has remained as true as possible to the tequila-making traditions it started with, and it shows in the popularity and quality of its tequilas. Aged in American oak barrels for no more than eight months, this tequila is light in colour with restrained but elegant flavours.

There are dried sultanas, a hint of cocoa, some florality, and notes of caramelized agave on the nose. The wood is dominant on the palate, with layers of tobacco and spice.

CAZCABEL REPOSADO

38% ABV	*REPOSADO*	AGAVE: 100%	TEQUILA ARTESANAL DE LOS ALTOS DE JALISCO

FLAVOUR

Cazcabel has recently opened a new distillery, to the tune of £37 million, overseen by master distiller Yadira Hernández Lozano. This *reposado* is aged for a minimum of nine months in American oak and is a bright and easygoing aged tequila.

Candied fruits, dehydrated apple, sweet clementine, and a touch of spice are all pleasant aromas, followed by runny caramel and vanilla essence on the palate. There is also some distinct and welcome white pepper and clove on the finish. It makes a reliable tequila for mixing.

CENOTE CRISTALINO AÑEJO

40% ABV	*CRISTALINO AÑEJO*	AGAVE: 100%	FABRICA DE TEQUILAS FINOS, JALISCO

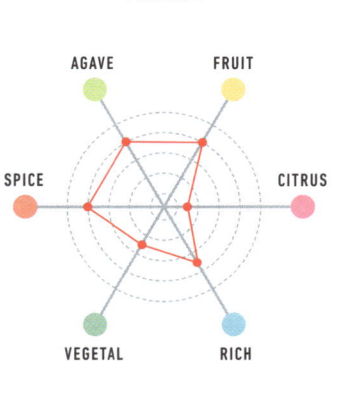

FLAVOUR

This *cristalino* is one of the best I've tried and is a real game-changer for the sceptics out there. Aged in American oak for more than a year, it has been run through an activated carbon filter to remove its colour but maintains all the character you'd expect from an aged tequila. It's immediately super bright and fresh – like clean sheets on a summer day.

It's floral and subtly sweet on the nose, with rose petals, pampas grass, and white peach, followed by vanilla, white chocolate, and cinnamon, with a backbone of savouriness on the finish.

CÓDIGO 1530 ORIGEN EXTRA AÑEJO

38% ABV	EXTRA *AÑEJO*	AGAVE: 100%	VARO DESTILERÍA, JALISCO

FLAVOUR

AGAVE · FRUIT · CITRUS · RICH · VEGETAL · SPICE

This expression from Código has been aged for six years in Napa Valley Cabernet French white oak wine barrels. The colour is eye-catching, almost like a rose gold, and gives a hint of what's to come. It is impressively bright for a six-year-old tequila.

Its aromas include dried figs, a slight savouriness of sage, and lots of lovely, warm spicing from clove and cinnamon. This carries onto the palate, along with red-apple skin, gooseberry, oak, and pear drops too.

DON JULIO ULTIMA RESERVA

40% ABV	EXTRA *AÑEJO*	AGAVE: 100%	LA PRIMAVERA, JALISCO

FLAVOUR

AGAVE · FRUIT · CITRUS · RICH · VEGETAL · SPICE

This very special extra *añejo* uses the last crop to be planted by Don Julio and his family in 2006. It has been finished for two to four months in Madeira wine casks, and sweet wine carries through beautifully.

Orchard and stone fruits like apricots and nectarines are matched with marzipan, manuka honey, and plenty of cooked agave on the nose. The palate is bursting with fruit-salad sweets, a dusting of baking spice, rancio (an oxidized-wine flavour), and fig leaf. The final texture is silky and clean with a lasting note of hazelnuts.

EL ESPOLÒN REPOSADO

40% ABV	*REPOSADO*	AGAVE: 100%	CASA SAN NICOLAS, JALISCO

FLAVOUR

Made by master distiller Jesús Susunaga, El Espolòn tequila is the brainchild of the late Cirilo Oropeza, who brought the brand to life in 1996. This *reposado* is aged for two to six months in American oak barrels and is packed with sweet, ripe fruit and dessert-like spicing.

There is a distinguishable ripe banana note on the nose, followed by tonka bean vanilla and cooked agave sweetness. On the palate, runny caramel is complemented with muscovado sugar, cinnamon, and warming clove.

FORTALEZA REPOSADO

40% ABV	*REPOSADO*	AGAVE: 100%	DESTILERÍA LA FORTALEZA, JALISCO

FLAVOUR

Guillermo Sauza runs his distillery as close to how his family ran it when it started production 150 years ago, and Fortaleza has gained fame as a top-quality tequila, with fans around the world.

Aged in American oak, this *reposado* is silky on the palate, while still remaining bright with lots of spice. On the nose, there's wild honey, dark chocolate, and crystallized ginger, moving into baked apples, menthol, allspice, and cracked black pepper on the palate. The cigar-box element makes it perfect for post-dinner drinks.

FUENTESECA RESERVA 18 YEARS 1995

43.5% ABV	EXTRA *AÑEJO*	AGAVE: 100%	TEQUILEÑA, JALISCO

FLAVOUR

Maestro tequilero Enrique Fonseca has created an incredible lineup of his own, which ranges in age from seven to 21 years. Distilled in 1995, this tequila has spent time in ex-rye Canadian white oak barrels at high altitude for six years, before being moved to the cooler climes of El Chapingo for the remaining 12.

The result is dominant oak on the nose, with some layers of spice and cola bottles, and more tannic and dusty peach notes on the palate. It is a brilliant example of an old tequila that has been well looked after.

MIJENTA TEQUILA BLANCO

40% ABV	*BLANCO*	AGAVE: 100%	CASA TEQUILERA DE ARANDAS, JALISCO

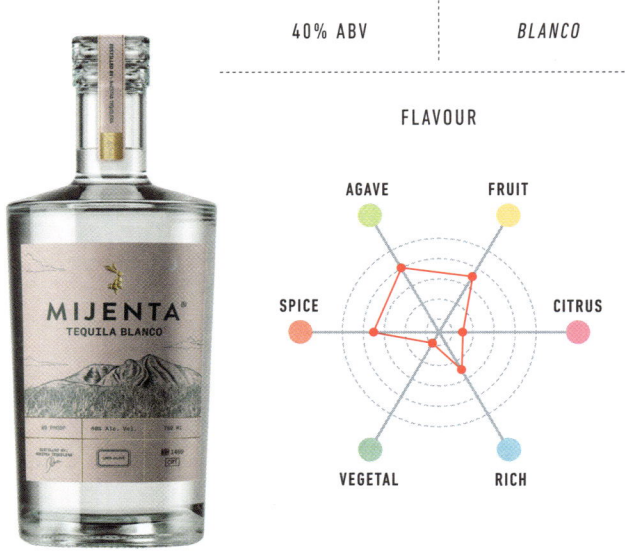

FLAVOUR

Made by *maestra tequilera* Ana María Romero, Mijenta has been synonymous with quality and sustainability since its launch in 2020.

This *blanco* is a celebration of the character that can be obtained from agave grown in soil with a high iron content, clay, lime, and other elements, which lend a minerality alongside fruit. On the nose, there's sweet melon, cooked agave, and a florality of honeysuckle, while the palate has more spiced notes, like cinnamon, with a mouthwatering quality on the finish.

TAPATIO AÑEJO

38% ABV	*AÑEJO*	AGAVE: 100%	LA ALTEÑA, JALISCO

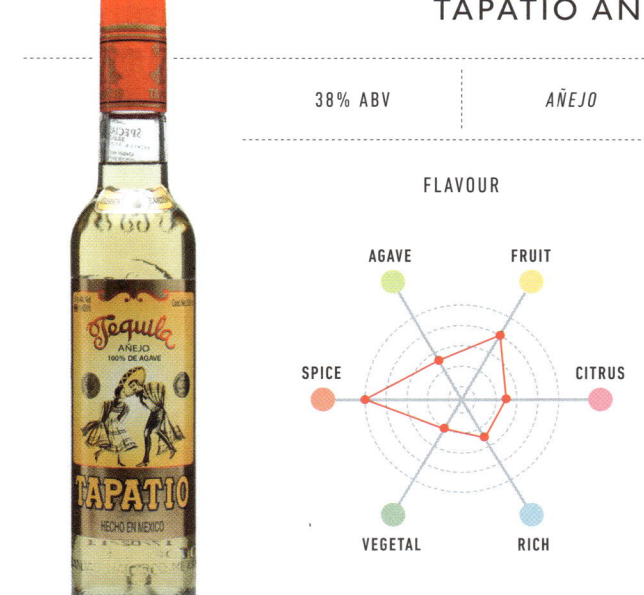

FLAVOUR

Made at La Alteña distillery, this *añejo* is part of the famous Tapatio brand, loved by bartenders. Double distilled and with no added water, this is bursting with character. It is aged in ex-bourbon barrels, and has a distinct duality of fruit and spice with a creamy texture.

On the nose, cooked orchard fruits appear along with an abundance of baking spices on the palate, freshened by a slight numbing herbal note. The finish comes with cocoa and a peppery back note. It would make a lovely digestif.

TEQUILA MI CAMPO BLANCO

40% ABV	*BLANCO*	AGAVE: 100%	LA COFRADÍA, JALISCO

FLAVOUR

Thirty-eight-hour steam cooks, natural open-air fermentation, and a month in ex-Napa Valley Chardonnay casks all add to the allure of Mi Campo's *blanco*.

It is packed with all kinds of fruit on the nose, like baked apples, banana fritters, and star fruit, with maple syrup and a hint of baking spice. On the palate, it is very silky, and there is more herbal spice and a touch of salinity on the finish. Mexico City artist Raúl Arias created the eye-catching label designs that make Mi Campo shine on the shelf.

TEQUILA MI CAMPO REPOSADO

40% ABV	*REPOSADO*	AGAVE: 100%	LA COFRADÍA, JALISCO

FLAVOUR

AGAVE · FRUIT · CITRUS · RICH · VEGETAL · SPICE

Fermented in open-air tanks among some fragrant citrus trees, and rested for three months in ex-red wine French oak barrels from the Napa Valley, this *reposado* is a beautifully balanced tequila that shines a light on both fruit and spice.

The nose is sweet cinnamon, chocolate powder, vanilla fudge, and allspice, while the palate ramps up the spiciness while also showcasing fruits like nectarines and tinned peaches. White pepper on the tip of the tongue and a salinity and smoke on the finish round off this *reposado*.

TEQUILA OCHO SINGLE ESTATE AÑEJO 2023 SAN JERÓNIMO

40% ABV	*AÑEJO*	AGAVE: 100%	TEQUILERA LOS ALAMBIQUES, JALISCO

FLAVOUR

AGAVE · FRUIT · CITRUS · RICH · VEGETAL · SPICE

Grown at the sun-drenched San Jerónimo ranch in deep, red, rocky soil, 1,200 tonnes of exceptionally mature agaves were harvested to make this single-estate tequila. It has been aged in ex-bourbon casks for the minimum time of one year.

You'll find baked apple, caramelized agave, and a back note of dark chocolate, as well as some smoke on the nose. On the palate, those fruits are more like caramelized stone fruits and baking spices, and toasted notes come too. An earthy and mineral backbone shines through.

TIERRA-NOBLE EXQUISITO EXTRA AÑEJO

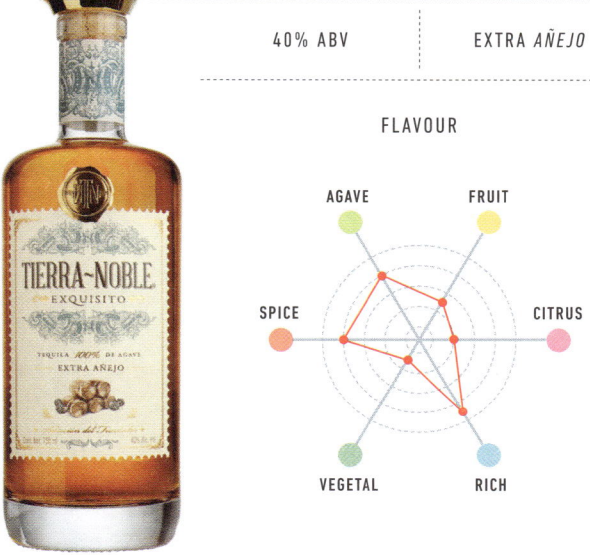

40% ABV	EXTRA *AÑEJO*	AGAVE: 100%	PREMIUM DE JALISCO, JALISCO

FLAVOUR

AGAVE · FRUIT · SPICE · CITRUS · VEGETAL · RICH

Want to know what a tequila made in one of the world's highest distilleries tastes like? Then try this premium expression from Tierra-Noble. Made in the highlands of the Sierra del Tigre near La Estacada, this amber extra *añejo* has been aged in French oak for up to 85 months, and the results speak for themselves.

A spectacular dessert tequila, the nose expresses the wood beautifully with bags of vanilla, coconut, dates, and salted caramel. It then moves into dark chocolate, ginger cake, and tobacco notes on the palate.

VOLCAN DE MI TIERRA REPOSADO

40% ABV	*REPOSADO*	AGAVE: 100%	AGROTEQUILERA DE JALISCO, JALISCO

FLAVOUR

AGAVE · FRUIT · SPICE · CITRUS · VEGETAL · RICH

The first thing to notice about this *reposado* is its colour. A deep, glistening amber, it's rather arresting on the eye. And on the palate too – aged in European and American oak casks, this *reposado* from Juan Gallardo's Volcan de Mi Tierra displays a multitude of fruit flavours.

A woody, marzipan character complements baked apples, sultanas, grilled pineapple, and prunes, before moving into more yellow-flesh fruits on the finish, with citrus peels too. A menthol cooling effect right on the end rounds this off perfectly.

EARTHY/MINERAL TEQUILAS

These two categories of tequila might be the hardest to describe but can also be some of the most delicious. Earthy characteristics are usually found on both the nose and palate, while minerality is mostly present on the palate, and can correspond with texture as well as taste. They're both the result of the soil the agave was growing in and the surrounding conditions, as well as distillation.

FLAVOUR NOTES

When we use the word "earthy" to describe tequilas, it can be a rather literal descriptor, like soil, forest floor, and clay, or it can refer to a deep and pleasantly agricultural character. Minerality is more difficult to put into words, but generally can mean rocks, a type of cleanliness, or petrichor (the smell of rain).

SOIL CLAY FOREST FLOOR

WET STONES SLATE PETRICHOR

MIXERS	COCKTAILS
DALSTON'S Pineapple Soda	**SHORT** Rosita, Verdita
DOUBLE DUTCH Pomegranate & Basil	**LONG** Bloody Maria, Paloma Negra
RAPSCALLION Cranachan	**RIFF** Gibson, Michelada

ARETTE ARTESANAL SUAVE BLANCO

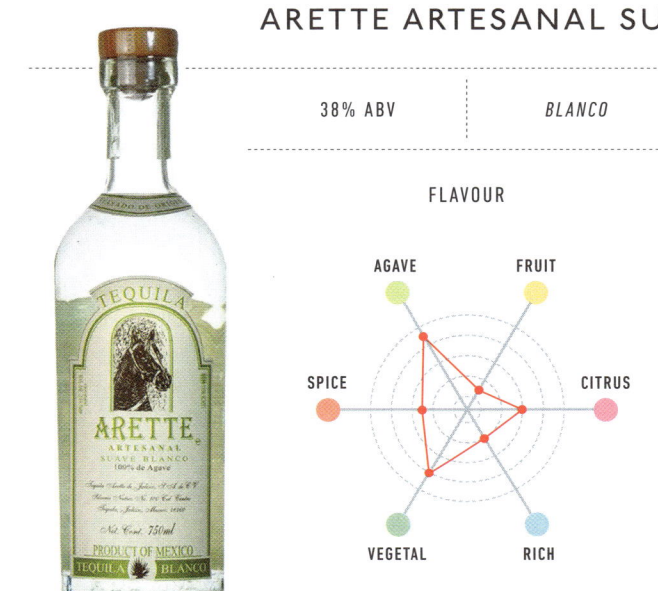

| 38% ABV | *BLANCO* | AGAVE: 100% | EL LLANO, JALISCO |

FLAVOUR

An absolutely stunning *blanco*, this expression is produced by brothers Eduardo and Jaime Orendain, fifth-generation tequila makers. Part of Arette's premium Suave range, it has been rested in stainless steel for six months before bottling, a mellowing technique that has paid dividends.

There is plenty of agave character, earthiness and minerality here – slate and stone might sound like strange flavour descriptors, but taste this, and you'll get it. There is also a brightness of citrus, green pepper, and a radish pepper heat. Savour this over ice.

ARQUITECTO

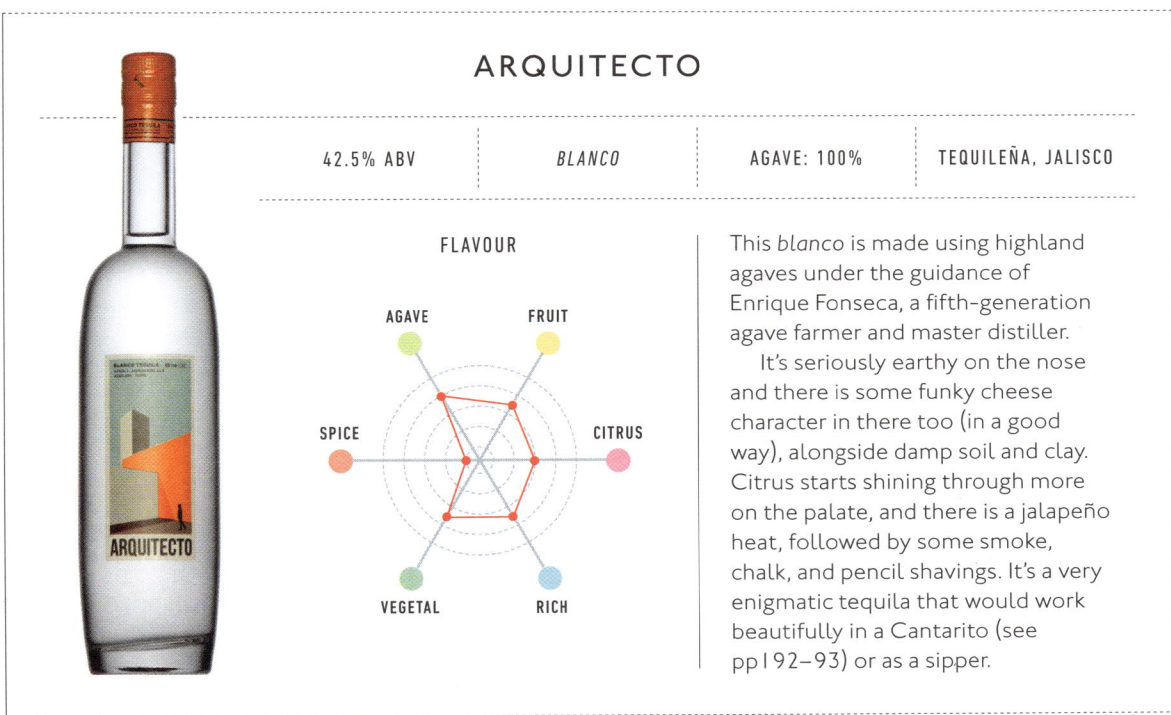

| 42.5% ABV | *BLANCO* | AGAVE: 100% | TEQUILEÑA, JALISCO |

FLAVOUR

This *blanco* is made using highland agaves under the guidance of Enrique Fonseca, a fifth-generation agave farmer and master distiller.

It's seriously earthy on the nose and there is some funky cheese character in there too (in a good way), alongside damp soil and clay. Citrus starts shining through more on the palate, and there is a jalapeño heat, followed by some smoke, chalk, and pencil shavings. It's a very enigmatic tequila that would work beautifully in a Cantarito (see pp192–93) or as a sipper.

ARTENOM SELECCIÓN DE 1414

41.2% ABV	*REPOSADO*	AGAVE: 100%	DESTILERÍA EL RANCHITO, JALISCO

FLAVOUR

Founded by master distiller Enrique Fonseca to showcase the skill of *maestros tequileros* at some of tequila's best NOMs (see p13), ArteNOM is here highlighting the work of Sergio and José Manuél Vivanco at the Destilería El Ranchito.

This *reposado* is an intriguing mix of salt and sweet. There's a minerality here, underpinned with sweet agave alongside burnt caramel, vanilla, brown butter, and salted caramel. On the finish, there is a chalky texture and some cracked black pepper that robustly rounds this tequila off.

BATANGA TEQUILA BLANCO

38% ABV	*BLANCO*	AGAVE: 100%	TEQUILA ORENDAIN DE JALISCO, JALISCO

FLAVOUR

Founded by Eduardo Orendain in 1926, Batanga Tequila shares its name with one of tequila's most famous cocktails (see pp190–91). The process from the agave fields to bottle is overseen by *maestra tequilera* Lorena Diaz, who has more than 23 years of experience in the industry.

There is a minerality to this tequila with some earthy character. On the nose, peppers, lactic acid, red brick, forest floor, and wet leaves are followed by a palate with paprika heat, artichoke savouriness, and green peppercorn spice, with menthol on the finish.

BATANGA TEQUILA REPOSADO

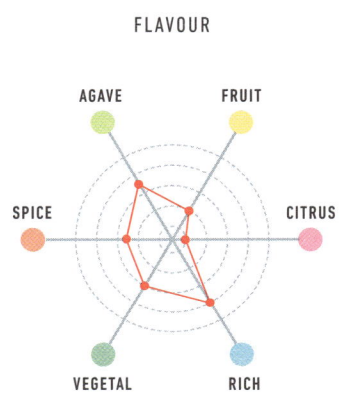

38% ABV	*REPOSADO*	AGAVE: 100%	TEQUILA ORENDAIN DE JALISCO, JALISCO

FLAVOUR

Batanga Tequila is overseen by *maestra tequilera* Lorena Diaz. Its *reposado* is rested for four to six months (double the minimum time needed for a *reposado*), and it would stand up well in cocktails, from classic tequila to twists on whisky.

On the nose, there's smoke, clay, a deep vanilla, orange oil, coffee, and liquorice, while the palate is creamy, not too spiced, but presenting earthy notes like cacao nibs and leather. The finish is long and slightly chalky – it's really good stuff.

CALLE 23 AÑEJO

40% ABV	*AÑEJO*	AGAVE: 100%	HACIENDA CAPELLANÍA, JALISCO

FLAVOUR

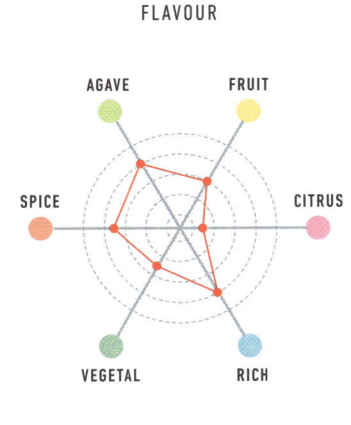

Made by French-born biochemist and engineer Sophie Decobecq, the owner and founder of Calle 23, this *añejo* has been made using agaves grown in Jalisco's highland region. It has been aged for 16 months in ex-bourbon barrels.

I love the earthiness of this *añejo* – coffee, bitter dark chocolate, toasted marshmallows, oak, and bonfire are delightful on the nose, as is the ever-present agave, which can sometimes get lost in aged tequilas. There is a heat of spice on the finish and an added slate minerality too.

EL RAYO TEQUILA PLATA

| 40% ABV | BLANCO | AGAVE: 100% | COMPAÑIA TEQUILERA HACIENDA LA CAPILLA, JALISCO |

FLAVOUR

Paying homage to the legend that a lightning bolt cooked an agave and turned it into tequila, El Rayo is a modern tequila and is suggested to be best drunk in a T&T (tequila and tonic). Its earthy and mineral character certainly lends itself to the serve.

Earthiness on the nose is made up of notes of slate, rocks, pencil shavings, and hedgerow florality, while the palate delivers a touch more sweetness with caramel, dark chocolate, charred fruits, and grilled spring onion. A chalky texture adds even more character.

GRAN ORENDAIN BLANCO

| 38% ABV | BLANCO | AGAVE: 100% | TEQUILA ORENDAIN DE JALISCO, JALISCO |

FLAVOUR

Anything that carries the name Orendain comes with an elevated expectation – the distillery has been making tequila since 1926 – and this blanco does not disappoint. Triple distilled, it is exceptionally silky and moves between sweet earthiness and cold minerality all at once.

The nose is deceptive with vanilla and baked orchard fruits right at the front, before moving into something much more moody and deep on the palate. Slate, mineral soil, and pine resin bring an oily texture that makes this a perfect sipper.

MIJENTA TEQUILA REPOSADO

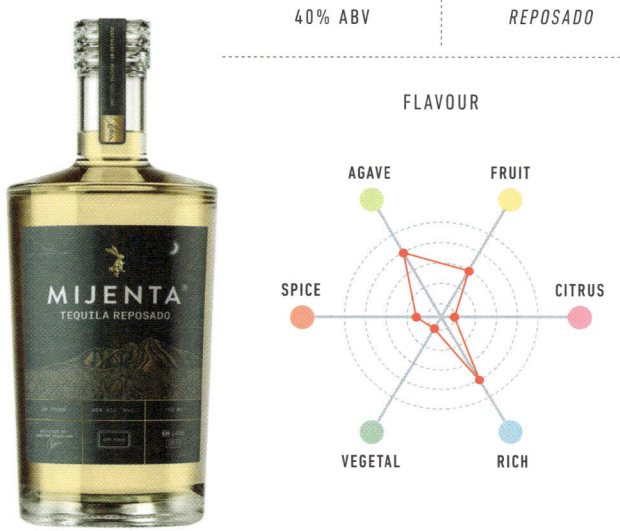

40% ABV	*REPOSADO*	AGAVE: 100%	CASA TEQUILERA DE ARANDAS, JALISCO

FLAVOUR

Made by *maestra tequilera* Ana María Romero, Mijenta is a brand that looks to the future while protecting tequila's past. Its *reposado* has been aged for up to six months in a combination of American oak, French oak, and French acacia casks, and the result is moreish and earthy.

There is a cigar-box character on the nose, as well as wet clay, sage, and a vanilla note. On the palate is a saline finish and intense dried fruit right on the end, including all the pips, stones, and stalks too. It's a surprising and enigmatic tequila.

TAPATIO BLANCO 110

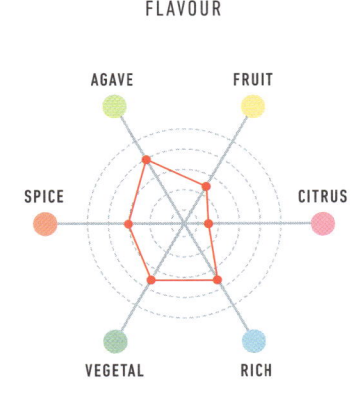

55% ABV	*BLANCO*	AGAVE: 100%	LA ALTEÑA, JALISCO

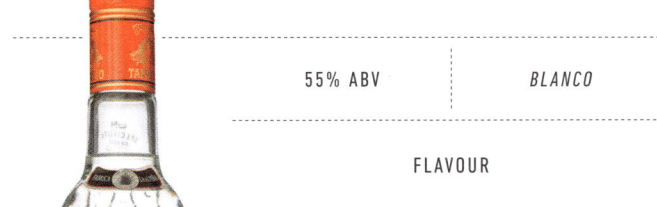

FLAVOUR

This *blanco's* name refers to its 55% ABV (or 110 proof), which really punches through when it comes to raising the aroma and flavour stakes.

It's beautifully earthy on the nose, with petrichor, a pleasant touch of sulphur, and lots of agave. The palate is spicy, hot, and briny, with some coriander herbaceousness that is replaced with charred peppers and aubergines. It has a beautifully oily texture and lots of black pepper on the finish. Powerful stuff – handle it neat if you can, but it's cracking with a mixer or maybe in a Daiquiri twist.

TEQUILA 30-30 BLANCO

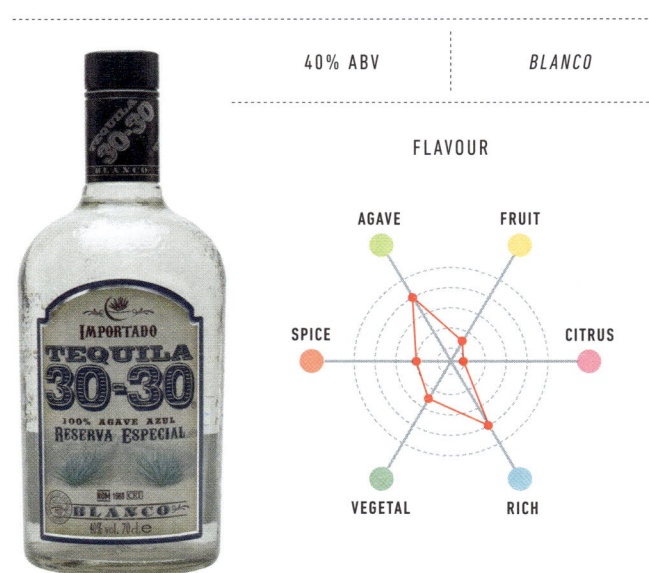

40% ABV	BLANCO	AGAVE: 100%	AGROINDUSTRIA GUADALAJARA, JALISCO

FLAVOUR

Made by Sixto Vera Garcia, Tequila 30-30 is owned by a Mexican family whose roots lie in agave farming. It takes its name from the type of rifle used to fight the French during their second invasion of Mexico.

This *blanco* has an expressive nose. Soil and pebbles are joined by dry clay and a lactic note, before heading into tree sap, Brazil nuts, and green olives. Cooked agave, brine, dried herbs, petrichor, and blackboard and chalk all culminate in a green peppercorn finish. A waxy, nutty texture rounds it off brilliantly.

TEQUILA OCHO PLATA PUNTAS 2023 MESA COLORADA

53% ABV	BLANCO	AGAVE: 100%	TEQUILERA LOS ALAMBIQUES, JALISCO

FLAVOUR

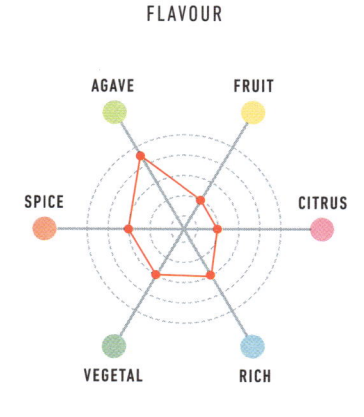

Showcasing a cut of a distillation at a higher ABV than a lot of tequilas, this distiller's cut from 2023 sits just above the heart cut. It uses agave from the Mesa Colorada ranch in the highlands of Jalisco, where rich, red soil is surrounded by volcanic clay.

The result is distinctly earthy and mineral, which is almost seasoned with black pepper and salinity too. There are heady green notes of celery and oregano on the nose, while the palate remains herbal and rather savoury. It's a bold and beautiful tequila.

TERRALTA TEQUILA BLANCO

| 40% ABV | BLANCO | AGAVE: 100% | DESTILERÍA EL PANDILLO, JALISCO |

FLAVOUR

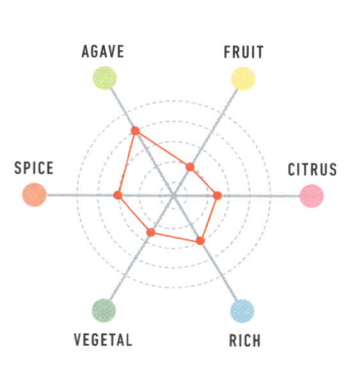

Terralta brings new meaning to the terms "earthy" and "mineral" with this *blanco*. Made using agaves crushed with a *tahona* and cooked in stone ovens, this tequila is a star on its own and also served with citrus.

You'll find petrichor, wet forest floor, pine needles, nettles, and wildflowers on the nose, while a sweeter, charred-fruit note sits at the back. On the palate, this is silky and velvet in texture, with a growing heat from white pepper, slate coolness, and sweet herbs like fresh mint and dill. It's delicious.

VOLCAN DE MI TIERRA B.T

| 38% ABV | BLANCO | AGAVE: 100% | AGROTEQUILERA DE JALISCO, JALISCO |

FLAVOUR

Founded by Juan Gallardo and part of Moët Hennessey's portfolio of spirits, Volcan de Mi Terra brings together the former's tequila heritage and the latter's premium approach to spirits. This expression celebrates the *tahona* and lowland agave and is as earthy as it gets.

On the nose, you'll find wet soil, petrichor, minerality, clay, cooked agave, and roasted nuts. On the palate, saltiness is matched with grapefruit and a touch of pink peppercorn. It's an exquisite sipper – and it looks good too.

SAVOURY/VEGETAL TEQUILAS

"Savoury" might sound like a strange word to describe a tequila, but while cooked agave can bring sweetness, its magic is that there are more juxtaposing notes there that have developed during the plant's time in the ground. Vegetal notes are twinned nicely here, as a lot of the flavours that come through, especially in *blanco* tequilas, are only heightened by fermentation and distillation.

FLAVOUR NOTES

Savoury here is usually correlated with darker and more astringent flavours like coffee, olives, or a smokiness, and is also used to describe an overall character of a tequila. Vegetal is more prescriptive and ranges from salad to grilled vegetables.

OLIVE COFFEE SMOKE

GREEN PEPPER ARTICHOKE CUCUMBER

MIXERS	COCKTAILS
DASH Cucumber & Mint Sparkling Water	**SHORT** Frozen Margarita, Tequila Mockingbird
PUNCHY Cucumber, Yuzu, & Rosemary Sparkling Water	**LONG** Bloody Maria, Paloma Negra
RAPSCALLION SODA Burnt Lemon	**RIFF** Caipirinha, Dirty Martini

---

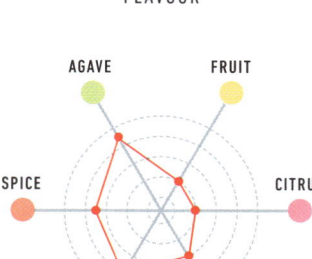

CASA NOBLE TEQUILA BLANCO

40% ABV	BLANCO	AGAVE: 100%	LA COFRADÍA, JALISCO

FLAVOUR

Founded by Jose "Pepe" Hermosillo, Casa Noble grows its organic agave in the mountains of western Jalisco and triple distils its tequila. Its *blanco* is a great match for food as well as for classic tequila cocktails, and it shines with greenness and a beautiful texture.

On the nose, there are notes of crisp and crunchy salad vegetables, with some soft florality and a touch of sweetness. These are followed by a burst of white pepper, pitted green olives, and a touch of warming spice on the palate.

CASCAHUÍN TAHONA BLANCO

42% ABV	BLANCO	AGAVE: 100%	TEQUILA CASCAHUÍN, JALISCO

FLAVOUR

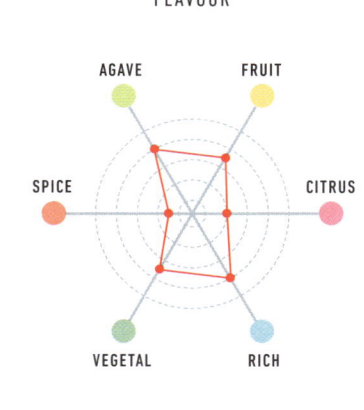

One of the more recognizable tequila brands in Mexico, Cascahuín has an impressive portfolio and knows how to have fun with its tequilas. This expression uses *tahonas* to crush the *piñas*, which is apparent in this *blanco*'s more vegetal taste.

There are super-creamy notes on the nose, with milk chocolate and a pleasant lactic, cheesy character. On the palate, a waft of smoke appears, with the chocolate turning dark, and a shift into coffee beans and green olives. It's a surprisingly savoury tequila.

CÓDIGO 1530 BLANCO

| 40% ABV | BLANCO | AGAVE: 100% | VARO DESTILERÍA, JALISCO |

FLAVOUR

Made using rainwater that has been filtered through volcanic rocks, Código 1530 may have a mere 10 or so years behind it commercially, but it has, in fact, been made for hundreds of years by five families in Amatitán.

This *blanco* is a mix of vegetal and citrus with a savoury edge. On the nose, there is mint, fresh grass, and some florality, as well as some pecorino character, before moving into orange peel, pine, vine leaves, and a slightly resinous texture. It's a good one for pairing with food and a hit in a Ranch Water (see pp204–05).

DON FULANO BLANCO FUERTE

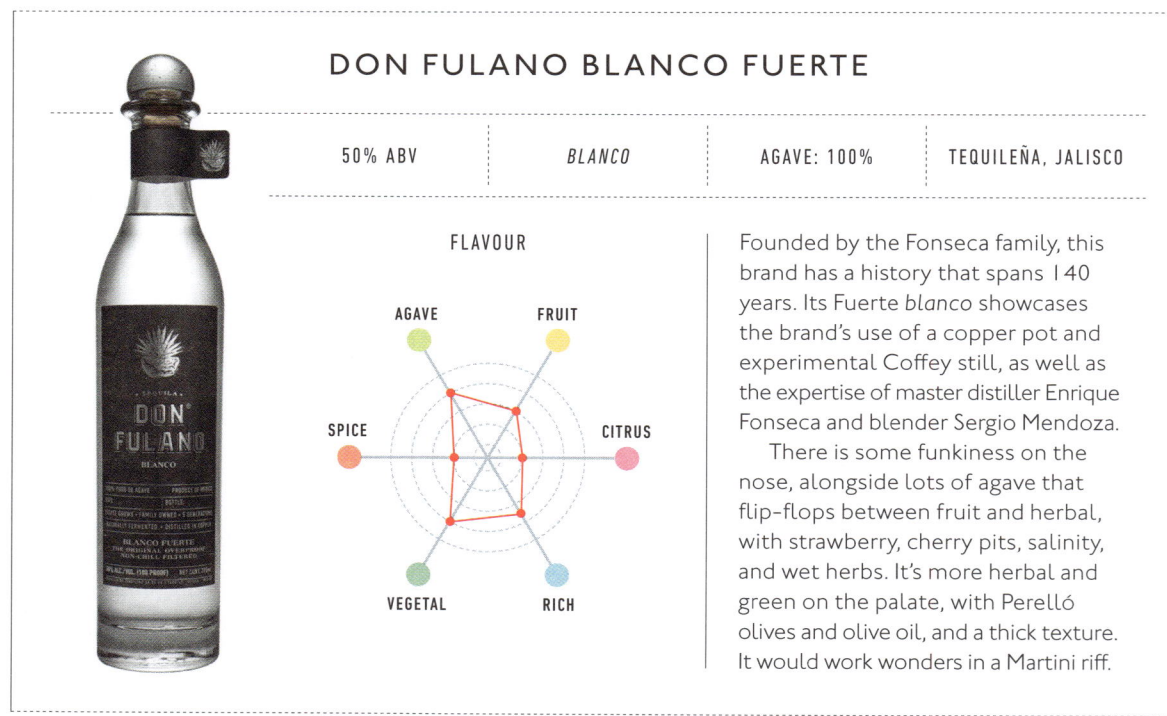

| 50% ABV | BLANCO | AGAVE: 100% | TEQUILEÑA, JALISCO |

FLAVOUR

Founded by the Fonseca family, this brand has a history that spans 140 years. Its Fuerte *blanco* showcases the brand's use of a copper pot and experimental Coffey still, as well as the expertise of master distiller Enrique Fonseca and blender Sergio Mendoza.

There is some funkiness on the nose, alongside lots of agave that flip-flops between fruit and herbal, with strawberry, cherry pits, salinity, and wet herbs. It's more herbal and green on the palate, with Perelló olives and olive oil, and a thick texture. It would work wonders in a Martini riff.

EL RAYO TEQUILA REPOSADO

40% ABV	*REPOSADO*	AGAVE: 100%	COMPAÑIA TEQUILERA HACIENDA LA CAPILLA, JALISCO

FLAVOUR

Named after the lightning bolt said to have cooked an agave and created the first tequila, El Rayo was founded not in Mexico but in Peckham, London, by Jack Vereker and Tom Bishop. This *reposado* is rested in ex-bourbon barrels for seven months and is delightfully vegetal.

There is initial sweetness on the nose, changing to salad notes like romaine lettuce, cucumber, green pepper, and olive oil. The palate is super clean with lemon zest, a heat that grows slowly from jalapeño, and a mildly oily texture too.

ÉLALA BLANCO

38% ABV	*BLANCO*	AGAVE: 100%	CASA TEQUILERA DE ARANDAS, JALISCO

FLAVOUR

A tequila brand owned by two Dutch women, Élala was born of a discovered love for the agave category. Amsterdam's first and only tequila, it is made in small batches in Jalisco.

There is a distinct green quality, with briny notes on the nose as well as olives, fennel, green peppercorns, and artichoke. On the palate, it is rich and creamy with a soft pepperiness that underpins its vegetal character. It would be a brilliant tequila for a riff on a classic Dirty Martini, and it would also work well across the gamut of traditional tequila cocktails.

FORTALEZA BLANCO

40% ABV	BLANCO	AGAVE: 100%	DESTILERÍA LA FORTALEZA, JALISCO

FLAVOUR

The Fortaleza brand may have only been established in 2005, but it has a loyal fanbase who can't get enough of its exceptional tequilas. With 150 years of family history in tequila-making, Fortaleza, run by Guillermo Sauza, has stayed true to its roots by using traditional methods such as small brick ovens, *tahonas*, and wooden fermentation tanks.

This *blanco* is one of the best on the market – it has an incredible butteriness to it, while also showing savoury notes such as olive brine, celery, and capers.

HERRADURA REPOSADO

40% ABV	REPOSADO	AGAVE: 100%	CASA HERRADURA, JALISCO

FLAVOUR

We have Herradura to thank for the commercialization of *reposado* – it was the first brand to properly introduce the category back in 1974. Aged for just a month, this is an excellent expression of a *reposado* and wins a lot of awards as a result.

There are plenty of dried fruits here – fig, dates – complemented by more savoury notes like sandalwood, burnt caramel, walnuts, and sage. The texture is resinous and oily, and there is a hint of cracked black pepper on the finish. It's a bold, nuanced tequila.

MADRE TEQUILA BLANCO

48% ABV	*BLANCO*	AGAVE: 100%	TEQUILA EL TEPOZAN, JALISCO

FLAVOUR

Any mezcal lovers might know the Madre brand for its artisanal mezcal range, but its first 100 per cent blue Weber agave tequila follows suit when it comes to quality.

Made by the Padilla family in San Julián, this tequila is delightfully savoury, with olive brine, mushrooms, and earthiness on the nose, followed by brighter vegetal notes like jalapeños and cooked sage on the palate. It finishes with cracked black pepper and a lovely waxy palate, reminiscent of Brazil nuts. The branding is a bold mix of tradition and modernity.

MIJENTA CRISTALINO TEQUILA REPOSADO

40% ABV	*CRISTALINO REPOSADO*	AGAVE: 100%	CASA TEQUILERA DE ARANDAS, JALISCO

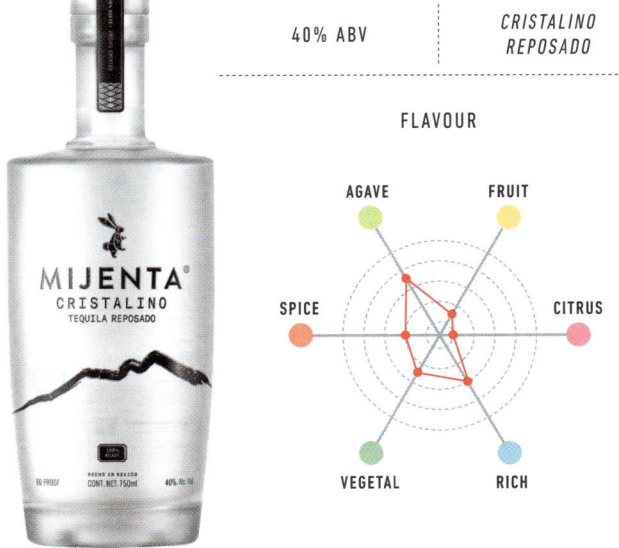

FLAVOUR

Mijenta pays attention to the details, from using spent agave fibres for its labels to protecting the craft of *jimadores* via its foundation. With *maestra tequilera* Ana María Romero, the brand has made a B Corp *reposado* especially for its *cristalino*.

Characteristic of the category, it is silky in texture and has some savoury notes, such as green coconut, coffee, and herbs like sage and thyme, especially on the finish. The agave character is still there – it often isn't in *cristalinos* – and a maple note lifts it with a touch of sweetness.

OLMECA ALTOS PLATA

38% ABV	BLANCO	AGAVE: 100%	CASA PEDRO DOMECQ, JALISCO

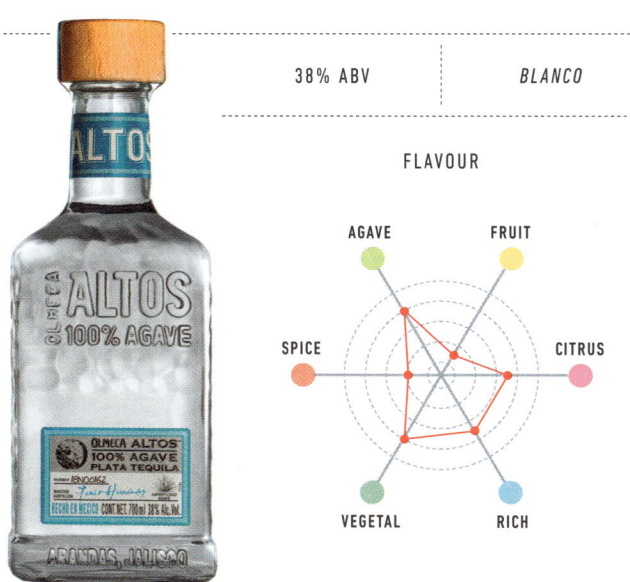

FLAVOUR

A bartender favourite, it makes complete sense that Olmeca Altos was founded by two bartenders, the late Henry Besant and Dré Masso, who teamed up with *maestro tequilero* Jesús Hernández to create their brand. The agave is slow cooked in *hornos*, milled using a *tahona* and roller, and made in small batches.

This is a beautifully clean tequila with coffee, milk chocolate, and lime zest, with some pepper bite on the finish and a back note of earthiness from mushroom and green olive. It is a brilliant all-rounder *blanco*.

SAN MATÍAS TAHONA BLANCO

38% ABV	BLANCO	AGAVE: 100%	TEQUILA SAN MATÍAS DE JALISCO

FLAVOUR

With a history dating back to 1886, San Matías is said to have been the first producer to bring extra-aged tequila to the market, in the early 1990s. This *blanco* uses agave crushed by the traditional *tahona* method.

The result is a savoury number that hits all the right notes: capers, olive brine, roasted aubergine, and grilled peppers on the nose, with a creamy texture and an umami greenness of spring onion, wild garlic, and preserved lemon on the palate. It would work wonders in a Martini riff.

TAPATIO BLANCO

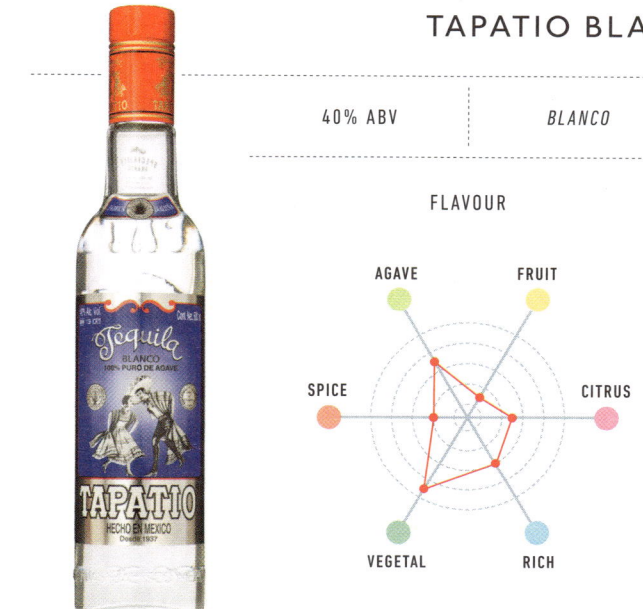

| 40% ABV | BLANCO | AGAVE: 100% | LA ALTEÑA, JALISCO |

FLAVOUR

Made at La Alteña distillery, founded by Don Felipe Camarena in 1937, Tapatio is still owned by the Camarena family and is testament to the near-century of tequila-making history behind it.

This brilliant *blanco* begins with freshly cut grass, green peppercorns, petrol, and crunchy green pepper on the nose, before a mineral flavour that finishes with some citrus oil, menthol, and liquorice root right at the end. It's ideal for mixing, sipping with some citrus, or with a Verdita (see p214).

TIERRA-NOBLE TEQUILA BLANCO

| 40% ABV | BLANCO | AGAVE: 100% | LA ESTACADA, JALISCO |

FLAVOUR

Made at 2,195m (7,200ft) above sea level, Tierra-Noble is the product of one of the highest distilleries in the world. It uses agaves from the Tequila Valley and Los Altos de Jalisco regions, and this *blanco* showcases the characteristics of both.

It is distinctive on the nose, with strawberry jam, shortbread, freshly cut mint, and a touch of curry leaf. On the palate, there are pickles with sweet agave, some pleasant jalapeño heat, and a welcome citrus hit of grapefruit oil. The finish brings some salinity and a slightly dusty texture.

CLASSIC
·······TEQUILA·······
COCKTAILS

IT MAY BE THE MOST familiar format to drink tequila, but how much do you know about your favourite tequila cocktails? Here we delve into everything you need to perfect your cocktail-making, from the importance of *mise en place*, the equipment, and easy-to-make syrups and infusions. From the famous Margarita and Paloma to the lesser-known Toreador and Ranch Water, we'll take a tour of some of tequila's most-loved cocktails, including ways to put your own spin on them. We'll look at how tequila can be switched into other classic cocktails to give them an agave-flavoured twist, as well as some of the modern tequila cocktails being served in the world's best bars today. And we've not forgotten tequila shots either – just don't expect to see them with lime and salt here.

MISE EN PLACE

The French method of *mise en place* is more often reserved for professional kitchens, but the practice is working its way into the world of cocktail making.

MILITARY PRECISION

Who'd have thought the French army would have a say in your cocktail hour? The military-like organization of its staff kitchens may have been the inspiration for French culinary heavyweight Georges Auguste Escoffier (1846–1935).

In the 19th century, Escoffier updated and simplified fine dining in France, as well as establishing the hierarchical *brigade de cuisine* system that is still used today in restaurant and hotel kitchens. He is also said to have popularized the method of *mise en place*.

Meaning "to put in place" or "to gather", *mise en place* refers to the method of organizing and prepping ingredients and supplies in advance. Historically, it has been more associated with kitchens and chefs, with inspiring restaurateurs often explaining its importance. Today, this practice is becoming more prevalent in the methodology of the bartender.

Having garnishes, bitters, citrus juice, sugar syrup, equipment, and most-used bottles in easy-to-access and commonsense places means that the ergonomics of making multiple cocktails at speed isn't unnecessarily difficult.

ERGONOMIC MATTERS

Take a look behind the stations of some of the world's most successful bars, and you'll see for yourself the level of thought and practicality that has gone into making bartender stations ergonomically sound.

The Tayēr cocktail bar at London's Tayēr + Elementary, for example, was designed by bar owners Alex Kratena and Monica Berg with Oslo's Behind Bars design agency. It is adaptable to each bartender's needs and ways of working, with bottles and ingredients arranged efficiently and flexibly in a series of hexagons. At Chicago's The Aviary, bartender stations are complete with clever time-saving equipment so bartenders don't have to wash their shakers between cocktails.

But why should you, the home bartender, care about all of this when you're not working a bar shift or serving multiple paying customers? The reason is that having your cocktail ingredients properly prepared ahead of your cocktail or dinner party is key to alleviating unnecessary stress. Just as it's important to prep your dinner ingredients, making sure your cocktail-making station is well organized for the evening ahead will make your Margarita game a doddle.

HANKY PANKY
The bar stations at Mexico City's Hanky Panky are set up so bartenders can serve their thirsty customers with speed and precision.

FOUR THINGS TO DO BEFORE YOU START SHAKING OR STIRRING

Ensure any cocktail party is stress free by prepping all your ingredients and equipment ahead of time.

LIQUID

Have enough of your wet cocktail ingredients to hand for your number of guests, and reduce the amount of different tequilas you need. Pre-squeeze and bottle juice ahead of time. Ditto syrups. And ensure you have plenty of ice. Easier still, pre-batch everything.

GARNISHES

Cut your wedges, rim your glasses, and slice or pick your garnishes well in advance and have them in easy-to-grab containers ready for use before your guests arrive. And if you're cutting chillies, do this separately to avoid cross contamination.

GLASSWARE

If you can serve your cocktails in one style of glassware, this will make life easier. Have two glasses per person, so that fresh ones can be served as used glasses are washed. If you're freezing glassware, this might only be possible for the first couple of serves.

EQUIPMENT

You can lose a strainer, stirrer, and more in a matter of moments when you're under pressure. Lay out your equipment ahead of time and always return it to the same place, rinsed, after use. If you have multiples of the same thing, just be sure to keep them all clean.

COCKTAIL-MAKING EQUIPMENT

A cocktail maker should never blame their tools, so gather together some quality kit, make sure you know where everything is, and keep it all ready for action.

PREPPING YOUR COCKTAILS

As well as glasses of course (see pp114–15), some essential pieces of equipment are important to get started.

KNIVES AND CHOPPING BOARDS
Making tequila cocktails often requires a lot of cutting (fruits, chillies, and so on). Your knife can also double up as a stirrer should you need it.

MEXICAN ELBOW CITRUS PRESS
This is possibly the most effective home juicer for citrus fruits. If you're juicing larger fruits like grapefruits, a larger lever presser might be more suitable.

ICE
The frozen stuff is more of a philosophy than a piece of equipment, but it's essential (see p187).

COCKTAIL MAKING

These items are fundamental to making a good cocktail.

JIGGER
This is the ultimate measuring device for spirits. Not all jiggers are built the same, so check for exact volumes and any inside marker lines. Usually, they're available in 30ml/60ml (1fl oz/2fl oz) and 25ml/50ml (¾fl oz/ 1½fl oz) sizes.

SHAKER
While professionals might favour a Boston shaker (two sections, one larger than the other), for use at home, I'd probably suggest using a three-piece cobbler (a shaker, strainer, and lid) or a French shaker (shaker and lid but no strainer).

HAWTHORNE STRAINER
These coiled strainers are made for fitting on top of a mixing tin or glass for straining your cocktails.

OTHER USEFUL EQUIPMENT

Not all these pieces of equipment are essential, but they will help to refine your cocktail-making skills.

Pestle and mortar These are useful for grinding or muddling any ingredients.

Glass bottles and pourers Store any pre-made syrups or pre-squeezed juices in glass bottles, and use pourers for stress-free pouring.

Cheese slicer Renowned American bartender Jeffrey Morgenthaler swears by the slightly left-field choice of a cheese slicer for cutting citrus fruits for their peel. It really does work and is much safer than a knife.

Mixing tin/glass If you're not shaking your cocktail or building it in the glass, a mixing tin or glass can come in handy.

Fine strainer This piece of equipment stops fruit or ice shards from making it into your final serve.

Bar spoon A long-handled spoon that is handy for mixing stirred cocktails, combining ingredients that have been built in the glass, or for adding small amounts of ingredients to the cocktail.

Tongs These are great for adding ice or garnishes to cocktails.

Bar picks A handy piece of kit if you have a particularly elaborate garnish.

Straws Use metal ones preferably or ones that won't contaminate the taste.

Jugs If you're serving in bulk, a large ceramic or glass container, or several, is essential.

Tray Avoid mishaps by using trays to transfer glasses and jugs from the kitchen to the party zone.

COOL TECH

BLENDER
If you need to blend ingredients or make a quick and easy Frozen Margarita, this will serve you well.

SLUSHY MACHINE
For the ultimate blowout, you can get these with multiple chambers for different types of tequila slushies.

RAPID CHILLER
These nifty gadgets can chill liquids in record time without dilution – a piece of kit for the cocktail connoisseurs.

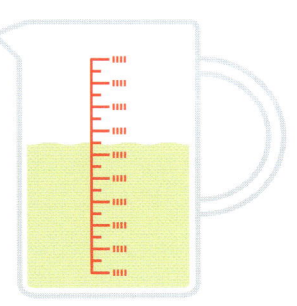

MEASURING JUG
This is useful for measuring ingredients in larger quantities if you're making cocktails in jugs or in batches.

BOTTLE OPENER
Essential for opening sodas, tonic, and other mixers.

REFINE YOUR COCKTAIL-MAKING SKILLS BY BUILDING A SET OF ESSENTIAL EQUIPMENT.

SYRUPS, INFUSIONS, AND ICE

Making cocktails at home needn't be complicated, and knowing how to make syrups and infusions and chill your drinks is all part of the fun, adding a personal touch to your creations. Here are some foolproof recipes to get you started.

SUGAR SYRUPS

Sugar syrups are great for adding sweetness, texture, and flavour in place of agave syrup, and they're super simple to make.

SIMPLE SYRUP 1:1

Simple syrup is a controlled and classic way to add sweetness to your cocktails.

METHOD:

1. Heat 120g (4oz) granulated sugar in 120ml (4fl oz) water until it dissolves.

2. Let the liquid cool, pour into a glass jar, and seal. It will keep for a month in the fridge.

CITRUS OIL SYRUP: OLEO SACCHARUM

This syrup is a good way of utilizing all those spent citrus peels. Add it to cocktails, or the candied peels can be great in punches.

METHOD:

1. Add leftover citrus peels to a jar.

2. Add granulated sugar to coat.

3. Toss and then muddle.

4. Seal the jar and leave overnight. It should keep for a week in the fridge.

GRENADINE

Use homemade grenadine in your Tequila Sunrise (see pp206–07).

METHOD:

1. Take equal parts pomegranate juice and granulated sugar, and heat in a pan with a couple of drops to one teaspoon of orange blossom water until the sugar has dissolved.

2. Let it cool, pour into a glass bottle, and store it in the fridge. It should keep for about a month.

INFUSING TEQUILA

Infusing tequila is an easy way of bringing more flavours to your cocktails.

1 Take your ingredient of choice, such as jalapeños (sliced into rounds), whole pink peppercorns, or grapefruit peel, wash if needed, and add to a clean, sealable container.

2 Add your tequila of choice and seal the container. Allow it to sit in the fridge for a few days and keep tasting to judge when you're happy with it.

3 Strain/filter through cheesecloth to remove solids and pour the infused tequila into a bottle.

JALAPEÑO
TEQUILA
20/09/2025

4 Label the bottle with the date and keep it in a dark and cool place. It will keep for about six months, or longer in the fridge.

LET'S TALK ICE

A cocktail without ice – to shake, stir, or be poured over – is no cocktail at all. Ice plays many roles when it comes to making cocktails. It keeps them cold, sure, but it also adds an extra aesthetic layer in the glass, and the ceremonial clinking we all know and love. But it is also key when it comes to dilution. Why do I want my drink diluted, you ask? Because it softens and opens up the flavours of your cocktail. Note that more ice doesn't mean more dilution – in fact, it means the opposite.

A lot of tequila cocktails call for ice for serving, such as Margs, Palomas, and Cantaritos, but you will also need ice for shaking and stirring. Make sure your ice is dry when you use it – that is, not already melting – for a slower rate of dilution.

While making ice isn't difficult in theory, good-quality clear (not cloudy) ice is widely available to buy and pays dividends over trying to make it at home.

If you can't find clear ice, silicone moulds are the best for making ice at home. Use filtered water to fill them: 2.5 x 2.5cm (1 x 1 in) cubes are the best all rounders, while ice balls are good for sipping tequilas or slow-drinking cocktails.

SALINE SOLUTION

Saline solution is perfect for adding salinity to cocktails in a more controlled fashion than simply adding salt.

1. Stir 20g (¾oz) sea salt with 80ml (2¾fl oz) boiling water until dissolved.

2. Filter through cheesecloth into an eye dropper.

3. Squeeze two or three drops into your cocktail to taste.

TO GARNISH OR NOT TO GARNISH?

That is the question. Although its popularity has waxed and waned over time, the cocktail garnish is a multifaceted and handy tool for elevating your cocktail game.

GARNISHES THEN AND NOW

The first appearance of garnishes in official records is said to be in American bartender Jerry Thomas's famous book *How to Mix Drinks: Or, A Bon-Vivant's Companion*. Published in 1862, it was the first-known cocktail book. Thomas references several garnishes, but most prominent is lemon peel.

Fast-forward to today, and the lure of the garnish ebbs and flows in bartending land. Garnishes can range from bacon rashers, ironic umbrellas, and stencilled scenes, to minimalist items such as flowers, peels, and single drops of oil (or nothing at all). Whatever form it takes, the garnish flip-flops in and out of favour over time and oceans, but it plays more than just a visual role in cocktails.

PEPPERCORNS

BITTERS

SALT

GREEN PEPPERS

WEDGES

PEEL TWISTS

PEEL COINS

SLICES

ZEST

SEASONING

As in cooking, adding seasoning to tequila cocktails is a way of enhancing flavour. Salt is perhaps the most obvious, used on the rim or in the mix, while pepper in its many forms can add some heat and bite. Green peppers or a sprinkling of peppercorns, for instance, add flavour and warmth. Bitters are also a final flourish, and my favourite is a mole bitter as a nod to tequila's Mexican heritage.

CITRUS

Citrus garnishes are the easiest to reach for and are the perfect bedfellow for tequila cocktails, which often use citrus juice. Wedges, slices, and zest are relatively easy to prepare, but if you're using peels, remove the pith to avoid any bitterness. You can use peel as coins (small circles) or twists, or simply express and drop them into your cocktail or discard.

GARNISHES CAN OFFER THE DRINKER AN EXTRA ELEMENT TO THEIR TASTING EXPERIENCE.

ADDED EXTRAS

As we've seen, aroma plays a huge part in how we perceive flavour, and garnishes can offer the drinker an extra element to their tasting experience. Citrus peels, for example, contain oils that, when expressed (squeezed) or gently pressed around a glass, can impart an incredible amount of aroma with relatively little effort.

With tequila cocktails specifically, garnishes often play an important role in signalling certain characteristics that the drinker can find in their glass. From chillies in a Spicy Margarita (see p196) to grapefruit in a Paloma (see pp202–03), and much more in between, there are plenty of ways to bring some extra flair to tequila cocktails. Here's how to execute some of the best.

RED, GREEN, OR JALAPEÑO CHILLIES

TAJÍN

DILL

ROSEMARY

CORIANDER

SAGE

CHILLI

Spicy tequila cocktails require chillies, so be sure to have small rings of red, green, or jalapeño chillies to hand, and cut them separately from other ingredients. Tajín is a classic Mexican spice mix made of mild chilli peppers, sea salt, and lime. It can be used as a rim by pouring it into a saucer, rubbing either a half or whole glass rim with lime, and gently rolling the glass in the mix.

HERBS

Some tequilas are especially herbaceous in nature, and these characteristics can be amped up in volume with the use of matching herbs. Use sprigs of fresh herbs, with the stalk securing the sprig in the liquid and the leaves on top. Don't go too crazy – battling through a jungle of leaves to get to your cocktail is not a pleasurable experience.

BATANGA

Made with four simple ingredients, this Mexican classic from the 1960s is as easy to make as it is delicious.

HISTORY

Invented by Don Javier Delgado Corona, owner of La Capilla bar in Tequila, Mexico, in 1961, the Batanga is made up of four simple ingredients – tequila, lime juice, salt, and cola. Among superfans, it is one of the category's most loved cocktails. It's a Cuba Libre-esque serve and said to be a variation of the Changuirongo – tequila mixed with sweet soda. The way that Don Javier made it, though, is what gives it its legendary status in drinks circles. It is said he mixed it with a wooden-handled knife that he used for chopping limes, chillies for salsa, and guacamole ingredients, adding an original and distinctive edge to the flavour.

WHAT MAKES A BATANGA?

It's a refreshingly easy drink to make in its most basic form, but make sure all your ingredients are singing, with plenty of salt, high-acid limes, and Mexican cola if you have it. If you want to make it the authentic way, be certain to mix it all together with a large knife in honour of the late, great Don Javier.

LIME JUICE

COLA

SALT

BLANCO TEQUILA

BOLSTER YOUR BATANGA

FERNET-BRANCA: Known as the "bartenders' handshake", Fernet-Branca is an *amaro* (bitter Italian liqueur) that contains around 27 botanicals, including cinnamon, myrrh, iris, and saffron, and adds a bitter edge to anything it touches.

AMARO MONTENEGRO: Made in Bologna, Italy, this *amaro* edges more on the delicate side with the addition of orange, cloves, and marjoram, making it a slightly sweeter, floral addition.

CINNAMON SYRUP: Drawing out those spice notes of the cola, and adding some warmth and sweetness, cinnamon syrup makes a great spiced addition to this classic cocktail.

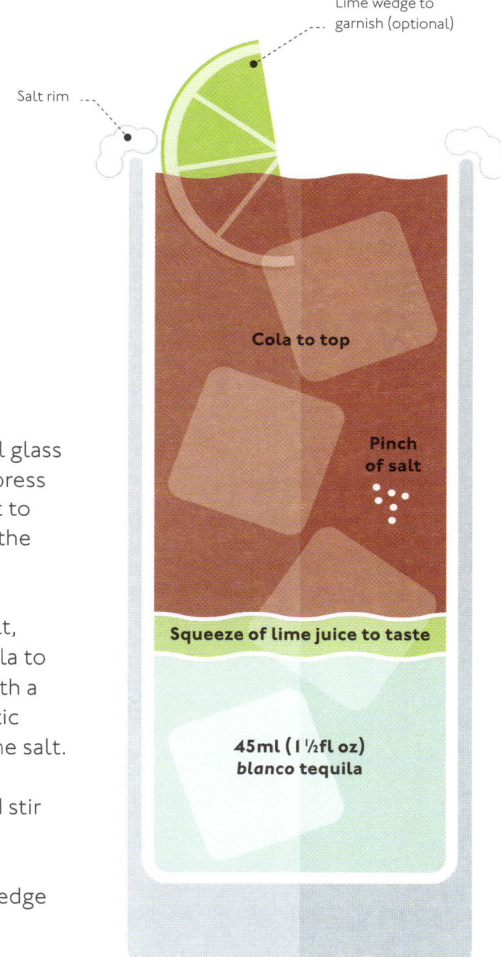

Lime wedge to garnish (optional)

Salt rim

Cola to top

Pinch of salt

Squeeze of lime juice to taste

45ml (1½fl oz) blanco tequila

METHOD

1. Rim your highball glass with lime juice and press onto a saucer of salt to create your rim. Fill the glass with ice.

2. Add a pinch of salt, lime juice, and tequila to the glass, and stir with a knife (for an authentic touch) to dissolve the salt.

3. Top with cola and stir again to mix.

4. Garnish with a wedge of lime if you like.

NOTE

IF YOU'RE NOT SURE ABOUT THE SALT RIM, TRY A HALF-RIM SO YOU CAN DIP IN AND OUT.

DON JAVIER IS SAID TO HAVE NAMED THE COCKTAIL AFTER A CUSTOMER WHO WAS *BATANGA* – SPANISH SLANG FOR "THICK IN THE MIDDLE", OR STOUT.

CANTARITO

This fruity Jalisco staple is served in a vessel that alone makes it worth ordering. Some recipes call for other citrus juices too, so don't be shy to experiment with your favourites.

HISTORY

Derived from the word *"cántaro"*, which is Spanish for "jug", the Cantarito and the container after which it is named (which can also go by the name *jarrito de barro*) are Jaliscan products through and through, much like tequila itself. And nothing feels quite so pleasing than drinking a Cantarito in its proper guise. The Jalisco favourite combines *reposado* tequila, lime juice, grapefruit soda, and orange juice in a beautiful clay cup, rimmed with Tajín (a Mexican seasoning made of chilli peppers, lime, and sea salt). It's served in bars, and even on the side of the road, across the region.

WHAT MAKES A CANTARITO?

The *cantarito* makes the Cantarito. Its physical makeup, appearance, and ability to keep its contents cool make it the perfect vessel for such a popular cocktail in the Mexican heat. If you don't have a clay cup though, a Collins glass is your next best thing. And don't forget your pinch of salt either. It really helps draw out those all-important citrus notes.

TAJÍN

REPOSADO TEQUILA

ORANGE JUICE

GRAPEFRUIT JUICE

LIME JUICE

GRAPEFRUIT SODA

SALT

OTHER JUICES TO EXPERIMENT WITH

BLOOD ORANGE Less acidic than a navel orange, blood orange brings a sweeter, more delicate edge, and could be useful if it's dancing with more acidic citrus fruits.

YUZU Super tart and sour, yuzu can be used to ramp up that acidity level if you feel like your Cantarito needs a push in that particular direction.

BERGAMOT Woodier and earthier than a lot of citrus juices, bergamot can add a more nuanced edge to a Cantarito and stop it being too sweet.

METHOD

1. Chill your clay vessel by soaking it in water at least 10 minutes before making your drink.

2. Rim your vessel with Tajín.

3. Shake the tequila, orange, grapefruit, and lime juice, and salt in a shaker over ice.

4. Strain into your clay cup over ice and top with grapefruit soda.

5. Stir and garnish with a wedge of lime.

Tajín rim

Lime wedge to garnish

Grapefruit soda to top

Pinch of salt

15ml (½fl oz) lime juice

20ml (¾fl oz) orange juice

20ml (¾fl oz) grapefruit juice

60ml (2fl oz) *reposado* tequila

NOTE

THE ADDITION OF CHAMOY SAUCE AND SALT ON THE RIM WILL AMP UP THE FLAVOUR EXPERIENCE.

THE ALKALINE NATURE OF THE CLAY IN THE CUP HELPS TO ROUND OUT AND BALANCE THE ACIDITY FROM THE FRUIT JUICES.

EL DIABLO

El Diablo is a mid-century classic that smacks of both fruit and spice and is woefully overlooked. See this as your opportunity to shine a light on it.

HISTORY

El Diablo ("The Devil") can chart its evolution back to 1937, when it featured in *The How and When*, a cocktail book by Hyman Gale and Gerald F. Marco. It appeared there as just Diablo and there was no tequila in sight – in fact, the recipe used white rum instead. But in 1946 in *Trader Vic's Book of Food and Drink*, we find the Mexican El Diablo, which used tequila. By the time it is simply known as El Diablo, it is recognized as the four-ingredient cocktail we know today, combining tequila, crème de cassis, lime juice, and ginger ale or beer. It's a lighter alternative to, say, a Margarita, but certainly no wallflower.

WHAT MAKES AN EL DIABLO?

The two main variables in El Diablo are, in fact, also its two most defining elements: the crème de cassis and ginger. Some recipes call for ginger syrup and sparkling water instead of ginger ale or beer, or Chambord or other blackberry liqueurs instead of crème de cassis. Whatever your riff, be sure to keep the fruit and spice punchy.

LIME

GOLD TEQUILA

CRÈME DE CASSIS

GINGER BEER

CRÈME DE CASSIS CHOICES

GIFFARD CRÈME DE CASSIS IMPÉRIAL The famous French brand makes some of the best liqueurs and syrups on the market. Its Crème de Cassis Impérial uses blackcurrants from the Loire Valley.

DE KUYPER CASSIS This classic Dutch liqueur is a versatile product and probably one of the easiest to get hold of in supermarkets. It's everything you'd expect from a classic cassis.

BRIOTTET CRÈME DE CASSIS DE DIJON The French artisan producer Briottet turns out some top-quality liqueurs, and its crème de cassis delivers not only on flavour but texture too.

METHOD

1. Add ice to a Collins glass.

2. Add the lime juice and a squeezed lime wedge to the bottom of the glass.

3. Add tequila and crème de cassis and stir.

4. Top with ginger beer while stirring continuously.

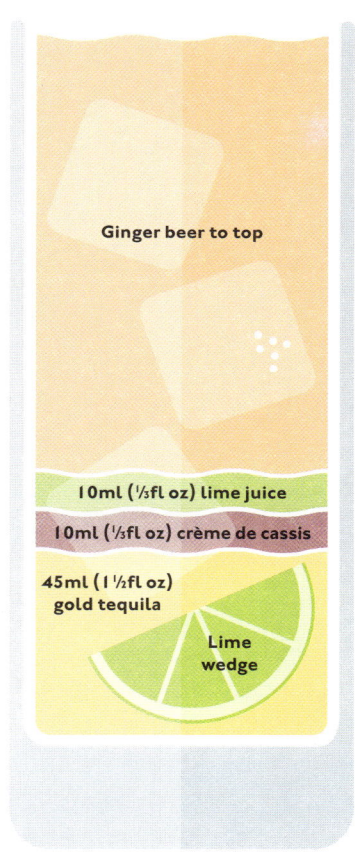

Ginger beer to top

10ml (⅓fl oz) lime juice

10ml (⅓fl oz) crème de cassis

45ml (1½fl oz) gold tequila

Lime wedge

NOTE

ADD SOME MORE FLAIR AND AROMA WITH A BLACKCURRANT GARNISH.

INSTEAD OF USING GINGER BEER, MAKE GINGER SYRUP BY HEATING SUGAR, WATER, AND FRESH GINGER TO BRING IT ALL TOGETHER. THEN ADD SPARKLING WATER.

MARGARITA

Myths abound about the origins of this most classic tequila drink. Whichever one you believe, it's undisputed that the Margarita is tequila's most famous cocktail.

HISTORY

Utter the word "Margarita", and any cocktail aficionado worth their salt will tell the tale of Carlos "Danny" Herrera. A Mexican bartender working in a Tijuana restaurant, Rancho La Gloria, in the late 1930s, Herrera, it is said, invented the cocktail for an aspiring actress, Marjorie King, who was allergic to any spirits other than tequila. They might also mention the name Margarita Sames, a Dallas socialite who claims to have invented the cocktail in 1948 in her holiday home in Acapulco. Or, it may be attributed to Jose Cuervo, who advertised tequila in the US with the tagline: "Margarita: it's more than just a girl's name."

WHAT MAKES A MARGARITA?

Sitting in the "sour" cocktail category (and often referred to as an evolution of the Daisy), the Margarita balances its hero spirit, tequila, with the acidity of lime and sweetness of the orange liqueur. It can be served straight up or with ice from the shaker and with a rim of your choice (salt or half salt).

LIME

ORANGE LIQUEUR

SALT

BLANCO TEQUILA

MARGARITA RIFFS

SPICY MARGARITA: For heat lovers, the Spicy Margarita is one of the most popular modern variations. This version can have the addition of chilli syrup, muddled jalapeños in the shaker, a chilli garnish, or a Tajín rim (mild chilli peppers, lime, and sea salt) to really up the ante.

FROZEN MARGARITA: The Frozen Margarita has become a summer staple around the world, and you'll need a blender for this one (or one in a nearby bar). This is also where you can have some fun with more exotic flavours, such as mango.

TOMMY'S MARGARITA: The classic Marg's most famous riff slightly changes the specs and replaces orange liqueur with agave syrup, thanks to San Francisco bartender Julio Bermejo, who was experimenting with the cocktail at his parents' restaurant, Tommy's, in the late 1980s.

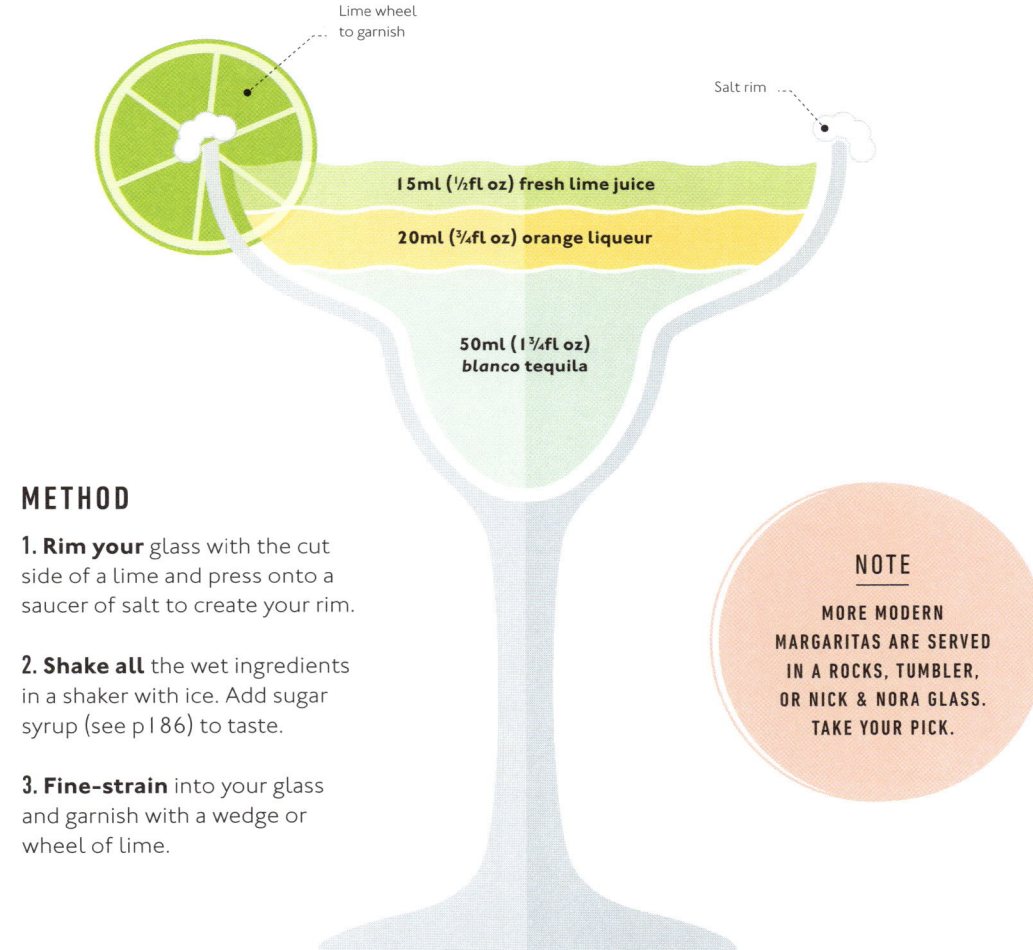

Lime wheel
to garnish

Salt rim

15ml (½fl oz) fresh lime juice

20ml (¾fl oz) orange liqueur

50ml (1¾fl oz)
blanco tequila

METHOD

1. **Rim your** glass with the cut side of a lime and press onto a saucer of salt to create your rim.

2. **Shake all** the wet ingredients in a shaker with ice. Add sugar syrup (see p186) to taste.

3. **Fine-strain** into your glass and garnish with a wedge or wheel of lime.

NOTE

MORE MODERN MARGARITAS ARE SERVED IN A ROCKS, TUMBLER, OR NICK & NORA GLASS. TAKE YOUR PICK.

THE WORLD'S FIRST FROZEN MARGARITA MACHINE WAS INVENTED IN 1971 BY DALLAS RESTAURATEUR MARIANO MARTINEZ.

CAFÉ ROYAL MATADOR

There are two very different but equally delicious tequila cocktails that go by the name of Matador. The Café Royal version is probably the original guise of this cocktail with its myriad faces.

HISTORY

The first records of this short and dry version of the Matador appeared in English bartender William J. Tarling's famous *Café Royal Cocktail Book* in 1937. Using equal parts tequila, curaçao, and dry vermouth, it's a Negroni-style cocktail that has been played with by bartenders in more recent years with the addition, in small measures, of other spirits, such as mezcal and rum.

See pp200–01 for Trader Vic's version of the Matador.

WHAT MAKES THIS MATADOR?

It uses equal parts ingredients, and while cocktails of a similar format might be more likely stirred down over ice, the original recipe calls instead for the ingredients to be shaken. The original doesn't specify a garnish, but an orange twist works wonderfully.

BLANCO TEQUILA

CURAÇAO

DRY VERMOUTH

BOOZY RIFFS

MEZCAL: This classic is an excellent base for numerous riffs, so why not add a small measure of mezcal to bring another layer of agave complexity to your Matador.

RUM: Bartender riffs on this classic abound, and rum, most often white rum, is a popular choice. Where your rum is from – Jamaica, Barbados, or Martinique, for example – will have a big impact on the flavour.

REPOSADO **TEQUILA:** While *blanco* is often used in the base of this cocktail, *reposado* tequila has become increasingly popular among bartenders for adding a deeper dimension.

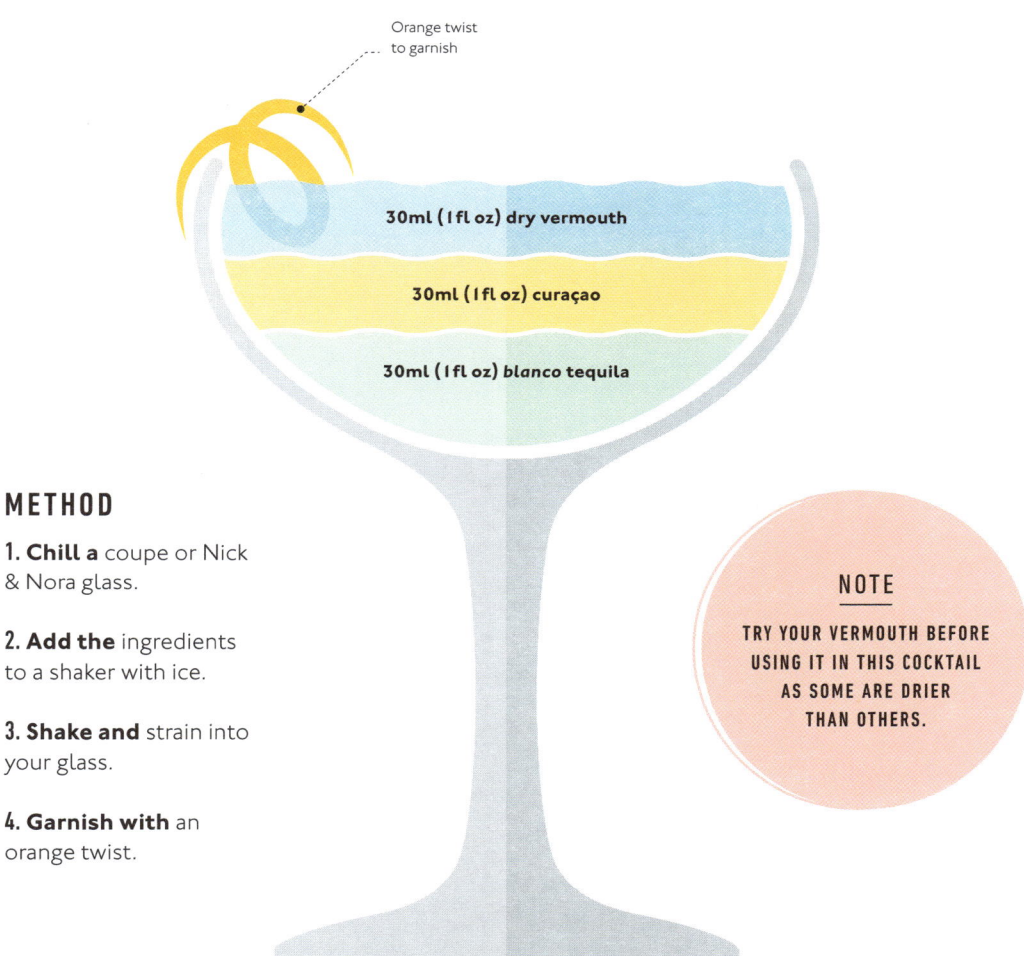

Orange twist to garnish

30ml (1fl oz) dry vermouth

30ml (1fl oz) curaçao

30ml (1fl oz) *blanco* tequila

METHOD

1. Chill a coupe or Nick & Nora glass.

2. Add the ingredients to a shaker with ice.

3. Shake and strain into your glass.

4. Garnish with an orange twist.

NOTE

TRY YOUR VERMOUTH BEFORE USING IT IN THIS COCKTAIL AS SOME ARE DRIER THAN OTHERS.

LONDON'S THEN-NEW ACCESS TO THE AGAVE SPIRIT MEANT THAT THE MATADOR WASN'T THE ONLY TEQUILA COCKTAIL IN TARLING'S BOOK.

TRADER VIC'S TEQUILA MATADOR

Written by American bartender Victor Bergeron, also known as Trader Vic, this recipe is a more tropical rendition of this tequila-based cocktail.

HISTORY

Trader Vic's Tequila Matador dates from 1972, 35 years later than the Café Royal version (see pp198–99). It appeared in Victor Bergeron's revised edition of his *Trader Vic's Bartender's Guide.* Bergeron founded a chain of Polynesian-themed restaurants, and his version of the Matador comprises a tropical twist with tequila, pineapple juice, and lime juice. It can be served long with ice, short without ice, or short and on the rocks. It's often described as a Margarita-style cocktail.

WHAT MAKES THIS MATADOR?

The pineapple juice is the defining factor in this version of the Matador, so make sure you do your research to choose the right one. Some might not be as sweet as you'd think, so there is always the option to add a small amount of sugar or agave syrup to round things off. A dried pineapple wheel adds a final aromatic touch.

REPOSADO TEQUILA

LIME JUICE

PINEAPPLE JUICE

BOLSTERING BITTERS

BITTERED SLING GRAPEFRUIT & HOPS: Fresh grapefruit peel along with floral, herbaceous, and bitter hops add another dimension to this cocktail. South Asian peppercorns and bitter cinchona bring some welcome bite too.

THREE FAMILIES AMETHYST PUNCH: A beautiful Sri Lankan-inspired bitter, it comprises Park Estate green tea cold brew and Ceylon arrack-based tea tincture, green peppercorns, dried mangosteen, caraway seed, liquorice root, and mangosteen and green tea distillates.

SEASN LIGHT: This alcohol-free bitter from the genius behind Seedlip has top notes of fresh cut grass, lime, and grapefruit peel, as well as bitterness from king of bitters (*Andrographis paniculata*) and a welcome salinity from kombu and sea salt.

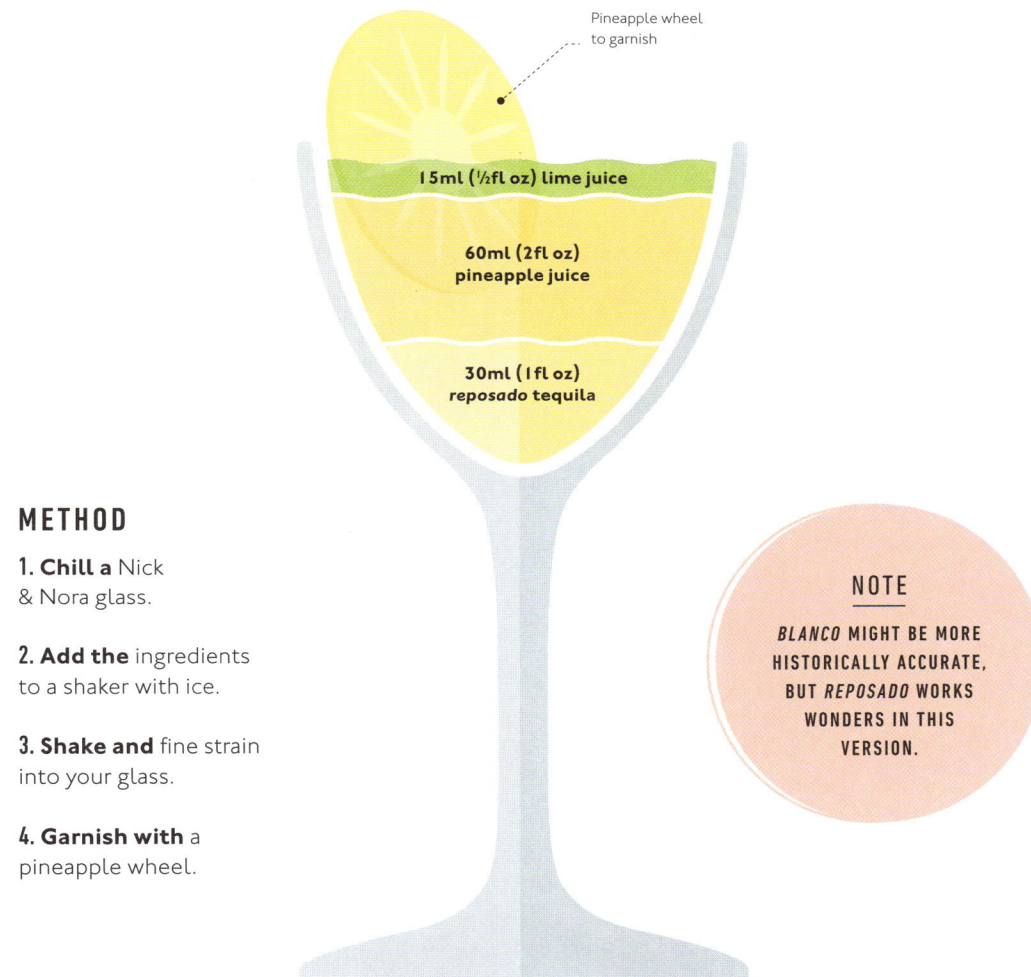

Pineapple wheel to garnish

15ml (½fl oz) lime juice

60ml (2fl oz) pineapple juice

30ml (1fl oz) *reposado* tequila

METHOD

1. Chill a Nick & Nora glass.

2. Add the ingredients to a shaker with ice.

3. Shake and fine strain into your glass.

4. Garnish with a pineapple wheel.

NOTE

BLANCO MIGHT BE MORE HISTORICALLY ACCURATE, BUT *REPOSADO* WORKS WONDERS IN THIS VERSION.

TRADER VIC IS SAID TO HAVE CREATED MORE THAN 200 SIGNATURE COCKTAILS, INCLUDING THE FAMOUS MAI TAI.

PALOMA

One of the rising stars in the world of tequila cocktails, the Paloma has evolved in recent times from its probable origins in the 1950s.

HISTORY

Combining tequila with grapefruit soda, lime juice, and salt, this pink number has an uncertain origin. Some credit legendary bartender Don Javier Delgado Corona from Tequila's La Capilla bar as the creator. Others say it was invented when a 1950s brochure for grapefruit soda brand Squirt suggested mixing it with tequila. The addition of lime juice and salt is rumoured to have occurred in Jalisco two decades later, and more contemporary versions have seen the grapefruit soda replaced with fresh grapefruit juice, sugar, and sparkling water.

WHAT MAKES A PALOMA?

The grapefruit soda. Some people use fresh juice with soda water and sugar syrup, but for an easier option, a good-quality bottled soda makes the Paloma a straightforward drink to serve at home. As with many tequila cocktails, have some salt handy.

PINK GRAPEFRUIT SODA

LIME JUICE

AGAVE SYRUP

BLANCO TEQUILA

SALT

GRAPEFRUIT SODA ROULETTE

SQUIRT: The most authentic option for this particular cocktail, Squirt was created in 1938 and may have been the catalyst for the creation of the Paloma.

JARRITOS: Tart and tangy with a welcome sweetness, Jarritos is a worthy contender of any soda vying for the top spot as the Paloma's ideal soda.

THREE CENTS PINK GRAPEFRUIT SODA: This soda was actually created by bartenders specifically with the Paloma in mind, so it's no surprise that it works sublimely.

Slice of pink grapefruit to garnish

Pink grapefruit soda to top

Pinch of salt

1 bar spoon agave syrup

20ml (¾fl oz) strained fresh lime juice

60ml (2fl oz) *blanco tequila*

METHOD

1. **Add all** the wet ingredients except the soda to a highball glass.

2. **Stir to** combine.

3. **Add ice** cubes and top with grapefruit soda.

4. **Add a** pinch of salt if needed.

5. **Garnish with** a pink grapefruit slice.

NOTE

GO FOR GOOD-QUALITY SODA OVER FRUIT JUICE FOR FOOLPROOF CONSISTENCY.

SOME SAY THE PALOMA IS NAMED AFTER A FOLK SONG FROM THE 1860S, "LA PALOMA" (SPANISH FOR "THE DOVE").

RANCH WATER

We have Texas to thank for this exceptionally easy, light, and sessionable cocktail, which requires a very specific brand of Mexican sparkling water, Topo Chico.

HISTORY

The origins of the Ranch Water cocktail could go back to as relatively recently as the late 1990s. In a nod to its name, it is thought that the Ranch Water might have been invented at Ranch 616 restaurant in Austin, Texas. Owner Kevin Williamson is said to have put it on his opening menu in 1998, and he is credited with training the team at Gage Hotel's White Buffalo Bar in Marathon, Texas, where it was officially first seen in 2010. Its association with ranches is due to its exceptionally light and refreshing nature, giving ranch hands something thirst-quenching but a bit boozy after a long day's work.

WHAT MAKES A RANCH WATER?

It's the use of Topo Chico sparkling water that really gives this cocktail its USP. Naturally carbonated, it has been bottled at the Cerro del Topo Chico spring in Monterrey, Mexico, since 1895. It's that carbonation, which is turbo-charged by a second, artificial one, as well as its slightly salty flavour profile, that give it its cult status, and the cocktail is often served straight from the bottle.

BLANCO TEQUILA

LIME JUICE

TOPO CHICO SPARKLING WATER

LIME WEDGE

MODIFY IT

JALAPEÑOS Want to spice things up a bit? Muddled jalapeños give this cocktail a more savoury, spicy edge.

TRIPLE SEC The addition of 1 to 2 teaspoons of triple sec will make this a richer and more nuanced cocktail.

AGAVE SYRUP For those with sweeter palates, adding some agave syrup to taste can help balance out the minerality.

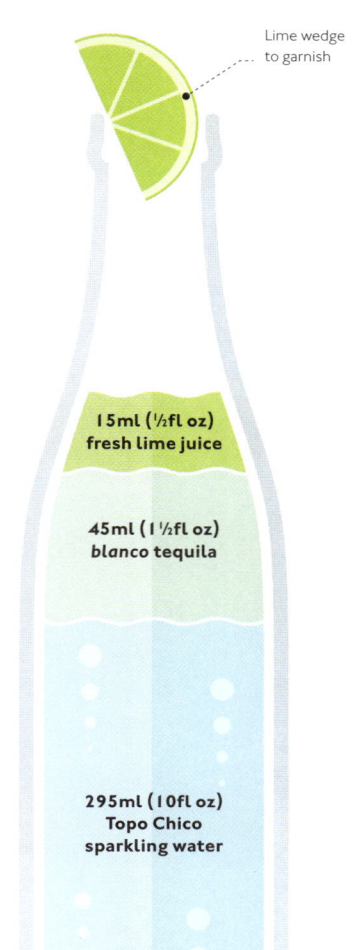

Lime wedge
to garnish

15ml (½fl oz)
fresh lime juice

45ml (1½fl oz)
blanco tequila

295ml (10fl oz)
**Topo Chico
sparkling water**

METHOD

1. Chill a 355ml (12fl oz) bottle of Topo Chico sparkling water.

2. Decant 60ml (2fl oz) out of the bottle.

3. Add blanco tequila and lime juice and stir gently.

4. Garnish with a wedge of lime.

NOTE

REPLACE TOPO CHICO WITH FRANKLIN & SONS 1886 SODA WATER, OR ADD SALINE SOLUTION (SEE P187) TO SPARKLING WATER.

YOU CAN ALSO SERVE THIS IN AN ICE-FILLED COLLINS GLASS, ADDING LIME JUICE AND TEQUILA BEFORE TOPPING WITH TOPO CHICO AND GENTLY STIRRING.

TEQUILA SUNRISE

A kitsch child of the 70s, the visually appealing and easily built Tequila Sunrise will give you plenty of modern-day satisfaction.

HISTORY

There are numerous versions of the origin story of the Tequila Sunrise. One goes back to the 1930s and takes us to Tijuana and the Agua Caliente racetrack hotel. But the version we all know and love is drenched in 70s nostalgia and combines tequila, grenadine, and orange juice. Invented by Bobby Lozoff and Billy Rice at the Trident bar in Sausalito, California, it got its reputation by passing the lips of none other than the Rolling Stones while on their 1972 tour (later dubbed their Tequila Sunrise tour). It may have fallen from favour since its heyday, but with good ingredients and in the hands of someone who cares, it still deserves our attention.

WHAT MAKES A TEQUILA SUNRISE?

While good ingredients are, of course, key, like most things in the 70s, its looks are what make the Tequila Sunrise so iconic. The layering of tequila, orange juice, and the final addition of the pomegranate-based grenadine to create the "sunrise" visual is what truly makes this cocktail so identifiable on first glance. Never forget the orange slice and cherry garnish on top.

REPOSADO TEQUILA

ORANGE JUICE

GRENADINE

MIX IT UP

ORANGE JUICE While you can keep this classic, think about swapping in more seasonal oranges throughout the year, such as blood orange (see p117), to add some variety to your Sunrise.

GRENADINE Shop-bought grenadine is great, but if you want to add some more personality to your cocktail, try making it yourself (see p186).

CHERRY A rich Luxardo maraschino, kitsch glacé cherries, or even cherries soaked in an aged tequila for added kick – how you garnish your Tequila Sunrise can take it up a flavour notch.

Orange slice and
cherry to garnish

15ml (½fl oz) grenadine

120ml (4fl oz)
freshly squeezed
orange juice

60ml (2fl oz)
reposado tequila

METHOD

1. **Fill a highball** glass with ice.

2. **Pour in the** tequila first, followed by the orange juice.

3. **Top with** grenadine but don't stir.

4. **Garnish with** an orange slice and a cherry.

NOTE

CONSIDER USING
A SLIGHTLY EARTHIER
TEQUILA TO OFFSET
THIS COCKTAIL'S
SWEETNESS.

THE COCKTAIL'S ADOPTION BY FIGURES IN POPULAR CULTURE MADE IT FAMOUS. THE EAGLES EVEN NAMED A SONG AFTER IT ON THEIR 1973 ALBUM *DESPERADO*.

TOREADOR

This apricot-forward precursor of the Margarita is a classic in its own right, and gives tart and earthy flavours in equal measure.

HISTORY

Not many people know that before the Margarita, there was the Toreador. If you haven't heard of it, consider yourself in good company: despite being delicious and a favourite among bartenders, one of the tequila category's original classics is little known. It first appeared in 1937 in the *Café Royal Cocktail Book* by London's William J. "Bill" Tarling, and appeared 16 years before even a whiff of the Margarita in print. The origins of its name are unknown, but its distinctive calling card is the use of apricot brandy liqueur alongside tequila, lime juice, and, these days, bitters. Tart and orange-hued, it's beautifully balanced.

WHAT MAKES A TOREADOR?

The apricot brandy liqueur is what really makes the Toreador shine – both in flavour and colour. Be sure to taste your apricot brandy before you use it, or find out where it sits on the sweetness scale, to understand how it will impact the overall balance of your finished cocktail. You can use any tequila but *reposado* is usually the best match for the apricot profile.

APRICOT BRANDY LIQUEUR

REPOSADO TEQUILA

LIME JUICE

DRESS TO KILL

DRIED APRICOT Dehydrated apricot wheels make a visual and fragrant addition to the oft-ungarnished Toreador.

TOASTED ALMONDS Toast some almonds and grind them into a fine powder. Brush some honey on your glass and roll it in the powder for a nutty addition.

THYME SPRIG A perfect herb to complement apricots, a sprig of thyme will add some herbal and more earthy aromas to your serve.

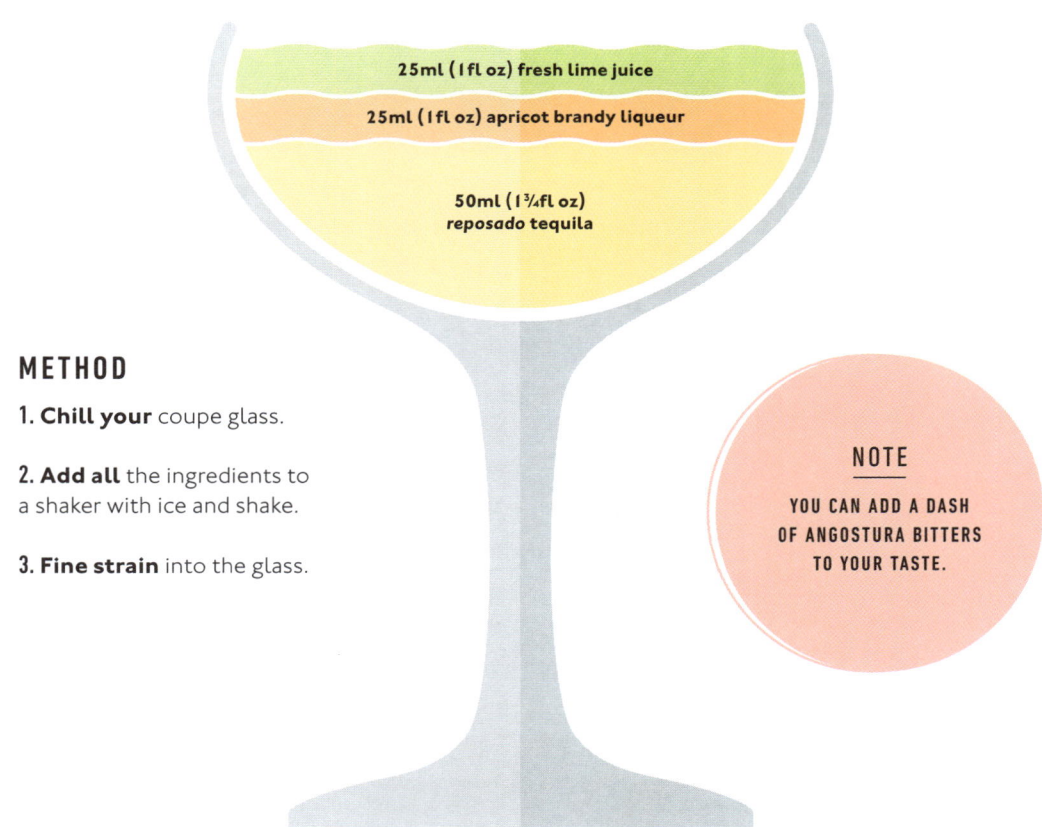

25ml (1fl oz) fresh lime juice

25ml (1fl oz) apricot brandy liqueur

50ml (1¾fl oz)
reposado tequila

METHOD

1. **Chill your** coupe glass.

2. **Add all** the ingredients to a shaker with ice and shake.

3. **Fine strain** into the glass.

NOTE

YOU CAN ADD A DASH
OF ANGOSTURA BITTERS
TO YOUR TASTE.

IF YOU WANT TO EXPLORE OTHER AGAVE SPIRITS,
A SUBTLY SMOKY MEZCAL WORKS WONDERS
AS A SWAP FOR TEQUILA AND RAMPS UP THE
EARTHINESS OF THE TOREADOR.

MODERN CLASSIC COCKTAILS

This side of the 20th century, prominent bartenders have created some of tequila's more modern classic cocktails. Here are four of the most revered.

LONE RANGER

Jeffrey Morgenthaler created this cocktail in 2012 for the brunch menu at Clyde Common at the Ace Hotel in Portland, Oregon, US. He wanted something breakfasty that wasn't the typical Champagne and orange juice sort of cocktail. Tequila was interesting and unexpected, and sparkling rosé was perfect for the spring timing of the menu launch. As for the name, his reasoning is lost to the ages, but it certainly stuck.

Lemon twist to garnish

45ml (1½fl oz) blanco tequila

30ml (1fl oz) lemon juice

15ml (½fl oz) rich simple syrup

60ml (2fl oz) brut rosé sparkling wine

METHOD

1. Add tequila, lemon juice, and rich simple syrup (2:1 sugar to water) to a cocktail shaker with ice and shake until cold.

2. Add the sparkling wine to the shaker.

3. Strain over fresh ice into a Collins glass.

4. Garnish with a lemon twist.

MEX MARTINI

It was around a decade ago that agave expert Megs Miller came up with the idea of the Mex Martini. The Martini was always her favourite cocktail, so she asked bartenders to make her their version of an agave Martini. After some research, she quickly found that bianco vermouth works the best with earthy agave distillates, and that putting agave centre stage in a stirred cocktail highlights all its amazing qualities.

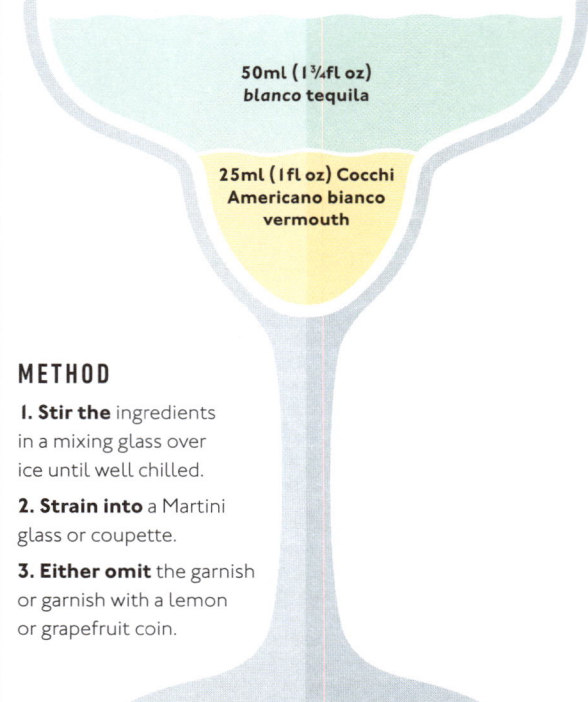

50ml (1¾fl oz) blanco tequila

25ml (1fl oz) Cocchi Americano bianco vermouth

METHOD

1. Stir the ingredients in a mixing glass over ice until well chilled.

2. Strain into a Martini glass or coupette.

3. Either omit the garnish or garnish with a lemon or grapefruit coin.

THE SIESTA WAS INSPIRED BY THE FORMAT OF THE HEMINGWAY DAIQUIRI.

NEW YORK MINUTE

Luke Whearty created the New York Minute for the autumn 2009 menu of award-winning Der Raum cocktail bar in Melbourne, Australia. He was head bartender there for a number of years and wanted to create a cocktail that combined three things he was passionate about at that time: coffee, agave spirits, and the classic Martinez cocktail.

SIESTA

It was at the Flatiron Lounge in New York City in 2006 that Katie Stipe came up with the Siesta. It was inspired by the format of the Hemingway Daiquiri. It swaps rum for an agave base with a touch of bittersweet Campari in place of Luxardo Maraschino liqueur. The Siesta has gained popularity all over the world thanks to the availability of ingredients, making it easy to replicate, and for its use as a gateway cocktail for those who may shy away from bitter spirits.

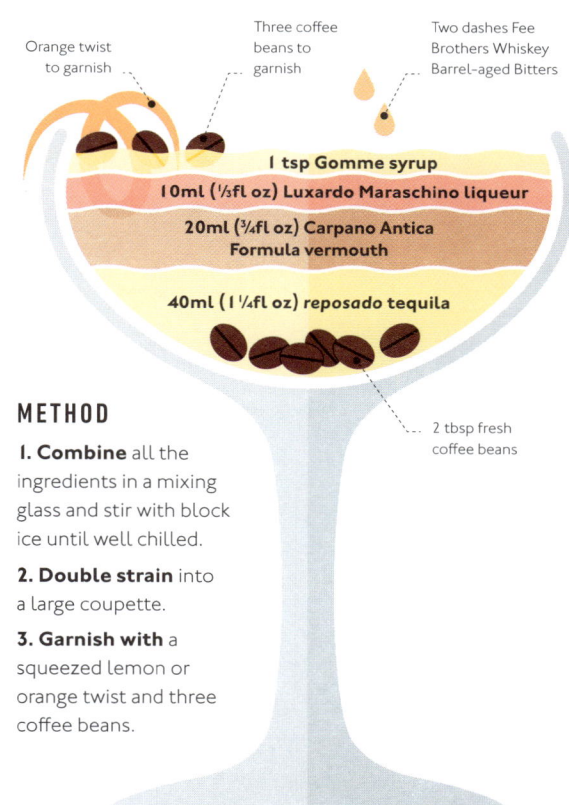

Orange twist to garnish

Three coffee beans to garnish

Two dashes Fee Brothers Whiskey Barrel-aged Bitters

1 tsp Gomme syrup
10ml (⅓fl oz) Luxardo Maraschino liqueur
20ml (¾fl oz) Carpano Antica Formula vermouth
40ml (1¼fl oz) reposado tequila

2 tbsp fresh coffee beans

METHOD

1. Combine all the ingredients in a mixing glass and stir with block ice until well chilled.

2. Double strain into a large coupette.

3. Garnish with a squeezed lemon or orange twist and three coffee beans.

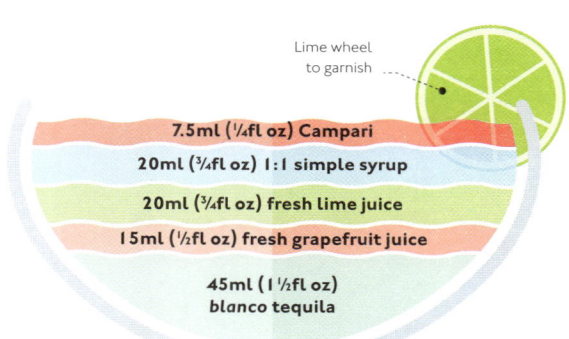

Lime wheel to garnish

7.5ml (¼fl oz) Campari
20ml (¾fl oz) 1:1 simple syrup
20ml (¾fl oz) fresh lime juice
15ml (½fl oz) fresh grapefruit juice
45ml (1½fl oz) blanco tequila

METHOD

1. Add all the ingredients to a cocktail shaker with ice and shake until cold.

2. Fine strain into a chilled coupe glass.

3. Garnish with a lime wheel or grapefruit twist.

CLASSIC COCKTAIL RIFFS

While tequila has its own gamut of classics, its versatility means it can also be used in cocktails based on other spirits. Just be careful not to mask the flavours of agave with dominant ingredients.

TEQUILA ESPRESSO MARTINI

Swap in *blanco* tequila (one from the fruit/spice or sweet/rich section) for the vodka in this classic London cocktail created by the late, great Dick Bradsell. Make sure you're using fresh espresso and serve in a chilled Martini or Nick & Nora glass.

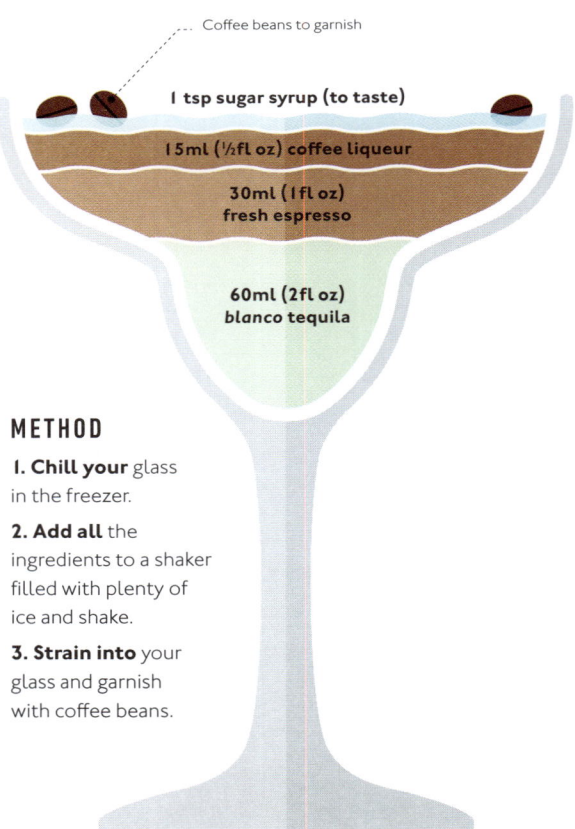

Coffee beans to garnish

1 tsp sugar syrup (to taste)

15ml (½fl oz) coffee liqueur

30ml (1fl oz) fresh espresso

60ml (2fl oz) *blanco* tequila

METHOD

1. Chill your glass in the freezer.

2. Add all the ingredients to a shaker filled with plenty of ice and shake.

3. Strain into your glass and garnish with coffee beans.

MEXICAN MULE

This is a twist on the versatile Moscow Mule, a 1940s Los Angeles-born cocktail. It combines the tequila-friendly flavours of lime, mint, and ginger to create a seriously refreshing and easy summer cocktail, served in a copper mug over ice.

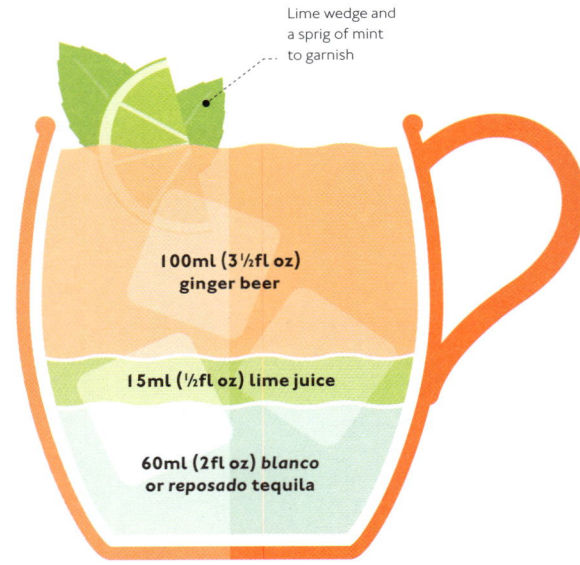

Lime wedge and a sprig of mint to garnish

100ml (3½fl oz) ginger beer

15ml (½fl oz) lime juice

60ml (2fl oz) *blanco* or *reposado* tequila

METHOD

1. Fill a chilled copper mug with ice and add lime juice and tequila.

2. Top with ginger beer and stir.

3. Garnish with a lime wedge and a sprig of mint.

THE MEXICAN MULE IS A SERIOUSLY REFRESHING AND EASY SUMMER COCKTAIL.

TEQUILA MANHATTAN

An aged tequila swap for American whiskey is needed to make this Manhattan adaptation, also known as a Distrito Federal (the old name for Mexico City). Use a tequila with distinct aged characteristics and some body to stand up in this short, strong serve.

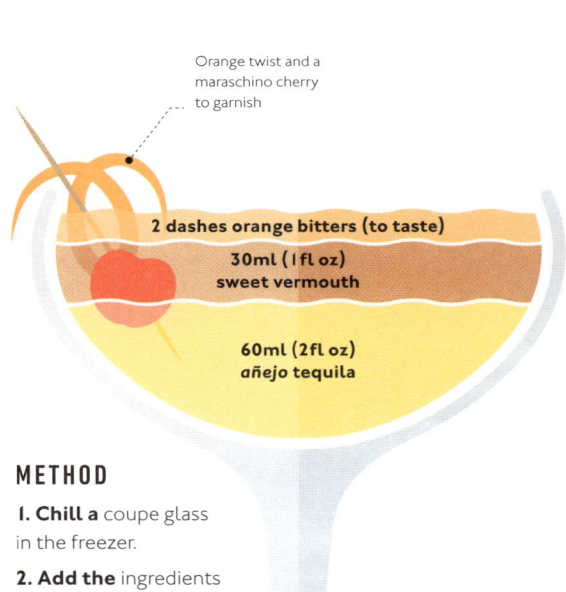

Orange twist and a maraschino cherry to garnish

2 dashes orange bitters (to taste)

30ml (1 fl oz) sweet vermouth

60ml (2fl oz) *añejo* tequila

METHOD

1. Chill a coupe glass in the freezer.

2. Add the ingredients to a mixing glass filled with ice and stir.

3. Strain into your glass.

4. Garnish with an orange twist and a maraschino cherry.

TEQUILA CORPSE REVIVER NO. 2

Delicately balanced, this is one of my favourite riffs on a classic. Equal parts tequila (in place of gin), triple sec, and aromatized wine, along with lemon and absinthe, work wonders with tequila in this twist on the classic Harry Craddock cocktail from the 1930s.

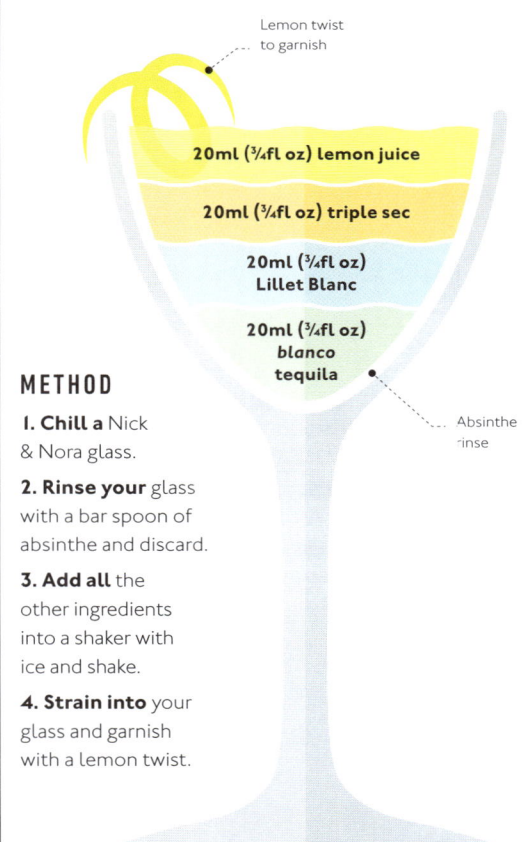

Lemon twist to garnish

20ml (¾fl oz) lemon juice

20ml (¾fl oz) triple sec

20ml (¾fl oz) Lillet Blanc

20ml (¾fl oz) *blanco tequila*

Absinthe rinse

METHOD

1. Chill a Nick & Nora glass.

2. Rinse your glass with a bar spoon of absinthe and discard.

3. Add all the other ingredients into a shaker with ice and shake.

4. Strain into your glass and garnish with a lemon twist.

SHOTS, SHOTS, SHOTS

Tequila shots with lime and salt are a ritual reserved for drinkers outside Mexico. But move aside lime and salt – tequila shots should be a celebration of the spirit, not a cover-up.

WHO DRINKS SHOTS?

Shots are arguably the origin of every tequila nay-sayer's aversion to the notorious party spirit. Whatever you call it – training wheels, lick-sip-suck – drinking tequila *cruda*, or tequila shotted with lime and salt, is not typically done in Mexico. (Hands up if you've woken up bleary eyed and less than bushy tailed in the aftermath of one of these nights…)

The ritual of drinking shots is said to have originated in 1918 during the outbreak of Spanish flu in Mexico. Doctors prescribed the trio of tequila, lime, and salt to ease patients' symptoms. This practice gradually made its way from Mexico to the United States, and the infamous tequila shot was born.

Thankfully, as tequila becomes better understood and more quality spirits are now proudly served in bars, the need to undertake such a ritual is falling out of fashion. But that doesn't mean that more nuanced tequila shots aren't a fun way to imbibe the spirit. Orange wedges, grapefruit slices, strawberries, and white pepper are all far superior alternatives to lime and salt among bartenders.

SHOTS AND CHASERS

There are also well-known shot and chaser combinations that stand up as some of the most popular ways to drink tequila. Served alongside a shot of tequila, a chaser acts as a go-between – you sip one and then the other, back and forth. So, the next time you're in the market for a quick hit of the good stuff, try making one of the following recipes and leave the lime wedge and salt alone.

VERDITA

A green shot that brings a hit of herbalism to proceedings, the Verdita is a classic tequila accompaniment, and it works well with mezcal too. I suggest you make a bottle of this, keep it in the fridge, and serve it at your next party.

INGREDIENTS

450ml (15fl oz) pineapple juice

50g (1¾oz) mint

50g (1¾oz) coriander

Chilli/jalapeño (to taste)

METHOD

1. **Add all** the ingredients to a blender and blend well.

2. **Strain into** a sterilized bottle and refrigerate.

3. **Serve in** a shot glass.

A FEW WELL-KNOWN SHOT AND CHASER COMBINATIONS STAND UP AS SOME OF THE MOST POPULAR WAYS TO DRINK TEQUILA.

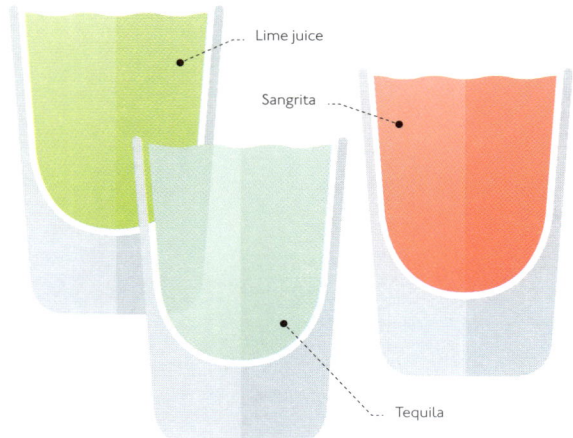

Lime juice

Sangrita

Tequila

SANGRITA

Meaning "little blood" in Spanish, the Sangrita is a red-hued shot. Despite appearing in a lot of recipes, it actually originated without the addition of tomato juice, which brings a savoury edge, but feel free to eschew it.

INGREDIENTS

60ml (2fl oz) tomato juice (optional)

30ml (1fl oz) orange juice

15ml (½fl oz) lime juice

15ml (½fl oz) grenadine

Ancho chilli powder (to taste)

Slice of jalapeño

METHOD

1. **Add all** the ingredients to a blender and blend well.

2. **Strain into** a sterilized bottle and refrigerate.

3. **Serve in** a shot glass.

LA BANDERA

Not one, not two, but three shots make up La Bandera. Meaning "flag" in Spanish, it is made up of the three colours of the Mexican flag – green, white, and red – and it is super simple to make.

INGREDIENTS

1 shot of lime juice

1 shot of tequila

1 shot of Sangrita (see left)

METHOD

1. **Pour lime** juice into a shot glass.

2. **Pour tequila** into a second shot glass.

3. **Pour Sangrita** into a third shot glass.

4. **Alternate sipping** between the three shots.

GLOSSARY

Abocado
The use of additives, called *abocantes*, in a tequila, such as glycerine or oak extract, to enhance colour and flavour.

Aguamiel
The unfermented sap that comes from the **piña**. It is fermented to make **pulque**.

Alembic
Another word for a pot still in which most tequila is distilled.

Autoclave
A drum-like pressure cooker used to cook agave **piñas**.

Bagasse
The leftover fibres or pulp from the agave **piña** once it has been crushed and fermented.

Brix
A measure of the dissolved solids in a liquid, most commonly sugar, where 1 degree Brix (°Bx) represents 1g of sucrose in 100g of solution. It's usually measured with an optical refractometer.

Charring
The application of flame to the inside of a barrel used to age tequila, which enhances flavour and colour.

Cloning
The propagation of new plants by cutting offshoots (called pups or **hijuelos**) from a parent agave and replanting them.

Coa
The sharp, spade-like instrument *jimadores* use to harvest agaves.

Congeners
Substances produced during fermentation that create flavour.

Corazón
The heart of the spirit cut from the still and used to make tequila.

Curado
A tequila flavoured with natural ingredients, such as coconut.

Diffuser
An efficient but controversial piece of equipment that extracts sugary juice from uncooked, shredded **piñas** by adding water and sometimes acids to the fibres.

Hijuelo
A baby agave plant cut from the parent agave and often replanted. *See also*: **Cloning**.

Hornos
Clay or brick ovens used to cook agave **piñas**.

Jimador
A farmer who harvests agaves used to make tequila.

Maestra tequilera/maestro tequilero
The (female/male) master distiller at a tequila distillery.

Mosto
The liquid that goes through the fermentation process.

Mosto muerto
The liquid that results from the fermentation process, which goes into the still.

Ordinario
The liquid resulting from the first distillation.

Piña
The heart of the agave, which resembles a pineapple and is used to make tequila.

Pipones
Large wooden vats used for ageing tequila.

Pulque
An alcoholic drink made by fermenting the sap of an agave plant.

Quiote
The flower stalk that grows from the top of an agave. *Jimadores* cut it down to divert sugars to the **piña**.

Reductive sugar
The total reductive sugar (ART) in an agave is its **Brix** score minus 20 per cent. It is used to determine if the agave is ready for harvesting.

Roller mills
Machinery used to crush agave **piñas** with water to extract the fermentable sugars.

Tahona
A stone wheel used to crush agave **piñas** and release sugars, often motorized today but pulled by donkeys in the past.

Vinasse
The liquid waste that is a result of the tequila distillation process.

INDEX

ABOUT THE AUTHOR

Millie Milliken is a multi-award-winning spirits and hospitality writer and editor based in London. She writes for some of the world's most respected drinks publications with a specialism in distilled spirits and cocktails, and has edited two books written by bartenders. She also runs her own content and events company, Wet Ink, which introduces consumers to spirits through unusual lenses. She was placed 23rd in Drinks Retailing's Top 100 Most Influential People in Drinks list, was awarded the Alan Lodge Young International Drinks Writer of the Year by the Spirits Business in 2022, and was the International Wine & Spirit Competition (IWSC) 2022 Spirits Communicator of the Year.
@millie_milliken

AUTHOR'S ACKNOWLEDGMENTS

While my name might be the one emblazoned on the cover, this book is the result of the hard work, generosity, and knowledge of people without whom it would not exist. First of all, I want to thank the DK team for guiding me through my first-ever book: to Izzy Holton for the Instagram message that started it all back in 2023; Cara Armstrong, who took it from a possibility to a reality; Dawn Titmus, my editor, who has made me interrogate every fact, name, and number and been a brilliant collaborator; Marta Bescos, who had the unenviable task of calling in all the photos – thank you for taking on this monumental task so diligently; and Vanessa Hamilton, thank you for bringing my ideas to life with such beautiful design and illustrations. A special mention to my assistant, Georgia Weaser, for calling in more than 200 tequila bottles (and dealing with the inevitable postal mishaps), which was not in your original job description – thank you and please never leave me.

The content of this book is the culmination of knowledge learned from people who live and breathe tequila in their everyday lives. I have Steffin Oghene to thank for organizing an itinerary for me on my latest trip to Mexico, unasked, and making sure I was looked after on my solo travels. Thank you to all the distilleries who took the time to show me around, answer my questions, and made me feel at home. I'd also like to say a huge thank you to Francisco Castillon, who rearranged his diary to personally drive me around tequila country, keep me safe for three days, and was a fount of knowledge during our long and story-filled stretches on the road.

Over the course of my career and in the lead-up to this book, there have been a multitude of people who have introduced me to the myriad wonders of this agave spirit: Jesse Estes, Megs Miller, Deano Moncrieffe, Gabriela Moncada, and Matthias Ingelmann, to name a few. Thank you must also go to all the brands (and their PRs, marketing teams, and ambassadors) who sent me bottles without expectation, or organized tastings to spare more floor space of my office. And to the bartenders who offered their cocktails for this book – and all the bartenders who have ever served me a perfect tequila cocktail – thank you.

Finally, thank you to my partner, Richard, for enduring the tapping of my laptop keys through the late nights and early hours of 2024, not to mention the unfathomable wall of tequila that currently resides in our flat (you can drink it now). Your support, as always, is invaluable. And to my family and friends, thank you for your patience – this book was written during holidays, weddings, long weekends, birthdays, and a very quiet Christmas, and preoccupied most of my waking hours for the last 12 months. Next tequila's on me!

PUBLISHER'S ACKNOWLEDGMENTS

DK would like to thank the tequila distilleries, The Whisky Exchange, and The Story for their kind permission to reproduce images of their products, Niyran Gill for the cover illustration, John Friend for proofreading, and Vanessa Bird for the index.

48bl Statista 2025: data from Sales volume of tequila in the United States from 2004 to 2024.

PICTURE CREDITS

The publisher would like to thank the following for their kind permission to reproduce their photographs:

(Key: a-above; b-below/bottom; c-centre; f-far; l-left; r-right; t-top)

The Advertising Archives: 47t; **Alamy Stock Photo:** ACORN 1 81b, Art Collection 4 41tl, CalimaX 42, Cosmo Condina Mexico 68, Dave G. Houser 43, Hugh Mitton 76, NTB 47bl, Zoonar/Konstantin Kalishko 34; **AWL Images:** Hemis 18; **Café Pacifico:** Two Dudes Ltd 55; **Cantina OK!:** NIKKI TO & BUFFET. 57; **El Tequileño tequila:** 54; **Getty Images:** Hulton Archive/Archive Photos/FPG 53, Hulton Archive/FPG 46; **Getty Images/iStock:** DC_Colombia 14, solarisimages 52, Germán Zuazo Mendoza 19; **Renee G. Gudiño:** 56; **Leyenda de México:** 51; **Mezcal Aguerrido:** 35; **Shutterstock.com:** Alejandro Franco García 41br; **Tequila Casa Dragones:** 50.

DK LONDON
Editorial Director Cara Armstrong
Project Editor Izzy Holton
Senior Designer Glenda Fisher
Senior Production Editor Tony Phipps
Production Controller Celine MacLeod
Jacket Designer Glenda Fisher
Jacket Coordinator Emily Cannings
Art Director Maxine Pedliham
Publishing Director Stephanie Jackson

Editorial Dawn Titmus
Design and Illustration Vanessa Hamilton
Picture Research Marta Bescos

First published in Great Britain in 2025 by
Dorling Kindersley Limited
20 Vauxhall Bridge Road, London SW1V 2SA

The authorized representative in the EEA is
Dorling Kindersley Verlag GmbH. Arnulfstr. 124,
80636 Munich, Germany

A CIP catalogue record for this book
is available from the British Library.
ISBN: 978-0-2417-2619-8

Printed and bound in Malaysia

www.dk.com